Poets
Prophets &
Pragmatists

Poets Prophets & Pragmatists

a new challenge to religious life

Evelyn Woodward

AVE MARIA PRESS
Notre Dame, Indiana 46556

Library of Congress Catalog Card Number: 86-72375

International Standard Book Number: 0-87793-349-9

Cover design: Elizabeth J. French

Printed and bound in the United States of America.

For My Friends—
My Community of the Heart

Contents

Preface_____9

1 ORIENTATIONS:
Pluralism, Poets, Prophets, Pragmatists, Story_____13

2 COMMUNITY:
One Story Uniting Many Stories_____45

3 A SPIRITUALITY NAMED EMPATHY:
The Life Blood of the Community Story_____97

4 CONFLICT:
The Tangle of Our Stories_____135

5 FORMATION:
Shaping and Blending Our Stories_____177

6 COPING WITH STRESS AND BURNOUT:
The Experience of the Overloaded Story_____209

7 CONCLUSION:
Endings and Beginnings_____245

Preface

This book is not my own. While it is true that I wrote the words and must take total responsibility for them, many other people have unwittingly been the source of them. For the past decade I have been engaged in counselling religious and in consulting with their communities and congregations. In addition, I have been associated with a team of professional colleagues whose discussions have raised questions, generated ideas and suggested models for action. My own struggles with the complex milieu of modern religious life have also been a powerful consciousness-raiser. The issues raised in this book have emerged from all of these experiences.

Most of all, I am indebted to those individuals who have invited me into their fragmented and painful stories. As we broke the sacramental bread of their life's word, I have grown more and more aware of the meaning of the prayer of Jesus, "I thank you, Father, Lord of heaven and earth, that you have revealed these things to the little ones." I am aware of having been in close contact with the truly wise, who, unaware of the depth of their wisdom, simply and freely stated their inner truth as they saw it. These are the anawim—sometimes impoverished in inner resources and skills, but large in spiritual stature, for theirs is the kingdom of heaven. I thank them all and offer back to them the reflections that have come from knowing them.

Many times, when listening as deeply as I could to the stories of all these people, I found myself becoming overburdened and in need of re-creation—emotionally, physically, spiritually and intellectually. There was always a place to go, a readily accessible community of the heart, my friends. In the early 1970s Brother Ron Perry, FMS, director of the Sydney Archdiocesan Counselling Institute, gathered together a small group of religious who were engaged in the practice of the behavioral sciences in the field of religious life, and this group became the nucleus of a reference group which has expanded in the ensuing years and has offered personal support and sustenance as well as professional consultation and exchange. An encounter with Dr. Michael A. Cowan in Chicago in 1978 has also led to the developing of a new network of friends and associates in the United States, an enriching, illuminating and growthful experience. Traces of all these people are present in this book, and I thank them all.

In proposing, as I do, that the gifts of poetic insight, prophetic challenge and pragmatic planning are key qualities of leadership in a pluralistic age, I do not imply that these are limited to ascribed leaders. Everyone engaged in active ministry is asked to exercise some degree of personal leadership, and whenever persons living together in dynamic community life influence one another, they are exercising some leadership functions. Hence, whenever the world *leader* is used in the text, it is used in the broader and more inclusive sense of the word. When I specify any of the three gifts, it should be assumed that a single person may combine several or all of them, but that they are more often possessed separately, or at least in different proportions. Since it is a happy combination of these gifts that offers greater possibilities for creative leadership, religious orders engaged in the process of electing formal leaders might well take into consideration the balance of these gifts on a general or provincial council rather than electing persons with very similar gifts.

There are many individuals who have helped with the reshaping of the manuscript, friends who have read and discussed single chapters and helped elucidate ideas. They are too numerous to list here. However, I hope that I will be permitted without slight to anyone to mention the sensitive listening of Sister Mary Stephane of my own congregation, the warmth and welcome of the Merewether Beach community, the constant support and encouragement of my family and of my friend, Sister Ursula Kauter, the incisive criticism of Father William Burston, Director of Centacare in Newcastle, NSW, the enthusiasm and responsiveness of Brother Anthony Duncan, OH, of St. John of God Hospital, Richmond, and the ceaseless labor of my secretary, Mrs. Patricia Graham, in the typing and retyping of the manuscript. Her loyalty is beyond measure.

Behind all of these proximate persons are the shadowy figures of my own larger story. In particular, the spirit of our founder, Rev. Julian Tenison Woods, has become enormously important and present to me as I have tried to reflect on many of the issues in this book. His own radical concern for people, for poverty and for the church, along with his painful willingness to challenge the institutional church while struggling to preserve his loyalty to it, have been much in my thoughts, and in some mysterious way I feel that I know him better now than

I did when this work was begun. His frailties and strengths are dearer to me. It is my fervent wish that those religious who read these pages in the spirit of empathy will find again, even more deeply, the grandeur, courage and illuminating vision of their own founders.

1
ORIENTATIONS:

**Pluralism,
Poets,
Prophets,
Pragmatists,
Story. . .**

During the last 14 years a steady procession of religious, lay people and clergy has passed through the doors of the consulting center where I work. I have sat for hours with seminar and workshop groups reflecting on issues relating to church, ministry and the quality of religious living. I have assisted at the chapters of religious orders and have been called upon to intervene in community conflicts and decision-making, to help revise constitutions and to shape new understandings of leadership and community life. In the process I have been changed and challenged. I have found myself overwhelmed by people's honesty, pained and sometimes outraged by their brokenness, exhilarated and encouraged by their resilience, humbled by their trust and caught up in their questions. In recent times those same questions, along with reflection on my own experience of religious life and new learning from various sources, have prompted me to seek patterns, to reflect on trends and to ask, "Where are we? Where to next? How do we get there?"

Any pondering of the first question immediately demands an exploration of where we have come from because the past has left its signature on the present. Ruminating on our collective and individual stories has become an important part of understanding religious life as a process in which all three tenses are at work simultaneously. We have been. We are. We are becoming.

Asking where we are also raises the question of the impact of pluralism on the erstwhile stable institution of religious life. Although it has existed from the beginning, pluralism has a massive impact today because of the ease of worldwide communication, the diminishing of absolutism in the church, and more exchanges between church and world. Religious life is a ship afloat on an ocean of time whose tides are presently governed by the swell of pluralism. Navigation on that ocean calls for special gifts.

These navigational gifts must be described as we ask, "Where to next? How do we get there?" In the reflections of this chapter, and of those that follow, particular attention is paid to aspects of leadership that are referred to as *poetry, prophecy* and *pragmatism*.

Poets are individuals and groups who intuitively and deeply understand the nature and quality of human experience with delicate accuracy and empathy of perception. They arrive at this understanding before the logicians, philosophers, theologians, psychologists and anthropologists apply the scalpel of their intellects to the facts. The poet sees, understands and raises to consciousness. The poet is a visionary.

Prophets are men and women who are gifted with the ability to take the vision of the poets and challenge others with its power, goading them to new consciousness and to a life rooted in the new consciousness. They are the challengers of religious life.

Pragmatists are those practical planners who can, without distortion, take the vision of the poets and the challenge of the prophets and, in collaboration with them, put together ways of living. They can dismantle old structures and indicate where new ones are called for. They are the planners and evaluators, the troubleshooters and inventors in religious life.

Where Are We?

Religious life today is in a state of flux. Some would say that it is in a state of disorientation and demoralization. New polarizations have arisen just when people thought their orders had begun to emerge from the chaos of pre-Vatican II and immediately post-Vatican II changes. If change is a fact of life, and religious life has been evolving for centuries, why all this fuss? What is it about the present state of religious life that makes for greater urgency, more varied interpretations of the signs, higher hopes and deeper fears?

I have two responses to this. The first is a feeling of challenging optimism. In all the change that has gone on I hear the possibility and the invitation to become "more thickly alive," to borrow William James' felicitous expression. I perceive not merely an invitation but a necessity to become less isolated and bound in by institutions and more deeply immersed in outward-bound ministries that reach to wherever the cry of poverty and justice draws us. This is an invitation to see Christianity itself more "thickly," viewing it not as a "timeless religion but as intrinsically conditioned by history even as it has a mission to shape history."[1]

To take a consciously active role in the shaping of the future is a call to be uncomfortable and displaced. We can no longer be satisfied to operate solely in institutional ministries, however dedicated and laudable these may have been. The call to be pilgrims is louder now than ever before.

My second response is a desire to understand our jumping-off point, to look back and see where we have come from. I believe that this will help us understand some of the present pain being felt by those in religious life. The letting-go of cherished securities will not then become automatically easy, but it may become a more conscious "dying" to a known way rather than a feeling of being overtaken and overpowered by change.

We often speak of the last 20 or 30 years as a single period of the life-history of religious orders, yet as I see it, there have been two major movements. The first of these I shall call the de-institutionalization phase; the second will be referred to as the phase of pluralism-awareness.

Immediately after Vatican II most religious orders, especially the female ones, concentrated on aspects of institutional identity that were to be surrendered. Often the first and most emotionally-charged emphasis was on external and relatively unimportant things such as dress and daily schedule. What was not readily recognized by many was the significance of emerging from behind veils, habits, clerical collars and enclosures. In fact, this represented a change in worldview. It was a move away from a separatist and even elitist manner of being toward immersion, participation and equality. It was a reflection of a changed ecclesiology, the death of post-Tridentine garrison Catholicism.

While for many this was timely, for many more it was endangering. It brought with it a change in religious-life identity that they did not voluntarily seek. What they had chosen years ago no longer existed. Whether they saw it consciously or not, they were endangered by the loss of institutional parenting. From the more autocratic or benevolent-autocratic styles of other times, authority now began to be linked constantly with the notion of service, respect for the freedom and initiative of individuals, subsidiarity and collegiality. People who had hitherto been dependent, and who had even been rewarded for their dependency, were now asked to engage in personal and communal discernment, to substitute accountability for blind obedience, and to cease to equate uniformity with unity. Affectivity began to be recognized as a respectable dimension of human existence and celibate living. Relationality began to be extolled to people who had never received any training in it. Little wonder, then, that new stresses were experienced and that polarization developed between the exponents of rapid change and those who tended to be more resistant to it.

At this time the floodgates of departure from religious life opened and a rate of attrition never before known was experienced in many religious houses. Numbers of applicants diminished, first among women religious and then among the male orders. Numerous secondary problems developed out of this. I

mention one of them in particular. In all the de-institutionalizing movements that had been taking place, the most resistant
was often in the area of ministry. Here, religious were slow to
change. The alterations and adaptations within communal living modified details of ministry, but for the most part institutional ministries, such as schools and hospitals, were maintained. As numbers began to decline and average age increased,
religious groups doubled their efforts to sustain commitments.
Gradually lay people became involved in their apostolates, more
out of situational exigencies than from a deeply internalized valuing on the part of religious of the partnership of laity and religious in the work of the church. Old monopolies have died
hard. New crises arose out of all this. Stress from overwork became a new reality. Conflict arose out of vestigial superiority
that led to the neglect of laity on staffs, or to assigning them positions that were ancillary or less responsible than those taken
by the religious, or to active hostility toward laity assigned to
leadership positions.

A miracle of our time is that in the wake of all this has
come some level of acceptance and internalizing. This growth
is, of course, uneven. Observation suggests that many older religious arrived at peaceful acceptance before the middle-aged
did. Religious in their 50s now often express fears about their
future and uncertainty about their perseverance in religious life.
They link this with their fear that there will be no one to offer
them care as they age. Gradually, in the light of all this, institutional apostolates are being painfully surrendered, and a dawning awareness of other ways of being present is emerging, with
new understandings of the significance not only of work but
also of leisure. In the midst of all this is a resurgence of the
need for prayer that is gradually becoming separated from a previous identification with religious exercises and specific *forms*
of prayer. Theologies and spiritualities are multiplying and even
learning to dialogue with one another. The harshness of earlier
conflicts is giving way to a gentler sense of the inevitability of
differences.

At the same time, a new and heightened awareness of the
extent and depth and challenge of the differences is also arising.
This is the phase I have called pluralism-awareness. Peter Berger
has pointed out that

> a religious worldview, just like any other body of interpreta-
> tions of reality, is dependent upon social support. The more
> unified and reliable this support is, the more these interpreta-
> tions of reality will be firmly established in consciousness.[2]

A glance at the "megatrends"[3] occurring in the world in which religious life lives and moves indicates the scope of the changes. Living in a situation of "high transience"[4] and greater contact with their social milieu, religious are much more sharply aware of their options. Greater emphasis on personal responsibility and accountability makes obedience a new and challenging reality. Greater opportunities for intimacy and social permissiveness in the area of sexuality make celibacy a different reality involving constant choices. The move away from institutions and the search for areas of appropriate ministry make poverty, along with homelessness and pilgrimage, an immediate and often painful choice; community becomes a reality to be carried in the heart rather than a place in which to live. No longer is there simply a series of either/or, good/bad choices to make. We must choose from a plethora of moral, social, ministerial, ecclesial, psychological and theological possibilities. Even as we recognize the need for religious to be on the cutting edge of the church we are confused by multiple opinions of where that cutting edge is. Just as we come to agreement that we must respond out of our poverty to the cry of the poor, we recognize that poverty in our world wears many faces. Plurality of life choices demands our attention at every turn. We must constantly bring to bear on current questions a gospel awareness that is new because the situation is new, at least for us.

It is a dangerous time. One temptation is to talk about the multiple possibilities without action, to analyze and plan but never to implement. The other temptation is to act without reflection or planning, to do our own thing in ways that lead to fragmentation and ineffective action. I believe that it is a time for wise and risk-taking action. Out of all the possibilities, we must choose. This is the dilemma but also the exhilaration of pluralism. There is no escape from it.

I believe that acceptance of pluralism as a fact of life marks the present phase of religious life. We have moved from preoccupation with some of the internal issues related to de-institutionalizing and are broadening our horizons to see the challenge of bringing the unity of the gospel to a pluralist world of which we are ourselves a part. What follows, then, is a description of the phenomenon of pluralism and some of its implications.

Pluralism

Pluralism has been with us since the beginning. In the very infancy of the church the Council of Jerusalem was convoked precisely to deal with the divisions that had arisen as converts joined the church.

> But certain members of the Pharisees' party who had become believers objected, insisting that gentiles should be circumcised and instructed to keep the Law of Moses. The apostles and elders met to look into the matter (Acts 15:5-7).

These were not merely differences of opinion that were to be examined. They were deep cultural divisions that indicated quite separate and distinct ways of seeing and being in the world. Shaped in a different historical and cultural milieu, the converts of Antioch were having distinctly Jewish customs urged upon them by the Pharisees. The manner of their belonging was under scrutiny, and the view of one significant group was that uniformity was desirable.

The Council of Jerusalem, influenced by Peter and James, decided that recognition and acceptance of differences was quite consonant with full membership in the community. Far from quashing differences and invoking the past as the sole arbiter of what was allowable, the elders of the council decided in favor of the innovation of the younger churches, allowing differences between Greek and explicitly Jewish forms of community and worship. Thus, from the beginning, it was declared publicly that uniformity is not a criterion of unity, nor is it required for full membership and belonging.

The steps leading to this decision are worth noting. As with every council and chapter, there was prolonged discussion. The arguments presumably were aired and the decision-makers gathered the necessary information, the first step of an authentic discernment process. When this had gone on long enough, Peter spoke. Having listened to all that had been said, he was in a position to offer a summary and a conclusion. First, with the intuitive understanding of a poet, Peter offers an overview steeped in empathy and compassion arising from his own painful past experience:

> "Why do you put God to the test now by imposing on the disciples the very burden that neither our ancestors nor we were strong enough to support?" (Acts 15:10).

The experience of the past is examined and remembered realistically. It is respected without being canonized or imposed arbitrarily on others.

Peter then proceeds to single out what does unite. He seeks

the core of their unity around which other differences may be permitted to exist and flower.

> "God, who can read everyone's heart, showed his approval of them by giving the Holy Spirit to them *just as he had to us.* . . .
> We believe that we are saved in the same way as they are: through the grace of the Lord Jesus" (Acts 15:8, 11).

This is the enkindling vision of the community. Once this is accepted and internalized, pluriformity in other things can not only be tolerated but fostered and appreciated as a means of further growth.

The discussion among the elders dies after this statement. Peter's summary is overwhelming in its wisdom and charity. There is no more room for disagreement.

Stimulated by the truth of Peter's insight, Barnabas and Paul lend weight to it by providing evidence of the Lord's election of the gentiles, enumerating the signs that the Holy Spirit is indeed present also among them: "And they listened to Barnabas and Paul describing all the signs and wonders God had worked through them among the gentiles" (Acts 15:12).

Then a pragmatist speaks. James points out the consonance of current events with the words of the prophets and makes a practical proposal embodying the poetic insight of Peter and sharp awareness of its confirmation by the prophetic tradition. The pragmatist sees the harmony of the poetic insight and prophetic challenge, and translates both into a program for action:

> "My verdict is, then, that instead of making things more difficult for gentiles who turn to God, we should send them a letter telling them merely to abstain from anything polluted by idols, from illicit marriages, from the meat of strangled animals and from blood. For Moses has always had his preachers in every town and is read aloud in the synagogues every Sabbath" (Acts 15:19-21).

James, therefore, takes account of tradition, selects what is still applicable to the present and advocates explicit communication of this to the people whose inclusion is under discussion.

The prophets, Judas and Silas, are elected by the assembly to accompany Paul and Barnabas to Antioch to communicate the decision of the assembly, passing it on not merely as a juridical statement but as a sacred expression of the action of the Holy Spirit in the heart of the community. There is a challenge and there are demands in the statement, conditions to be met and injunctions to be obeyed. They are presented as minimal essentials selected to avoid unnecessary burdens. This letter from the Council was welcomed in the spirit that inspired it:

> The community read it and were delighted with the encouragement it gave them. Judas and Silas, being themselves prophets, spoke for a long time, encouraging and strengthening the brothers (Acts 15:31-32).

Clearly they combined the prophetic functions of criticism and energizing which will be discussed later in this chapter.

This vignette within the early church presents an image of the interaction of poets, prophets and pragmatists in the single task of leading a pluralist community. It has been argued recently in relation to the church's mission to the Third World that there is urgent need for a return to the more pluriform spirit of the first 400 years of the church's history.[5] Perhaps the same may be said of religious life.

Pluralism as a fact of life presents us with a constant challenge. Recognizing the variety and unfinishedness and imperfection of reality, we find ourselves invited to live within it in ways that engage it creatively, seeking harmonies and connections where they may be genuinely forged, recognizing differences that cannot be harmonized and finding ways of being at ease in their midst. It invites a humility before the complexity of a universe in which we are conscious that something always escapes.

The image of a jazz band has been used to describe this shifting, baffling reality. Each individual player appears to be doing his or her own thing with virtuosity, and yet their individual efforts are united in a brilliant whole. When such an image is applied to religious life, pluralism becomes less a problem to be dealt with than a solution to the problem of polarization. Polarization, which most religious have tasted in one form or another in recent years, is a separation by differences that are entrenched and obstinately clung to and defended. Where polarization exists, groups form to protect cherished ways of seeing the world or some aspect of it. All other possibilities are seen as inimical to their position, and the only form of communication that is possible is debate. In recent years some communities have foundered and lost their focus through such an experience. Pluralism consciously embraced is a way of dealing with the differences much more creatively, for pluralism recognizes and allows the differences while attending meticulously to the artistry of the combined melody. Such pluralism, however, must be authentically evangelical. The focus of the charismatic founder on a particular and core aspect of the gospel remains at the heart of our differences as the one in the midst of the many, just as the recognition of the presence and election of the Holy Spirit made it possible at the Council of Jerusalem for differences to be not only tolerated but sanctioned and blessed.

Pluralism has been around from the beginning, but it is more sharply obvious in a time of global communication and high transience. Those joining religious life now are drawn from diverse backgrounds which have carved different ways of seeing the world. Many religious groups now admit converts, older persons, those from a variety of ethnic backgrounds and cultures, those who were married and widowed, those who have had wide experience of the work place and perhaps the loneliness of being out of work and unable to find appropriate employment. Coming from their diverse viewpoints, these individuals are joining groups where there are older members whose experience of life has been more stable, more predictable and perhaps narrower. When these worlds of experience meet, the demands for adjustment and acceptance are high. Pluralism makes heavy demands.

Pluralism calls for the ability to live with ambiguity. It demands the surrender of the monistic belief that where there are differing approaches to reality, somebody must be right and the others wrong. The conflicts that may be created by the differences are not dealt with by reverting to the rigid structures of earlier times, even though the human tendency is to regress to autocratic decision-making and appeals to authoritarian leadership. The challenge to wider and deeper communication and mutuality is clarion clear. What animates it is respect for the inviolable dignity of the human person accompanied by a sense of being "not-yet" people, people-in-process, in the making along with the world itself. This, in turn, carries with it a sense of possessing a minimum of certainty and a great deal of uncertainty, a thirst for knowledge and understanding that is at the same time wary of facile absolutes. Such a person is also aware of the possibility of bad faith and sensitive to the injustices of the past and the possibility of their replication in different ways in the present.

Implicit in all of this is the need for tolerance and patience in a situation fraught with complexity, ambiguity and imperfection. Formation in religious life these days must, of necessity, help people grow toward an openness to differences that eschews the immediate remedy or the superficial solution. Learning how to live along *with* may be more appropriate than to live *for*. Radically new definitions of ministry will emerge from this. Power will be re-examined in the light of the evangelical core-belief system, and in its light will be transformed from unilateral power to mutual influence and willingness to be influenced. Authority will be more faithfully an internalizing of the church's understanding of it as service rather than the handing-down of decrees from on high, even though the church's sinful practice is sometimes at variance with its idealistic words.

Pluralism carries with it also the challenge to deal with conflict well. Conflict is inevitable, but it need not be destructive. The greatest destruction happens when groups avoid directly facing large differences in experience, which, if left unexplored, may open up unbridgeable gaps, or where there is conflict that undermines the central unity of vision. The unifying vision needs to be distinguished from the structures of community. The latter *serve* the former and outgrow their usefulness at more or less regular intervals. If they have been canonized as the essence rather than the ancillary props of community, they will resist change.

> One aspect of history is perfectly clear: the religious group as a sociological entity, whether at provincial or local level, needs a structure if it is to function effectively in society. However, the structures must be fluid and flexible. In fact they must be seen to work toward their own destruction in the responsible, creative and loving interaction of free persons, open and alert to the voice of the Spirit, vowing primary allegiance to Jesus, their Lord.[6]

In the preservation of the seminal vision and the creative sustaining of ambiguity and respect for differences, the combined personal and communal gifts of poetry, prophecy and pragmatism are called for.

Poets

At the heart of pluralism is the commonality of basic human experience, love and pain, laughter and tears, strength and vulnerability, resilience and fragility, hope and fear. In a religious community where there are distinct and recognizable differences about how the spirit of the founder is to be culturally realized in the present and about the nature of communal living and religious life itself, there is nevertheless the common human experience of struggle to grow, to become, to seek meanings and to minister. The poets of the community "see into" this.

The gift of the poet is recognition given utterance. Poets

live with eyes and ears wide open to the nuances of life, sensitive to the almost imperceptible gentle breezes that signify movements of the human spirit. Perception impels them to give tongue, so urgent is it. Out of their own heightened awareness, they raise the consciousness of those who read or hear them.

What is the difference, then, between the way the poet sees and the way the rest of us see? I believe that there is a kind of penetration in the vision of the poet that many of us lack. Where I see a formless block of stone, the artist sees a sculpture. Where I see a person or object as a means to an end, the poet sees these as worthy of appreciation. Where I see usefulness, the poet sees value. The poet evokes rather than analyzes. Poetry is less a matter of logic, certainty or pedantry than it is a matter of metaphor, image and invitation to originality of vision. The claustrophobia of our tunnel vision of reality cries aloud for newness and release. Art, and here I am speaking specifically of the poetic art, is for just such release into newness.

In its various moods the utterance of the poet may gently illumine what we have hitherto seen only darkly, or it may in more trenchant moments strip us of illusions, cut away masks and pretensions and leave us naked to some aspect of reality. It is, as Tanner says in *Man and Superman*, the work of the artist to

> show us ourselves as we really are. Our minds are nothing but this knowledge of ourselves; and he who adds a jot to such knowledge creates new mind as surely as any woman creates new men.[7]

Poetry, of necessity, springs from contemplation. Over recent years, new emphasis on meditation, stillness and centering prayer in religious life has underscored the need to re-focus on contemplation. At its worst, this is a form of self-preoccupation that *closes* our eyes to meanings by shutting us into the walled world of our own needs. At its best, it is an opening up to a world of ever-renewing meanings out of which poetry and prayer are born. Poets are men and women who can see beyond themselves, aware of their own inner life and experience but capable of generalizing from it and empathizing.

Living in the midst of strenuous pluralism, the poet of the religious life experiences and reflects on the confusion and the needs, the pain and the invitation, the central values and the peripheral. He or she, perhaps unwittingly, challenges the theologians, psychologists and social scientists to think again in new

ways about the same realities. Never totally trammelled by institutional ways of seeing, the poet is a de-institutionalizer constantly offering fire to melt our frozen vision. Like the author of
Proverbs, the contemporary poet knows that "without a vision
the people perish" (Prv 11:14), and the knowledge impels the
poet to focus on some quality of life, struggling to find meanings in the events of the human journey.

Innocence characterizes the vision of the poet. In an address to Latin-American poets in Mexico City in 1964,[8] Thomas
Merton claimed that the poet cannot be a cunning person, for
his or her art depends on an innocence that would soon be destroyed by being in business or politics or even academia. Merton insists that the hope that rests on calculation has lost its innocence. Even the calculated use of the "magic of words" is
foreign to the poet, for it

> is the businessman, the propagandist, the politician, not the
> poet, who devoutly believes in the magic of words.
>
> For the poet there is precisely no magic. There is only life in
> all its unpredictability and all its freedom. All magic is a ruth-
> less venture in manipulation, a vicious circle, a self-fulfilling
> prophecy.[9]

Later, Merton adds that poetry is the flowering of ordinary possibilities and the fruit of ordinary and natural choice. Obedient
to life, the poet holds out to humanity "fruits of hope that have
never been seen before. With these fruits we shall calm the resentments and the rage of man."[10]

How, then, is the poet's influence felt in religious life?
Since the poet is one who is unencumbered with the competitiveness and manipulations of institutional living, he or she can
look without vested interest at life itself as it is lived there,
searching for a liberating vision. The poetic religious, then, is a
person deeply in touch with the original vision of the founder
and constantly engaged with the interplay between the charism
and the immediacies of life which the charism is to illuminate.
Thus the freedom of the poet is to remain outside the temporal
imprisonments of institutional living and to span past, present
and future, bringing the light of what is best in our history to
bear on our struggles in the present and pointing to the unknown future with hope.

The poet does not do this with the charismatic fervor and
challenge of the prophets, but rather through an invitation to
look beyond immediacies to deeper realities. So the call of the

poet, knowingly or not, is a call to silence in the face of reality, to contemplation:

> Let us be proud of the words that are given to us for nothing; not to teach anyone, not to confute anyone, not to prove anyone absurd, but to point beyond all objects into the silence where nothing can be said. . . .We are the ministers of silence that is needed to cure all victims of absurdity who lie dying of a contrived joy.[11]

Within the structures of religious life throughout the ages there has been an inveterate impulse toward fixity. Institutionalizing brings norms, expectations, definitions, ways of including and excluding, judgment and proclamation. The poet embraces the insecurity of living on the margin of this, affected by it deeply, but not caught in it. Where the institution has answers, the poet has appreciation of questions and paradoxes. So, when an individual or group in a religious congregation manifests loneliness or anger or rebellion, the institutional response is often to analyze and to come up with the swift answers: *They have brought this on themselves. If they were not so much in search of distraction and could live more simply, then this or that would not be happening.* The poet, on the other hand, registers the quality of the loneliness or anger, gives it color and imagery, brings it to attention more sharply than those who experience it can do. The poet seeks the meaning without yielding to the temptation to facile solutions. The poet is a person who loves,

> mad with secret therapeutic love which cannot be bought or sold, and which the politician fears more than violent revolution, for violence changes nothing. But love changes everything.[12]

The poet, being a person of discernment, recognizes falsehood and injustice and brings them to attention with the simplicity of an image or the scalpel of irony. No long-haired dreamers, poets do not float ethereally away from the realities of daily existence but respond to the call to novelty and movement and fluidity, challenging stagnation wherever they see it, sometimes with a simple, silent living of the innocent life in the midst of guile and manipulation, sometimes raising their voices to point to other realities. They are uncomfortable people to be with.

The poets in religious life, then, will call the rest to examine and reflect on the realities of the present in the light of past and future. They will challenge both premature progress and stagnant fixity. They will recognize from the depths of their appreciative vision the sinful instrumentalism that is part of most institutions, including the church. They may not label it as such, but they have the power to invite us to conscious awareness of it. Above all, the poet will present us with the good, where it is seen, responding sensitively to the manifold experience of a group of individuals attempting to live true to a vision that can easily be clouded, distorted or lost. Poets will not do this by exhortation or rhetoric, but by the double witness of an innocent life and the power of the word. Under the influence of the Word, they will be persons addicted to silence in which they struggle to interpret the word spoken in them. Aware of their own finitude and fallibility they will be people of deep self-doubts that call them to faith in the existence of a truth and a good greater than any human plan can devise. Beyond the temporality and limitations of any experienced reality, they will seek ultimate meaning, knowing that

> For most of us, there is only the unattended
> Moment, the moment in and out of time,
> The distraction fit, lost in a shaft of sunlight.
> The wild thyme unseen, or the winter lightning
> Or the waterfall, or music heard so deeply
> that it is not heard at all, but you are the music
> While the music lasts. These are only hints and guesses,
> Hints followed by guesses; and the rest
> Is prayer, observance, discipline, thought and action.
> The hint half guessed, the gift half understood, is
> Incarnation.[13]

Out of the silence and the spoken word of the poets is born the role of the prophets.

Prophets

> True prophecy is a dynamic movement which combines criticism of the oppressive present, graced remembrance of the past, and the liberating exhibition of alternative futures to convert potentially destructive energies into the saving waters of life.[14]

What the prophet does, then, is listen attentively to the overarching vision of the poet, appropriate it and out of it draw energy to criticize and re-orientate the community. The poet is a person with respect for the goodness of the past and a dream for the future. The prophet seizes these and brings them into dialogue with the domesticating influence of institutions and cultural moments in time. To do this is a more internally consistent and integrated process than merely espousing causes. It is not flag-bearing protest so much as a persistent call to a way of being in the world that is different from that of the dominant culture. Not every angry man or woman is prophetic. Not every social crusader is faithful to the wisdom of the past, nor does every attempt at social remediation lead *per se* to a better future.

Jeremiah, for example, railed against specific wickedness, but at the core of his prophetic message is a call beyond the ritual exactitude of the day to personal conversion of heart. Not only does he sharply name the transgressions and dishonesties of his day, but he calls to inner conversion, points to another way of being, promising that the outcome of this will be a happier, more honorable life in which "the nations will bless themselves by him, and glory in him" (Jer 4:2).

Jeremiah urges not merely a change of the immediate behaviors that prompt his criticism, but a return to the best of the tradition, a way of life in keeping with the original vision of a life related to Yahweh:

> "Stand at the crossroads and look,
> ask for the ancient paths:
> which was the good way? Take it
> and you will find rest for yourselves" (Jer 6:16).

Criticizing and energizing must go hand in hand, for criticism without energizing may be merely destructive and purposeless anger, while energizing without criticism may lead in inappropriate or false directions. Brueggemann[15] holds the opinion that criticism is a faculty common to liberals, while energizing is often a contribution of conservatives. Given the polarities that emerge in a pluralist religious life, with the recognizable categories of liberalism or radicalism at one pole and conservatism at the other, the prophets are needed to straddle the gap and keep the two gifts in communion with one another for the sake of preserving the clean lines of the vision and practical fidelity to it.

Far from being lonely and isolated figures on mountaintops, prophets in religious life are those who can sustain the dialectic between the poets' vision and their own ability to challenge their fellows to live within its ambit, energized by its promise for the future. When I speak, then, of the gifts of poetry, prophecy and pragmatism in a pluralist situation, I am clearly speaking of them as gifts that are in constant dialogue. The challenge, criticism and energizing of the prophets are a result of having glimpsed the vision made explicit by the poets, and of matching up the vision with what is happening in the present and how it may carry a community into a viable and lively future. It is the prophets of religious life who take the vision first enunciated by the founder and kept alive and contemporary by the poets, and challenge present fidelity to it in ways that ensure that religious life remains a radical reality within the church, refusing to have its teeth drawn and its energy for living on the cutting edge of the church tamed or anesthetized.

It is a sociological fact of life that institutions experience a subtle shift of goals over time. While still stating goals in the original terms, they experience goal-displacement; what is actually happening is different from what is said to be happening. The vision then runs the risk of being only a nominal vision, while daily life bears witness to something other than the primitive commitment. For example, many religious orders originally founded to serve the poor and the damaged have gradually shifted over time to a fairly comfortable involvement with middle-class needs. At times this is defended casuistically by redefining poverty or pointing to the very real fact that the poverty with which the founder was concerned no longer exists. The poet reasserts the original vision in the context of the present and the prophet challenges the community to reform its fidelity to the vision in ways that continue to make it an alternative community. I venture to say that the goal-displacement that inevitably happens over time in religious life is always in the direction of tameness and safety and institutionalizing of the vision. It is the task of the prophet to recognize and criticize what is false in such displacement and to hold up the promise of a future dignified by a return to the radicalness of the vision (charism) in the shifting circumstances of the present. It is the prophet's task to seek new ways of living out that vision so as to leaven the environment with counter-cultural witness. The call of the prophet is always to insecurity and to a way of being that is larger than the present mode of being.

Precisely because the prophet is entrusted with the reversal of a state of affairs characterized by static triumphalism and its partner, the politics of oppression and injustice, he or she is genuinely responsive to the word spoken in scriptural revelation and in continuing experience. When one examines the lives of the Old Testament prophets, it is always "Yahweh who speaks," and this Yahweh is a God who sets his people free. Aware of being endowed with God's freedom, the prophet, often reluctantly, seeks out those areas of human experience where lack of freedom spawns exploitation, manipulation and injustice, naming them and calling for social action to overturn them. The prophet, then, is not merely an articulate social reformer. Neither is he or she solely a person who cares about God deeply and fervently. Rather, the prophet is one who is aware of an immanent God at the heart of all human experience. The theology preached by the prophet necessarily issues in social action characterized by compassion, justice and respect for the varieties of human experience.

This came home to me sharply on a recent occasion when I was asked to present my thoughts on the scripture readings during the liturgy. The reading was from Jeremiah, chapter 7, in which Jeremiah is instructed by Yahweh to stand at the gate of the temple and deliver the following biting message:

> Yahweh Sabaoth, the God of Israel, says this: Amend your behavior and your actions and I will let you stay in this place. Do not put your trust in delusive words, such as: This is Yahweh's sanctuary, Yahweh's sanctuary, Yahweh's sanctuary! But if you really amend your behavior and your actions, if you really treat one another fairly, if you do not exploit the stranger, the orphan and the widow, if you do not shed innocent blood in this place, and if you do not follow other gods, to your own ruin, then I shall let you stay in this place, in the country I gave for ever to your ancestors of old (Jer 7:3-7).

The presence of this God is conjoined with honest social justice. The prophet warns against empty worship that acknowledges the sanctuary of the Lord but has no overflow into mercy and compassion. The sanctuary of the Lord is no comfortable enclave for those who seek safety while oppressing and destroying others. The message is clear. Worship that is unaccompanied by freeing social action is empty and false. Conversely, it may also be claimed that social action unconnected with worship has no nourishment other than human courage and altruism.

Musing about the reading, I was also struck by the incredible transformation of Jeremiah from the whimpering and reluctant individual of Jeremiah 1 to the man of courageous and dangerous challenge in chapter 7. How did he get to be so different? The answer is there in the story of his call. "Do not say, I am only a child. . . . There! I have put my words into your mouth" (Jer 1:7-9). A consciousness of speaking the word of

Yahweh frees this shaky little man to grow into a prophetic giant. Always the challenges are preceded by "Yahweh says this"
or "the word of Yahweh was addressed to me saying . . . ," typical presages of prophetic utterance. Clearly Yahweh did not dictate the words to be said in the way that I might dictate a letter
to my secretary. The prophetic gift is a gift for discernment. The
discernment comes from being attuned to the word, the word
of Yahweh, spoken through the deep, half-remembered history
of a people and a culture, a transforming word that makes a
prophet out of a stammerer, the word of the God who lives at
the heart of a present unfolding experience. So the prophetic
religious is one who is constantly re-attuning to the message of
history, the core vision of a congregation and of religious life as
dangerous memory, to the word of scripture and the word being revealed in the present history-in-the-making of everyday
experience. He or she feeds on the word:

> When your words came I devoured them:
> your word was my delight
> and the joy of my heart;
> for I was called by your Name,
> Yahweh, God Sabaoth (Jer 15:16).

There is a shadow side of the call to prophetic witness. It
brings the burden of loneliness and pain. Though deeply committed to the relational life of the community, the prophet nevertheless stands apart, experiencing the paradox of engagement
and objectivity. Prophetic indignation brings upon the prophet
the ire and resentment of smaller individuals unwilling to bear
the full light of prophetic truth and challenge. This puzzles and
hurts:

> I never sat in the company of scoffers amusing myself;
> with your hands on me I held myself aloof,
> since you had filled me with indignation.
> Why is my suffering continual,
> my wound incurable, refusing to be healed? (Jer 15:17-18).

The answer to Jeremiah's plaintive question lies in the word
compassion. The prophet is not one who speaks merely with
the voice. The life and action of the prophet bespeak an identification with the marginal and oppressed. Their loneliness and
pain become the loneliness and pain of the prophet, from
which there is no escape. No wonder, then, that the prophets,
both of our deep story and of our present circumstances, are

stoned and rejected. Their very presence suggests newness and challenge to conversion.

In the pluralist situation within religious life these days, the authentic prophets (that is, those who genuinely combine criticism with hopeful energizing, as distinct from those who merely shout angrily) call the community to see the potential dangers of denying the differences in ways that may lead to polarization. Thus they challenge to unity amid diversity as distinct from mere tolerance of individualism. They insist on the centrality of the uniting charism as a binding reality. They also point out the richness of harnessing a variety of gifts and outlooks in a concerted witness to an alternative vision.

At the same time, prophets are aware of potential hazards, warning of the dangers of setting up enclaves that compete against one another and being critical of those areas of communal living that are beginning to "catch" the dominant consciousness and ignore those who are marginal. They are protective of every person's belonging and sensitive to movements toward exclusion. They goad people out of the tendency to settle, to lose the pilgrim spirit, to institutionalize works and to carve out safe niches, to fashion modern golden calves and lose sight of the journey.

The prophets of religious life, whether they are formal or informal leaders, are acutely aware of the tendency to choose safety over life, and thus they themselves are often to be found in the brave vanguard that challenges the church itself to move off comfortable middle ground to those places where the Word must most urgently be proclaimed. At the same time they needle individuals and groups and whole religious congregations away from the tendency to be self-preoccupied at the expense of ministry.

Acutely aware of the temptation to settle into a having mode of existence rather than a being-in-relationship mode which counters the dominant materialistic consciousness, the prophets are loud in their call to poverty. This is less a moralistic and judgmental outcry or a pedantic defining of what religious may and may not possess than a constant re-focusing on what is central to individual and corporate witness and what is counter-witness.

It is possible to go on and on adding to this list. The prophetically conscious members of every community will do just that in their own peculiar situations, seeing also that prophetic awareness is not limited to religious life, but flourishes in other places as well.

The gift of prophetic consciousness is not one that removes the recipient of it to a separate and distinct role or requires a kind of part-time engagement with it. It is pervasive and finds a channel of expression within whatever ministry a person exercises. It demands and invites insightful and planned action and therefore calls upon the gifts of pragmatists to translate the challenge and energy of prophecy into the immediate context of the systems within which it is uttered. Pragmatists are important shapers of a life that responds to vision and challenge.

Pragmatists

Pragmatism is often heard as a dirty word. Understood only in terms of instrumental action, it is interpreted as using people, riding over them, gratifying immediate needs and whims at the expense of deeper values. *The Concise Oxford Dictionary* defines *pragmatic* as "meddlesome" and *pragmatism* as "officiousness, pedantry or matter-of-fact treatment of things." Philosophically, pragmatism is a doctrine that estimates any assertion solely by its practical bearing upon human interests.

This is all, however, a very truncated understanding. The word has its origin in the Greek *pragmatikos*, which means "active" or "versed in state affairs." It has been variously interpreted as meaning "emphasizing practical values" and "concerned with practical consequences or values." With these meanings in mind, I take up the word here and re-define it as "practical planning capacity to translate into organized action the vision of the poets and the challenge of the prophets." Thus I am suggesting that the pragmatic people in any community can best use their gifts by being open to receive the deeply empathic insights of the poets and the grief-filled challenges of the prophets, and to give them shape in planned action. They cannot, therefore, be insensitive or selfish. Rather, the kind of pragmatism I am speaking of is a way of being that involves humble receptivity, an appropriation of the empathy modelled by the poets and prophets and the delicate melding of their empathy and the skill of initiating and planning change. To do this, they have to be humble and cooperative. They can never operate independently of the poets and prophets. Always, their programs of action must be tested against the vision and the compassion of their partners.

The kind of pragmatism I speak of is a *unifying* gift. Perhaps I can illustrate this with an example. I have been working

with a group of religious women who are painfully beginning to
see that they have overinstitutionalized their founding vision,
and that this has led them to become static and even irrelevant
in their locality. They run efficient schools. They live a highly
organized and regular religious life. But their average age is increasing. They are uneasy at the rate of attrition, especially from
the ranks of the younger and more articulate and talented group
in their 30s and early 40s. The members of this group who remain are uncertain and edgy about their continuance and the
shape of their future. Burnout is high, and is spoken of as a new
phenomenon among them. At chapters and gatherings of the
whole group, fears are sometimes hinted at of a new polarization emerging, no longer about aspects of community life,
dress, relational freedom and social behavior, but about ministry
and the ways their ministry currently models or fails to model
the founding charism. There are poetic individuals with insight
into the pain and the possibility of the situation. They are able
to empathize with the disorientation of many and to hail the
need for a return to the pristine vision of the early days. There
are prophetic individuals who in word and deed model a freedom and social awareness that challenges the group to an
awareness of how entrenched they have become.

Over time there has developed an uneasy recognition that
some kind of change is necessary, but as one sister said:

> "I'm trained to be a teacher and nothing else, and every
> year I'm appointed to a school and I accept the appoint-
> ment meekly. When we come to these meeting days, I hear
> people putting my awareness into words, but I don't really
> feel much better—less alone, maybe, but not much better—
> and I don't think I will feel much better until somebody can
> point out some directions for us, and until leaders can make
> it possible for us to move out more."

This statement accurately describes the process taking
place. A general but not universal malaise is present. Some individuals with poetic empathy are beginning to be articulate
about the pain of the malaise and even to trace its origin. Others
with the gift of prophetic criticism and hope for the future are
challenging to change. What appears to be lacking is a pragmatic approach to how and in what direction change should be
planned.

One hopeful movement is happening, however. One member of the group has taken the initiative to study social work

and to research areas of poverty in the local area. She has discovered a poverty-stricken region with almost total neglect from the church and has sought the permission and commission of the group to set up a small communal group there, living in housing similar to that occupied by most of the region's inhabitants and engaging in ministry to them in organized but non-institutionalized ways. She has done her homework with admirable thoroughness, consulting with members of other church groups and with social welfare and health and education agencies, seeking a shape for mutual cooperation in serving the people of the district. Having amassed demographic and housing details together with estimates of probable developments in the area over the next decade, she has turned her attention to the role of a religious community there. Listing the various ways in which such a community might offer credible witness to gospel and communal values there, she adds an interesting claim:

> "We have no vested interest and hence are able to act as mediators within the wider community: between political parties and community groups; between public housing tenants and private home dwellers; between families 'at war' in our street."

Here she is describing an appreciative rather than an instrumental approach to the task. She proceeds to speak of the ministry of genuine presence that she and a group of sisters might offer, but she is quite articulate also about what might be received by being part of such a venture. By receiving, she does not envisage reward or favor but refers simply to what the poor have to offer to those who are willing to be receptive and equal.

This sister is a pragmatist capable of taking uncoordinated insights and challenges and building them into a practicable program of action. Far from the original definition of pragmatism as meddlesome or interfering, her pragmatism is a direct outgrowth of the poetic and prophetic movements of others within the congregation. She is modelling a way of acting that moves away from an institutional apostolate in the direction of greater freedom, and probably also greater responsibility since the accountability her group of co-workers will exercise will be greater than that of colleagues working within the more predictable limits of institutional roles. It is interesting to note also the intrinsic connection that exists here between the founding vision and the gathering together of a group for ministry. It may perhaps be claimed that the needs that clamor for such a ministry, and the contemplation and organizing of the ministry itself, are the impetus to re-grasp the vision of the founder in the present.

Pragmatists within the community or congregation are persons who are willing to take risks and think outside the usual parameters. Most of us are unaware of just how deeply we are influenced by the system and sub-culture we live in. Pragmatists are often men and women with enough ingenuity and originality to recognize the limits of an old language of religious life and of structures that are the lived reflection of that language. They are capable of a freshness that at once respects the past and leaps off from it in new and creative and life-stimulating directions.

Far from living up to common misapprehensions that they are insensitive and manipulative, pragmatists who are seized by the vision of the poets and impelled by the energy of the prophets are men and women who can see patterns and produce programs not in a merely businesslike way (although they are certainly efficient), but in a manner that is deeply respectful, careful, and creatively in touch with the insights of their companion leaders. Nevertheless, they do have the toughness to see their programs implemented, to model them and to be accountable for success or failure. They are people who respect and understand the working of organizations. They are students of innovative leadership. They value and use models of systems creatively and responsibly, and at the same time they retain enough sensitivity to individuals and local communities to empathize with the pain of changing and of letting go.

If the programs and planning of the pragmatists are to be effective, there has to be an ability to work with mutuality alongside the more visionary members of the congregation, constantly checking programs for innovation, preservation and change against the major thrust of the vision which is itself always to be authenticated against the original gospel insights of the founder. For many pragmatists the greatest personal costs are in remaining patient with the abstractions of the vision and in seeing their particular contribution as part of a team effort, especially when their inner urge is to go ahead and launch into action unimpeded by the questions and reflections of poets and prophets. Thus, pragmatists are men and women of asceticism.

One implication of such collaborative and integrated action is the necessity that pragmatists be people who are just as deeply listening as their counterparts. Unless they have genuinely tuned in to the very heart of the vision and challenge, the actions that they plan may become ends in themselves. Listening that flows into the seminal spirituality of empathy will eliminate competitiveness and protect the integrity and cohesiveness of joint leadership.

Part of the genuineness of integrally collaborative leadership by the pragmatists is that sometimes they will perceive the necessity to relinquish a part of their plan, or at least to modify programs in the light of consultation with the poets and prophets. Mutual trust will require constant communication and respect for division of labor and talents. Energy will be seen to flow back and forth among leaders in ways that enable, encourage and create.

In many ways pragmatists are bridges. They sustain a clear-sighted view of goals and ways to reach and implement them. At the same time, however, they constantly bear in mind the needs and wants of those who are involved in such implementation, while simultaneously keeping their unclouded gaze on the charism of the congregation. They are men and women who invite members of their institutes to live out of the charism, and who insert the practical life-shape of the lived charism into the daily life of their communities. Pragmatists live in the now. They are concerned with the appropriation into the present lived moment of a charism born in the past. They also look to the future, seeking ways of projecting the inspiration that called their group into being into a world that, at that past moment, did not exist. Thus they are students of trends and projections as well as of present needs and poverty.

Imbued with a sense of service, and recognizing that their gifts are for the service of the charism and of the group to which they belong, pragmatists are people of humility. They show themselves constantly willing to submit their plans to the collective scrutiny of the poets and prophets and also of all whom they serve. They are not weak, however, and resist the impulse to be blackmailed by other people's fear or anxiety. Sometimes they will insist on small trial implementations of their programs in the knowledge that merely describing and talking are inadequate to convince many who might, however, be led to see the value of their plans if they are permitted to watch them take shape in action.

To be a pragmatist, then, calls for enormous strength. It means being able to handle paradox and contradiction. It means being clear and logical as well as sensitive and empathetic. It means being respectful and understanding as well as tough and determined. It means being cooperative as well as independent, practical as well as idealistic. It means being able to recognize the cross planted firmly and inevitably at the heart of the gift.

Since the pragmatists will often be persons who take the risk of being on the cutting edge of action, on the fringes with the fringe-dwellers and unorthodox in the eyes of those who cannot operate outside the safety of institutional works, they must be people who can handle intimacy and loneliness, building support groups for themselves to give them stimulus and energy. They also will be contemplators of the word. In particular, they will be persons and groups for whom the Matthean assurance looms large:

> "For I was hungry and you gave me food, I was thirsty and you gave me drink, I was a stranger and you made me welcome, lacking clothes and you clothed me, sick and you visited me, in prison and you came to see me. . . . In truth I tell you, insofar as you did this to one of the least of these brothers of mine, you did it to me" (Mt 25:35-36,40).

All those who prize religious life and take responsibility for it are concerned with molding the present and future chapters of a story whose roots are in the gospel and more recently in a particular founding insight into the gospel, a story which is, however, still unfinished and in the process of continuing to be written. In a particular way, those with poetic, prophetic and pragmatic gifts, no matter how small or how local, are also charged with the unenviable task of correcting course, of criticizing past and present deviations from the direction in which that story seems called to journey. Aware that every exodus, like the first, is toward freedom, they are men and women who constantly seek to loose bonds and to follow the God who promises life. They constantly reflect on the various levels of meaning present in the corporate story and are aware of the variety of individual stories woven into the collective fabric of the group's story.

Story

Again and again in the discussions in this book I take up the notion of story to describe our experience of ourselves and our world. At this time in religious life we are faced with a new exploration of community and of the interaction between our community and the world. We are forced by new developments in our story itself to do this. Events such as the recognition of the centrality of the laity within the church, or of the place of women in unfolding history, of the decline of many religious orders and the emergence of pluralism in theology and the very self-understanding of the church, all contribute to the challenge to ask again and again, "What kind of story are we in?"

There is no single answer. Stories have layers. There are individual stories and there are communal stories. There are stories of what is happening right now or of what has happened within our remembered history. There are stories shrouded so deeply in the mystery of the past that only images, distant music or echoes, can be recalled. We somehow recognize that these stories have shaped us and become so much a part of the fiber of who we are that they lie buried in our collective unconscious, intimations of immortality that we hint at from time to time as we sit around our campfires staring into the leaping flames and weaving tales of our origins. These stories are present to us in folklore and poetry, in ritual, music, symbol and faith.

In "The Narrative Quality of Experience," Stephen Crites distinguishes between the "mundane" level of our story and the "sacred" level. Each of us lives and grows and struggles in a world of relationships, events and objects. I grew up in a particular family and a particular place, and I inherited many of my family's ways of understanding reality. I was educated in a particular way and place, and absorbed understandings that have consciously and unconsciously shaped my experience of who I am and of who others are. Many of the characters in this mundane story are no longer alive or proximate geographically. They have, however, a presence that is tangible in its effects in both simple and complex ways. I had the privilege recently of being near my father as he remembered parts of our mundane story that had till then been lost to me. I had taken him back to the place where he was born and to which he had not returned for at least 70 years. The almost unchanged little hamlet was a shrine of stories for him, and as we passed the old flour mill, the church on the hill, the village school, the park and other familiar landmarks, characters emerged from the past: Aunty Sarah driving a pony-trap for miles to visit; Uncle Jack who owned the inn; other people who in indirect ways have shaped the way that my father and his children see their world.

This mundane story is not all in the past. It is still in the process of creation. New events unfolding their meaning or being explored in search of their meaning, new relationships, new loving, new conflict, new ideas and knowledge—all of these are shaping and reshaping the story to which I put my signature.[16]

Constantly acquiring new characters and new chapters, these stories are also the very stuff of mutuality which begins in the respectful sharing of stories and deepens into the transforming of one another's stories by challenge and most of all by the creativity of love.

When individuals bring their mundane stories into religious life, the diversity of stories is challenged to become a shared communal story. Because our stories represent different and unique experiences of the world, when the stories are gathered together pluralism inevitably exists. This has always been so, but it is more noticeable now when the stories of those joining religious life are much more markedly different. The qualitative difference between the stories is greater, and thus we become more sharply aware of the gaps in our understandings of reality and of the need to find commonalities and to establish mutuality. Of all the ages of religious life, perhaps this is the one in which the sharing of stories is most important. Of all the ages of religious life, perhaps this is also the one in which recovery of our contact with the uniting story of the founder's vision offers possibility of bonding the divergent stories into a single communal story.

There is another layer of our story, however, that is more difficult to tell. Crites refers to this as the "sacred" story. He claims that these stories are anonymous and communal and "lie too deep in the consciousness of a people to be directly told: they form consciousness rather than being among the objects of which it is directly aware."[17] We testify to these stories rather than tell them, their resonances echoing through our songs, stories and actions.[18]

In this book I am concerned with both the sacred and mundane stories. The resonances of faith from the deep Christian story lie at the heart of religious life with its local and church-wide history. The embeddedness of the founder's life within the context of this sacred story conceived the particular gospel emphasis that finally gave birth to a particular religious congregation in a particular place and time. As that religious group struggles with its evolving story in new times and new places, surrounded by new needs and new challenges, it struggles to hold its unfolding contemporary experience against the story of its beginnings in ways that allow creative novelty and adaptation. In order to do this the founding story has to be constantly revisited and retold in ways that continue to sustain, illumine and germinate meanings. In the return to where we began we find new knowing:

> With the drawing of this Love and the voice of this Calling
> We shall not cease from exploration
> And the end of all our exploring
> Will be to arrive where we started
> And know the place for the first time.[19]

For community consideration

A. Who are the visible poets, prophets and pragmatists of your order and how do they affect you?

B. What is the vision that unites you?

C. In what particular areas of the life of the order are prophets called for right now? Why?

D. Prepare together a list of questions and issues relating to the communal and ministerial life of your order that you would like to present to the poets and prophets and pragmatists as a mandate.

For individual consideration

A. What are your strengths for leadership? Into which grouping (poetic, prophetic, pragmatic) do they fall primarily? How do you use them in practice? Check out your perception of yourself with someone who knows you well.

B. What parts of your early story, or your formation story, do you still need to be reconciled with?

C. In what ways did the communal story of the order influence you to join it? In what ways do you perceive the passion of its early days still alive in the present?

Notes

1. William Burrows, *New Ministries: The Global Context* (Melbourne: Dove Communications, 1980), p. xiv.

2. Peter L. Berger, *The Heretical Imperative: Contemporary Possibilities of Religious Affirmation* (Garden City, NY: Anchor Books, 1980), p.24.

3. John Naisbitt, *Megatrends: Ten New Directions Transforming Our Lives* (New York: Warner, 1982).

4. Alvin Toffler, *Future Shock* (London: Pan Books, 1970), p. 51.

5. Burrows, op.cit., p.ix et passim.

6. Diarmuid O. Murchu, *The Seed Must Die . . . Religious Life: Survival or Extinction?* (Dublin: Veritas Publications, 1980), p. 108.

7. George Bernard Shaw, *Man and Superman* (Harmondsworth, Middlesex: Penguin, 1903), p. 62.

8. Thomas Merton, *Raids on the Unspeakable* (New York: New Directions, 1966), pp. 155-161.

9. Ibid. p. 159.

10. Ibid. p. 160.

11. Ibid. p. 160.

12. Ibid. p. 160.

13. T. S. Eliot, "Dry Salvages," *Four Quartets* (London: Faber, 1959), p.44.

14. Thomas E. Clarke, "A New Way of Reflecting on Experience," James E. Hug (ed.), *Tracing the Spirit: Communities, Social Action and Theological Reflection* (New York: Paulist, 1983), p. 25.

15. Walter Brueggemann, *The Prophetic Imagination* (Philadelphia: Fortress Press, 1978), p. 13.

16. Gary Jarvis re-names "mundane" stories as "signed personal histories" in his thesis, "The Affective and Social Nature of Biblical Faith" (Collegeville, Minnesota: St. John's University, 1983). The renaming is significant in that it underscores the greater control and conscious ownership we have over the shaping of our personal stories, as distinct from the inherited deep story.

17. Stephen Crites, "The Narrative Quality of Experience," *Journal of the American Academy of Religion*, 39 (1971), p. 295.

18. Ibid. p. 311.

19. Eliot, op. cit. p. 59.

2
COMMUNITY:

One Story Uniting Many Stories

Community is the process of becoming united through the common experience of a core vision. It is the leap of the human spirit in response to the impetus and inspiration of a shared story, a merging of individual stories without losing them, a way of seeing the world, a way of being in the world. When I feel myself drowning in the syrupy ocean of words often used to describe the reality of religious community, I yearn for the pure, clear water of a scripture text that embodies the central vision, and I return again and again to read:

> So if in Christ there is anything that will move you, any incentive in love, any fellowship in the Spirit, any warmth or sympathy—I appeal to you, make my joy complete by being of a single mind, one in love, one in heart and one in mind. Nothing is to be done out of jealousy or vanity; instead, out of humility of mind everyone should give preference to others, everyone pursuing not selfish interests but those of others. Make your own the mind of Christ Jesus (Phil 2:1-5).

The heart of the story is the mind of Christ recognized by the founder and still being communicated, discovered and created within the experience of the community. It is process, spirit, developing life, life meeting new and original moments for which there are no ready-made answers or responses. It is ongoing creation. The mind of Christ, then, is the enkindling experience.[1] The heat thrown off from it will be felt in the unity of central convictions, the tenderness and sympatico of the community's life together, a stance of appreciative awareness before the mystery of each other's reality, and a common purpose or impulse to action stimulated by the core vision. Because we are in the middle of our story, and not at its beginning or end, we are constantly breaking new ground, bringing to bear on contemporary needs and invitations to ministry our inherited understanding and experience of the founder's vision and the plurality of our insights, talents and social consciousness.

Stories exist within stories, and stories spawn stories. Founders of religious orders were men and women fascinated by the person of Jesus Christ and the implications of his life, not just as a historical event in the world's past, but as a dynamic reality penetrating and subsuming the present, challenging to both mysticism and social action. The enormous range and depth of the Christ-story were dealt with by focus on particular aspects of it evoked by the milieu in which the founders lived. They saw areas of human life where there was a crying need for the Christ-story to be told. They went into the dark places of human existence, poverty, ignorance, illness, degradation and misery, telling the story in words of proclamation and deeds of compassion. The founders were men and women who operated habitually out of the "strenuous mood."

> The capacity for the strenuous mood probably lies slumbering in every man, but it has more difficulty in some than in others in waking up. It needs the wilder passions to arouse it, the big fears, loves and indignations; or else the deeply penetrating appeal of some one of the higher fidelities, like justice, truth or freedom.[2]

For the founders, the strenuous mood arose from their faithful contemplation of the gospel and their sensitivity to their own social milieu. Thus their following of Christ had both a mystical and a political element. It began in a contemplative vision and overflowed into the expression of love enjoined by the gospel:

> "For I was hungry and you gave me food, I was thirsty and you gave me drink, I was a stranger and you made me welcome, lacking clothes and you clothed me, sick and you visited me, in prison and you came to see me" (Mt 25:35-36).

There was a necessary connection between the vision and its enactment that is akin to Meister Eckhart's description of life itself as a kind of boiling over, a welling-up from inner depths and overflowing into something external as well. The wilder passions generate social energy.

Community means participating in this. It means sharing the contagion, catching the strenuous mood, burning with the same fire. It means standing within the same story and looking at life from there—sharing, catching, burning, standing, looking. Community is *process*, not *thing*. It is being caught up in a movement rather than creating a social structure. Its emphasis is not on ourselves but on the original vision and on being catapulted outward by that vision.

A lot of language used to describe and write about community leaves me cold. Frankly, I am irritated by the emphasis on "caring and sharing," not because these realities are repugnant but because their interpretation is repugnant. Too often they are presented as weak and sentimental "warm fuzzies" for the gratification of members, for safety and security. I do not believe Christianity is a safe religion, and I do not believe that religious life is a kind of enclave or refuge for the weak and needy, though all of us who embrace the call of the gospel and the charismatic vision of a particular founder readily admit to weakness and need.

I firmly believe that embracing the founding vision means being in unity in a world torn by disunity. There is powerful witnessing in this. Understandably, over the recent past there has been a preoccupation with the quality of relationships among community members, a reaction to previous emphasis on work at the expense of and to the detriment of the communal vision. Unfortunately reaction sometimes freezes into partial vision, and people forget what they are reacting against, and that it was not all bad! One extreme reaction is to put the entire emphasis on *being* in community and to neglect *action* which is the energized response to the seminal vision. What results is something characterized by pious, ecclesiastical, institutional navel-gazing! Vanier's warning that we are called together just as we are is timely. He goes on to say:

> If we are always looking for our own equilibrium, I'd even say if we are looking too much for our own peace, we will never find it, because peace is the fruit of love and service to others.[3]

With all our diversity, with disagreements about the how, where and when of our lives, we are nevertheless held together by the *why*.

> May they all be one,
> just as, Father, you are in me and I am in you,
> so that they also may be in us
> so that the world may believe it was you who sent me
>   (Jn 17:21).

At the heart of every founder's vision is a call to energetic, tough and unifying love that is a personal appropriation of the central dynamic of the life of Jesus, namely, the communion between him and the God he called Father.

It is clear, then, that the quality of the relationships existing among us is a powerful witness to the unifying and bonding created by embracing the central vision. I do not believe that those relationships exist merely for our satisfaction, but that they have an intrinsic connection with mission. It is quite possible to build a closely bonded group with heavy emphasis on loving and mutually satisfying relationships, and at the same time to witness to a corporate loneliness that forces us to huddle together in the dark for comfort. If this is the case, it is interesting to conjecture what it is we witness to, perhaps to lonely spinsterhood or bachelordom or even to the fear of marriage.

If indeed community is fuelled by the charism of the founder, if it resides in the experience of a common way of looking at reality, we do not create it but are called into it. We are held by it in dynamic unity even though we differ radically on many other things and must constantly work at the preservation of our central unity and the resolution of conflicts arising from our personal, historical, social, psychological and intellectual differences.

> One of the most critical witnesses the world looks for from religious life today is evidence of people who do not hide in enclaves of natural similarity but who can find in our many differences a graced unity of love focused in a shared vision.[4]

We do not build community. Community is. But we do build structures that nurture our attention to the vision, and we seek ways of protecting the values inherent in the vision, of keeping them alive and central. It is a mistake to confuse the essence of community with the structures that sustain it. Structures may change, adapt, develop, outgrow their usefulness and relevance and be replaced. The vision will remain, finding new challenges to meet, more dark places to illumine, new stories in which to express itself.

One of the movements among religious congregations who take their revitalization seriously is to seek new insights into the charism of their founder in order to discern new directions for themselves that are faithful to the deep story in which they are communally grounded. I deliberately make the connection between the charism and the search for directions, for it is simply a historical exercise to romanticize about the charism of the founders unless this is seen to have a direct impetus for our present life together and its overflow in ministry. Pleasant nostalgia about our past and its heroic beginnings is a far cry from the vocation to be a "kind of shock therapy instituted by the Holy Spirit for the Church as a whole."[5] But it is very easy, having institutionalized a form of ministry, to become so safe and comfortable in it that religious life itself loses its cutting edge and its loud proclamation of the radicality of the gospel fades to a whisper.

Johannes Metz asks a number of questions that challenge us to examine the vitality of the founding charism among us: Do we know where the "marginati" are, the fringe-dwellers whose plight demands on our part hunger and thirst after justice? Where are the lost hints and traces of religion that require reinforcing and fanning to flame? Do we even know? Are we brave enough today to take the raw and unpopular initiatives of our founders in new situations? Are we loyal enough sons and daughters of the church to be critical of its sinfulness and to recognize its poverty and the areas in which religious life might recall it to fidelity? Are we so comfortably ensconced within our own territory that we are satisfied with what is instead of being constantly uneasy about what-is-not-yet-and-should-be? Metz challenges religious life to exercise a shock effect in the church, to offer prophetic criticism, to avoid creeping passivity, bourgeois prosperity and dubious provincialism. He deplores the "levelling down of the religious orders to conform with the institutional church," the conformity that allows us to be the uncomplaining (or inactively complaining!) tools of dioceses which take advantage of our economic dependence to employ us as unsalaried functionaries. Perhaps his most challenging question is:

> Where in our world is there really to be found today what in my view is the necessary and fruitful tension (indeed the living antagonism) between the religious orders and the institutional Church? Where are the tensions that marked the early history of most religious orders, to name but two examples, in the cases of Francis of Assisi and Ignatius of Loyola?
>
> Have not the religious orders moved too far into that middle ground where everything is nicely balanced and moderate; so to speak adapted to and tamed by the institutional Church?[6]

I read such a challenge as a timely invitation to take up again each order's connection with the spirit of the founder, a cross-carrying spirit that sees a huge mission entrusted to the community and a parallel recognition that we are not able to fulfil it adequately because it is no less than communicating the transforming power of Christ. The paradox of the cross is planted squarely in the personal and corporate experience of inadequacy and helplessness, and the shocking reassurance of the gospel:

> "In all truth I tell you,
> whoever believes in me
> will perform the same works as I do myself,
> and will perform *even greater works,*
> because I am going to the Father" (Jn 14:12, emphasis added).

What are the ways in which we hang on to our bourgeois comfort and middle-ground respectability? I suggest that when we confuse the essential, binding vision that constitutes community with the structures meant to nourish it, we may canonize the structures at the expense of our connectedness with the vision. We may do this in a number of ways.

1) It happens occasionally that community is regarded as a spatial entity rather than as a process of increasing union in a common story. Let me illustrate:

Recently a member of a community whose thrust is predominantly educational sought permission to take up a post as secretary of an institute that performs educational work in parishes and dioceses and religious communities. She laid out for her superiors the nature of the group she would be joining and the "fit" between the community's outreach into ignorance and poverty and the nature of the work she would be taking on. Her talents were appropriate to the proposed work, and she saw herself as very clearly impelled by the general thrust of her community. The superior's first question was: "But, sister, what will you do *when you come back to the community?*" Clearly the questioner saw the work, which would take the sister to another city, as a form of departure from the community.

Partly, at least, there is a semantic problem here. The word *community* is commonly used to denote a group of people. I am insisting that it is *not* the group of people but the fiery vision that unites them, the quality of their bondedness, that is the essence of community. In the example just given, the petitioner cannot take the people with her, at least physically, but she certainly can take with her the union of vision and commitment that forges the essential bonds of community.

Such unity and connectedness require nourishment and a form of in-touch-ness that permanent geographical absence and lack of contact may make difficult. I once asked a religious friend how he kept alive his consciousness of brotherhood with his confrères while he was living alone at some distance from them. He replied that he had a network of relationships with members of his province, and that they were constantly in communication with one another, sometimes for simple exchange of friendly chat, at other times to share somewhat more deeply their common concerns and beliefs and values. He expressed the conviction that if those contacts kept the vision alive, he could continue to live fruitfully where he was, extending the sense of connectedness to those others with whom daily life brought him into contact. As an observer, I was awed at how thoroughly he did this. He gathered a small but ever-enlarging group from his neighborhood and from his academic colleagues, and in their frequent meetings I recognized the "catching" of his view of life, the challenging of it, the mutual give-and-take of insight, inspiration and discovery, the sharing of meanings, the melding of stories. Far from having left the community, he was living out of the very heart of it in a way that spread the contagion!

If we are too insistent on geographical togetherness we shall pass up opportunities for a leavening ministry that cannot be contained by city limits or monastery walls. If we can let go of the physical nearness and take the risk of loneliness and personal and individual responsibility for our lives as carriers-of-community, we may indeed have found a way of being true to the pioneering spirit of the founding charism. We shall also be faced with the challenge of finding ways of being in contact with one another and of creating new ways of celebrating our relatedness in community.

2) Related to the geographical definition of community is the tension between fixity and mobility. The gospel view of discipleship frequently mentions a kind of nomadic detachment. The disciple is one who travels from one place to another, accepted in some, rejected in others, carrying neither purse, nor scrip, nor shoes, constantly in exodus, because the Word is to be taken to the ends of the earth.

In contrast to this image is the history of most congregations, which have especially at those rich times of vocational abundance accumulated land, buildings, and perhaps a monopoly in a particular district of an apostolate such as teaching or nursing. But if we are constantly seizing opportunities to move to the cutting edge of the church, to be where the call for justice is loudest, we will be a pilgrim people, never allowing ourselves to "build here three tents." The vision that inspires us is not enshrined in a place, a mountaintop, but in ourselves as we struggle to give it new shape and visibility in a shifting market place. Leaving our boats behind is not something we do once when we join a particular congregation. It is a daily event if we are faithful both to our original story and to the call of our current story of involvement. We are community-carriers.

3) Another way of staying carefully and safely on middle ground is to deal with pluralism within and without by adopting a single way of looking at reality. The past has a way of get-

ting a stranglehold on the present by preventing us from engaging in propositional thinking. We adopt a single view of what it is to be a good Marist Brother, or a good Sister of Mercy or a good Redemptorist. We may easily look at how we are to be involved in ministry solely out of how we have done this in the past, with insufficient attention to the demands of the present, and little real appreciation of the differences that could enrich.

Propositional thinking, on the other hand, is the constant and uncomfortable asking, how else might we be in our world? If our founders were in our shoes now how might they bring their passion for gospel values to bear on this or that situation? Do we have symptoms of tunnel vision and what are they? Can we think new thoughts, take risks, delight in our diversity? What prejudices have we perhaps institutionalized? What stubbornness cries out for conversion? What gifts are available to which we merely give the nod at present but which might be a source of new energy for us? In another five or 10 or 20 years, what will this group look like? How do we want it to be? How do we get there?

4) A fourth guarantee of mediocre living is to over-sacralize the past. The present is holy too, and we are invited to hallow it further. Taking account of tradition does not mean to be institutionally hamstrung. Neither does the need to be a meaningful presence *now* necessarily mean ignoring our inheritance. Our deep story, originating in the past, is dynamically present to us here and now. It is, however, hand-in-hand with the developing story of our time, our culture, our human understanding of relationship, our technology, all the influences that impinge on us now and which our founders never envisaged. Our evolution, personally and communally, must take account of all that we hold dear and holy in our past, all those learnings from the past that need to be surrendered now as nonessential, and the invitations and lures to novelty that call us out of "then" into "now."

Communally, we are all lit from the same candle, and every moment of our life from then on derives light from that first spark, but depends for height and color and heat and intensity of its flame on present conditions. Our fidelity to our common bond must take account of both. The long memories of the elders of the tribe, our storytellers, will preserve for us the traditions, and the poets, prophets and pragmatists will offer us insight, challenge and programs for life in the now.

5) Loyalty to the church has often been a value that has kept us safely on middle ground. I want to suggest that loyalty

to the kingdom might perhaps be a good substitute. One of my friends once remarked in a somewhat cynical moment that Jesus came to establish a kingdom and what we did was build a church. Later discussion of this revealed an acute awareness that all institutions, the institutional church included, tend to assume unilateral power, a ponderousness that can slow and even deaden responsiveness, implicitly giving priority to efficiency rather than effectiveness. By contrast, the founder of the kingdom came "that they may have life and have it to the full." Blind conformity masquerading as loyalty to the church may at times shield religious from being a needling presence in a parish, a diocese or country, from being a continuous and living reminder to the institutional church of its original purpose. Founders were men and women who respectfully confronted bishops and popes and were sometimes rewarded for their risk-taking by the wrath of the institution, excommunication and ridicule. But eventually they were vindicated by the visible fruit of their efforts.

I am not speaking of a deliberate stance of angry criticism *vis-a-vis* the church, but of a sensitive thirst for gospel values that registers unworthy attitudes and refuses to adopt them. Juxtaposing the fighting words of the beatitudes with the pastoral practice of a sinful human institution can be a healthy, if disquieting, exercise, and the most visible needling a religious community can offer the institutional church is the quiet modelling of behavior that is in tune with and arises from those same beatitudes.

Religious life, incarnation of each founder's dream, is called to give hands and feet to the mystery of church, to keep it alive, to shout challenge in places where it seems moribund. Creative disobedience can sometimes be profoundly loyal. It is never safe.

6) Finally, I want to mention the difference between maintaining institutional works and a more flexible adopting of corporate works. The difference, as I see it, involves the freedom to change and encompass diversity and pluralism of works. Institutional works, such as teaching in high schools, give way to the corporate work of education more broadly defined. Working in hospitals may give way to concern for the sick and poor wherever they are to be found, recognizing that illness is holistic and not merely physical. Hence some members of an institute may be involved in social or psychiatric care in poor areas where hygiene and standards of living are depressed. Others

may administer hospitals and enable others not necessarily members of their religious community to perform works of nursing and so forth. Others may take on salaried jobs to provide sustenance and support for those who engage in works of charity that cannot provide a livelihood. The corporate choice of a particular apostolic emphasis, such as service in the areas of poverty or injustice or ignorance, allows for a variety of forms of involvement. A diversity of gifts, talents and insights may then be harnessed to this broader view of mission. The charism may flower in areas it might never have irradiated when it was locked into an institutional shape. I believe this is one of the current challenges of pluralism to religious life.

A probably painful outcome of taking on corporate rather than institutional works is the difficulty then of holding all the diversity together creatively. Old structures of community living will have to be surrendered, and new ones found. There will be fewer structures. Because we are often geographically apart, our times together will be more than gatherings out of obligation rather than desire. We shall be challenged to suffer loneliness and to walk the path of converting it to solitude. We shall be invited to journey from institutional dependence to adult responsibility that does not always have institutional "parents" to fall back on when the going gets rough. A new and salutary uneasiness and insecurity may take hold of us. We may be grasped by a new awareness of the particular moment of history in which we live, and we may feel called by it to new and original action.

> It is difficult to describe, or even to list, the many different ways in which consecrated persons fulfil through the apostolate their love for the Church. This apostolate is always born from that particular gift of your Founders, which, received from God and approved by the Church, has become a charism for the whole community. That gift *corresponds to the different needs of the Church and the world at particular moments of history*, and in its turn it is extended and strengthened in the life of the religious communities as one of the enduring elements in the Church's life and apostolate (emphasis added).[7]

It remains, then, to discuss ways of being in relationship that will sustain and nourish the central motivation and vision that power our way of being in and for the world. I turn, therefore, to an examination of mutuality as it operates within community life, and then, in the following chapter, to empathy as a basic spirituality for life together.

Mutuality: Appreciative Awareness of Our Many Stories and Our Single Story

> i need to talk
>   and walk
>   with another
>
> i need to express myself
>   say things. . .
>
> this is a movement of life
>   life that is in me
>   and needs to flow out. . .
>
> i must speak . . . and dance
>   sharing things i love and hate
>   my hopes, my joys, my fears, my griefs . . .
>   giving myself
>   giving my life
>   giving life.[8]

Mutuality is the capacity to receive with respect and understanding the reality of another, and to offer to the other or others our own reality without pretense, game-playing, indirectness or manipulation. As such, it is far more than a mere skill. Based for religious on the recognition that relationship is incarnational, mutuality is a deeply held *value* that, in action, images the love of God. I speak of it, then, as a valued way of being in the world that, nevertheless, does require the appropriate skills as well as values and attitudes. It is for me a spirituality, that is to say, a directedness of spirit that governs our approach to others, be they friends, foes or passing acquaintances. It is a spirituality that lies at the heart of the dynamics of life together and makes of ministry a receptive as well as a giving process.

Growth does not take place in a vacuum. It is a relational process. But not all relating is mutual. When we look into the mirror of another person's eyes, we may do so in fear or with the expectation of finding rejection or anger or disapproval there. Sometimes the experience is like looking into one of those crooked mirrors that delight children by distorting their image. The social psychologist George Herbert Mead speaks of our looking-glass self, the self that is reflected back to us, but distorted by us by filtering it through old messages and memories. Learning mutuality means seeing others in a particular way and revealing who we are in trust that we will be received with respect. This may require struggling free of some of the distortions bred into us by our history.

Somewhere I read an old Hasidic story that illustrates the kind of "seeing" I am talking about:

> An old rabbi gathered his disciples around him and, as rabbis do, he posed them a question.
>
> "Tell me" he said, "how do you know when there is enough light to see?"
>
> After a pause, one of the disciples ventured, "Rabbi, there is enough light to see when, in the early dawn, I look out across the fields and can distinguish an oak from a sycamore tree."
>
> The rabbi shook his head.
>
> Another of the disciples suggested, "Perhaps, Rabbi, when through the morning mists I can tell the lambs from the kids as they romp in the meadow, then, maybe there is enough light to see."
>
> Again the rabbi disagreed.
>
> Finally, a third disciple said, "I know! When I look at the river in the early morning and can see the current moving in it there is enough light to see."
>
> Slowly, the rabbi looked up and said, "No. But I will tell you. When I look into the eyes of another person and recognize there my brother or my sister, *then* there is enough light to see."

Arriving at the rabbi's vision is not an immediate achievement for most of us, but a gradual process of letting go, of unlearning as well as learning. The best "school of mutuality" for me has been the experience of two relationships in my life that have modelled it for me. The first is a friendship of over 30 years' duration that has been a steady and rock-like reality for us all that time. It is a relationship that began through a common interest in religious education and a simple admission by the other sister that she needed some help with some of the graphics for her lessons. I tentatively offered what skill I had, and we spent many hours planning lessons and developing ideas for illustrating them, and then I would do the illustrations for her. So we began by sharing ideas and skills. In the process, however, we began almost inevitably to let each other know what we deeply believed, first in terms of what should be taught and how it should be taught, but then, in ever-widening circles, our disclosures took in aspects of our religious life, loves and hates, difficulties and fears. At first the relationship was, therefore, characterized by a *professional* mutuality; that is, it was an exchange directly related to and confined to our shared professional interests. Later it became the mutuality of *friendship*, when the quality of the shared information and the manner of our receiving this from one another shifted ground and deepened.

When I trace the steps of this process—something I certainly did not do at the time—I now recognize that we began with small and often unrelated snippets of information about our common task that revealed details about ourselves. I remember that my companion used to express a feeling of surprise that I, a high school teacher, took time to help her, a primary school teacher, and that I often responded with real respect for the work she did. Thus I picked up hints from her that she maybe felt a little inferior. We told stories to one another, stories from our respective classroom happenings and eventually stories of our families and backgrounds. At times, as the relationship developed, we supported one another through some of the hard times that were fairly common in the restrictive religious-life atmosphere of the late 1950s. I am aware, and probably was then too, that we were well on the way to developing one of those deplored and railed against "particular friendships" that religious at the time were enjoined to avoid like the plague!

Over the years the friendship continued, surviving separation, changes in occupation, education and life experience, including for both of us the development of other close and nurturing relationships. Different opportunities for personal education and development came our way, and we pursued different interests and, I believe, different rates of growth. It was never a heavily emotion-laden relationship. Nevertheless, it was a friendship that expressed its love in a steady fidelity in small ways: anniversaries and special occasions remembered, letters sporadically exchanged. It was and is a rock against which the waves of much of my life splash and break. I do not and have never doubted its mutuality, and I believe that my companion models for me a strong and challenging fidelity. She has taught me much of what I am writing here, though I am sure that when she reads it she will smile with modest incredulity.

This friendship is a placid state of expectation that we will accept each other unmistakably for what we are. It is unsentimental and fairly undemonstrative. We can challenge each other with a degree of safety which in my experience is rare. It is a relationship that demonstrates for me the truth of an assertion by Greeley:

> There comes a time in a relationship between friends when the risks of self-revelation have become minimal, when one can, for all practical purposes, be certain that the mutual giving in a friendship relationship will not stop. The turning point has been reached, and the friends will be friends forever. It takes a long time for a relationship to develop to this state, and those who prematurely announce that their commitment to one another is definitive and irrevocable are only deceiving themselves. . . . When a friendship has become irrevocable, the demands it makes on the friendship partners are not lessened, but the friends are able to be confident that they have passed the point of no return.[9]

The second relationship is a more recent one, and it followed something of the same path. It began in a professional encounter in which I was a student (on study leave in another country) seeking supervision and tuition from someone for whom I had a feeling of awe and distant, slightly nervous respect. Over quite a short period of time we told each other part of our background and life stories, shared insights, discovered common interests and puzzled over some of the same questions. Through all of this, I maintained my distance, at least in my own awareness, by treating the other person as a professor and myself as a student. For me there was no thought of friendship at the outset, nor of any other kind of mutuality. I was there to receive, and he was there to instruct, and that's what it was all supposed to be about. I developed a genuine liking for him, but this was so deferential that it did not approach any sort of closeness. I remember, however, that one day after a discussion long forgotten now, my "professor" stopped in his tracks as we were walking down the street toward the university and, turning to face me, said, half-smiling but unmistakably serious, "Evelyn, would you *please* stop relating to me as a teacher. You are a student in my class and also an experienced professional person. I respect your knowledge and your need to learn, but I want you for a friend." I walked the rest of the way to school that day in a daze, a little scared, a lot elated!

In the past few years a degree of closeness has developed between us that I would never have thought possible. It *wasn't* possible. The possibility has somehow been created as we risked each new step of relating. What I have learned is new capacity for intimacy that is entirely consonant with my choice of celibacy as a way of life, and a belief in my own worth that has grown more and more confident as my friend has demonstrated it to me. I have also learned to take new risks of self-disclosure and, best of all, have learned that challenge in a relationship, far from being destructive, can bring new and exhilarating depths of discovery.

Andrew Greeley once called self-revelation "the tension between terror and delight."[10] On the one hand is the reluctance to tell anyone about oneself out of fear that the other person will be disappointed and go away, and on the other hand is the need to be open and to give as much of oneself as possible. The friend I have just been describing has taught me to give. He taught me by giving.

In the development of these two relationships, there is a common starting-place, namely, self-disclosure and respectful receiving of it. This is where all mutuality begins. In the first chapter of St. John's gospel two of the disciples of John the Baptist tag along after Jesus until he finally turns and demands to know what they want. Their reply is simple: "Rabbi, where do you live?" Jesus' response is equally simple. "Come and see," he says. And so begins an association in which he constantly invites them to come and see, gradually letting them know who he is and where he has come from. In effect, all mutuality begins with the invitation, "Come and see." Not all mutuality results in friendship. It is, however, possible to value mutuality as the cornerstone of working relationships, and as the key to communal relating. It does not thereby imply an equal degree of closeness with everybody. I am inclined to think that a communal group where everybody is emotionally equidistant might be boring! Mutuality means relating to each person with respect and empathy, offering self-disclosure that is appropriate to the type of relationship envisaged. It enables a degree of openness to differences that makes pluralism an acceptable challenge in religious life.

Mutuality is a process that proceeds in identifiable stages, although we usually do not stop to map exactly where we are in the process. It is not a linear but a spiralling process which cycles through three main stages. Each stage is characterized by exchange. The first and most basic stage involves the exchange of self-disclosure and empathy, the second includes the exchange of challenge and examination of the challenge, and the third is characterized by the exchange of immediacy and exploration of the relationship.[11] I shall discuss each of these with particular reference to the social milieu of religious life.

STAGE ONE:
TELLING AND HEARING STORIES

> Love
> will never be anywhere
> except where equality and unity are.
> Between a master and his servant
> there is no peace
> for there is no real equality.
> And there can be no love
> where love does not find equality
> or is not busy creating equality.
> Nor is there any pleasure without equality.
> Practice equality in human society.
> Learn to love, esteem, consider all people
> like yourself.
> What happens to another,
> be it bad or good, pain or joy,
> ought to be as if it happened to you.[12]

At the beginning of mutuality we make ourselves known to one another. Equality begins in our respect for one another's stories. This is demonstrated in our willingness to disclose appropriate parts of our story and to listen with empathy to the stories of others.

From the beginning we are natural self-disclosers. Before we have developed language, we have learned to communicate that we are hungry, wet or in pain. Mothers can frequently distinguish between an infant's cry for attention and a cry that indicates that something is wrong. We smile, laugh, frown, shriek and wail. Already immediate bits of our experience are being told. When we have words, we quickly learn to say, "Mommy, I'm hungry," or "Daddy, please carry me." Inner recognitions are outwardly expressed. So, in adulthood, it is not the ability to be self-disclosing that has to be learned. Rather it is the skill of discriminating what is appropriate and inappropriate in this or that context. It is the skill of timing and proportion. And it is sometimes the unlearning of inappropriate reticence that we may have learned as time and history have unfolded.

There are some general rules about self-disclosure.[13] For present purposes, I list a few questions that are useful to me in assessing the appropriateness of disclosure.

(a) *What is the context?* If this is a work situation where the relationship is geared toward getting a job done or a decision made, it may be quite inappropriate to launch into disclosure of the details of a personal rejection experienced before

I came to work this morning. Such a disclosure may be entirely unrelated to the context and therefore in this instance out of place. If, however, because of the feelings of rejection I am still carrying I find my usual application to the task impaired, I may choose to mention that I am not at my best today because of an upset that happened outside the work situation. Usually the non-verbal signals of cadence and inflection, gesture and facial expression will indicate that this is a limited disclosure which does not invite extension. It is appropriate because it explains present behavior which may otherwise be puzzling to the other and potentially destructive of a working partnership.

In the context of a friendship or supportive relationship, I may choose to disclose more of the episode because whatever is important to either of us is seen as germane to our communication with another. Self-disclosure is for the sake of the quality of the relationship. In the workplace, ideas, fears, suggestions, information, hesitations, strengths and inabilities related to the work and the distribution of work are appropriate disclosures. In a relationship where greater emotional closeness is envisaged, additional disclosure will be deemed appropriate and past experience of a deeper quality may be risked.

(b) *Am I saying too much?*   It is possible to overwhelm another with the outpouring of a wealth of detail and history. Good self-disclosure is gradual and respects the other person's readiness to receive it. It proceeds incrementally over time. Part of the problem of the too-much-all-at-once disclosure is that it may, by implication, invite the other person to do the same when there is neither readiness nor willingness to do so. Thus a potentially creative relationship is aborted. Similarly, to invite another to "tell all" may be construed as an invasion. I remember instances in which people have said with great good will that they had decided to make a friend of me and wanted to know *all about me*. I know that my immediate instinct was to run a mile, and that my immediate reaction was to exercise great caution and reticence in what I did tell. The only time that I can think of when it is appropriate to tell a lot about oneself all at once is in a crisis, when the usual rules do not operate. It is common for persons suffering grief or trauma to pour out details that they might otherwise have been somewhat more private about.

(c) *Am I saying too little?*   Relationships need nourishment. Relationality can no more exist on fresh air alone than bodies can! If I am over-cautious or too reticent, I will send messages that say "Keep off the grass!" This may not be the message I want to send. In fact, the real message may be quite the opposite. If my shyness and reticence come from self-doubt, I may be crying for the reassurance of relationship, but it is axiomatic that non-verbal cues are highly ambiguous, and so it is likely that others will read my silence inaccurately. In addition, some balance is required to maintain mutuality. If the other person is constantly the one who risks disclosure, and I am always the quiet and receptive one, it may not be long before the other person begins to feel slightly foolish. I am not suggesting that mutuality happens in measured doses. It is not, "You tell me a bit and I'll tell you a bit," but it *is* two-sided.

(d) *Am I disclosing some things too soon?* I remember a group situation many years ago where the participants were strangers to one another and the first contribution one person made was the statement, "I'd better tell you all right now that I am a homosexual." I remember that the rest of the group backed off in fright. Nobody made any response to the speaker at all. He was left sitting there high and dry in splendid isolation. The information itself was quite admissible in the type of group this was, but it was offered too soon, before the group members even knew each other's names. The timing was all wrong. Later the individual was able to say that he was so conscious of his homosexuality and so endangered by the possibility that someone might guess it, that he needed to say it early, impelled as he was by great anxiety. Later there was empathy and receptivity to this. In the beginning there was only unresponsive fear. The general rule is that disclosure begins with the more obvious and external and proceeds gradually to the more hidden, each step tested in the context of the warmth and readiness of the relationship to receive it, and each new step always involving calculated risk. There are some things about my inner self, for instance, that I will readily disclose to a friend but will never disclose to the community "broadcaster." The risk is just too great.

(e) *Am I making a disclosure too late?* What might have facilitated our relationship a month ago may be inappropriate now. This often applies to the disclosure of feelings, and more will be said about it later. Suffice it to say here that to tell you about feelings I had in relation to you last month may be less creative of relationship than communicating them to you at the time when they actually occurred. In a work situation, for instance, it is more important to let you know I feel incapable of a particular task at the time when I am asked to do it than a week after I have tried and failed.

(f) *How do I disclose?*   Self-disclosure is not merely a matter of communicating information about myself. It is clad in words and signals. Self-disclosure and emotional blackmail are two quite different processes. Self-disclosure for the sake of the relationship (at whatever level is appropriate) is an appreciation of the other as listener and of the relationship as worthwhile. Emotional blackmail is instrumental in quality and manipulative in intention, at least subconsciously. As such it has nothing to do with the basic respect and equality of mutuality, and may, if it is a habitual stance that remains unaddressed, be an impediment to creative relating.

Self-disclosure is only half of the exchange that begins to build a relationship of mutuality. It must be met by receptivity and appreciation of the other that is often called empathy. Because I believe that empathy is robbed of its magnitude when it is seen only as a skill, it will be spoken of later as the basic spirituality underpinning community relationships. For the moment, however, it seems timely to pay some attention to those skills that are indubitably an expression of empathy. The first of these is listening, a combination of attitude and skill.

I cannot receive another's story into mine unless I can first hear it. There is more to this than registering a procession of words and decoding them and recoding them within my brain. Receptivity to the story is sometimes envisaged as being a screen on which another's story is projected. I prefer to think of the story being etched permanently rather than projected in disappearing frames. When I really listen to you, I register meanings, intensity, significance—emotion as well as content. The asceticism of listening is in the self-emptying that is its prerequisite. I cannot genuinely hear you if I am full of opinions, ready with arguments and rejoinders and good advice, or glutted with prejudice. All of these things deafen me to the full impact of your disclosure. Really listening means entering your story, registering its meanings and levels as completely as I can without analysis and evaluation, and catching its emotional impact.

The other half of listening is responsiveness. It is not much use to our relationship if I listen attentively but do not communicate to you either *that* I have heard or *what* I have heard. Much of my response will be in non-verbal signs, by now well-known because most of us have been exposed to skills training of various sorts. I nod, sit facing you squarely, utter sounds that signify receptivity. It is possible, however, to *do* all the right things externally and still leave the other person with a feeling of not being deeply heard.

> Once, during a conference that was for me of some significance, I found myself being uneasy and disturbed by the direction the decision-making was taking. I expressed this publicly without evoking much response. I went away from each session with an increasing sense of alienation and even anger. Finally, I said to myself, "You often counsel others feeling caught like this. Take your own medicine and ask for some help." So I sought out the facilitator of the conference. He generously made time available almost immediately, and I revealed my anxiety. I remember that I spoke with urgency and some pain, feeling near to tears. The facilitator responded to me with factual accuracy and impeccable *skill*. But I went away feeling unheard and unhelped.

Pondering this later, I discovered that the man had indeed done all the "right" things, but that I was left with an impression of someone sitting so far outside my experience that he observed, quite accurately, from afar. I felt like an object. What was missing, I think, was the warmth of someone who took the risk of walking right *inside* my experience and touching it with understanding. I know I was not looking for a cure or for intellectual agreement or endorsement of my position. All I wanted was for someone to *be* there, and when I had finished telling my story I looked around and there was no one there except a face saying the correct words. I hope that I am not being unjust to the facilitator. I can find many reasons why this situation developed as it did. But what I want to illustrate is that real empathy is an entering in that is warm and close and more than a correct text-book accuracy.

So far, I have outlined in general the first stage of building mutuality. I turn now to situating that within a religious community with its particular emphases, filters and rules.

Continuing education, renewal programs and the inclusion of psychological knowledge within training syllabuses have all helped to raise the consciousness of many religious communal groups about the significance of creative relationships among them. There is, however, if my observation is correct, still a lot of reluctance and reticence in engaging more than superficially with one another. A number of factors contribute to this.

1.   Low Self-esteem, Inherited From Past Repressive Regimes, Still Persists

Almost every religious who approaches my office and seeks counselling reveals uncertainty and hesitancy about personal worth. When this is situated within the context of building mutuality it is an impediment. One sister stated it cogently at a recent meeting with me:

> "Some of the younger people in the community have invited me to go with them during the holidays to a lakeside cottage they always go to. . . . Half of me would like to go and the rest of me is too scared. They seem to find it so easy to get close to one another. Sometimes it even seems a bit sentimental to me. They share a lot of what they think and they're always going on about how they feel. If they expected me to do that—and they might if I'm there for three whole weeks—I don't think I could do it. I'm not like that usually, but if I said how I felt sometimes I don't think they'd want me any more. They'd probably laugh at me or at least find out that they were mistaken about wanting me to be with them."

This is an expression of a common belief: If I really let you know who I am, will you still respect and like and accept me? The fear behind the question is that the answer will be negative; there is an inner suspicion of worthlessness.

When a person cannot risk saying who he or she is, mutuality cannot get off the ground. I know no simple answers for those inhibited by their fear but I am unwilling to give up the hope of building mutuality there. If there are some in the group who can join in modelling simple and low-key self-disclosure and quiet, undemonstrative empathy, I believe that they occasionally draw in those who appear afraid. We can offer as unthreatening an image of mutuality as we can without demanding a level of participation that is likely to make the fearful feel exposed and in danger. Here is an example of the beginning of such a process:

> There is a community grouping of four, two of whom have some ability to share information about themselves. The other two, Julie and Marita, tend to sit back and let the first two, Greta and Jane, make decisions and carry the whole interaction. As the group gathers to discuss some impending changes in the administration of the nursing home they are running, Greta, the chairperson, outlines the problem and

adds, "I'm a bit nervous about it, because it's new and I don't know how I'll cope with it." (She makes a simple disclosure about a personal feeling that is not too intense and is likely to be shared by some or all of the others.)

Jane, after looking around to see if the other two are about to speak, comments, "I've thought and thought about it. In my head I know that it's the right thing to do, but I have some echoes of your feeling, Greta. You put your finger on how scary it is to face something unknown." (She accurately perceives the feeling expressed by Greta, and adds her own disclosure to it.)

There is a silence for a while. The other two nod after each statement but do not speak. Greta notices this.

"I can see that you share the nervousness too, Julie and Marita. I guess the question is, Do we go ahead just the same? If we are all nervous about this, do we need another person to join us? Should we give up the enterprise totally, or should we join hands and leap in?" (Greta briefly acknowledges the non-verbal signals from Julie and Marita before offering some alternatives.)

I believe it is as simple as that. Picking up a sign of how the reticent or fearful person feels or thinks and stating it simply and with understanding without putting a spotlight on the other person may provide small pockets of safety for him or her eventually to risk a larger contribution. In the discussion above, in fact, Marita eventually said with some wonder in her voice, "I didn't think *you* would be scared, Greta. I though I was the only one who felt like that." She made a relational statement, and added a confirmation of her own fearfulness. This may be a small advance. I am an optimist who sees signs of hope in it. Genuine empathy knows that people who are nervous, afraid and doubting of themselves must begin disclosure in small ways which are received gently and fairly unobtrusively but with the warmth that creates new possibilities.

When the halting and minimal self-disclosures of a fearful person are received with genuine respect, the small "successes" encourage new efforts at risk-taking and begin, however haltingly, to establish a sense of worth, a recognition of having something worthwhile to offer to the other person or to the group as a whole. This is the beginning of real relationship and the birth of the possibility of friendship.

Friendship is only for those who believe that they do have something worth revealing to a friend, and there is an intrinsic value in them which others ought to find attractive. The trouble with most human friendships is that one, or usually both, of the partners really are not convinced that they have anything to offer.[14]

What Greeley asserts about friendship here, however, is equally applicable to the search for mutuality that does not necessarily envisage friendship as the goal of its process, but rather seeks a basically decent relationship that enables predictable life together, creates and sustains an atmosphere in which each person's membership is valued and protected, and generates energy for valued ministries.

I do not know of many ways of assisting a person to shed the load of doubt carried from recent or more distant history. Therapy may be of value, but I believe the best therapy is often what happens in a good communal group where affirmation is one of the ways empathy expresses itself. It may create a climate in which a crippled person can learn to stand upright for the first time. It is a slow and often disappointing process, producing no immediate and miraculous transformations. Miracles of growth follow the usual pattern of all growth. They are slow and sometimes invisible. There is asceticism in waiting.

2. Confusion About Needs and Community Expectations May Impede the Growth of Mutuality

People come into communal groups with different histories and different needs. If there is a tradition of not speaking about these needs then there is little hope of clarification, and people continue to act out of the needs without making them explicit. Evelyn and James Whitehead ask a number of questions about the functioning of a group that are pertinent to this discussion:

1. What is the major focus of this group?

2. How fully is the individual member expected to be involved with this group?

3. How appropriate is it for the members of this group to share with one another on an emotional level?

4. How is behavior regulated in this group?

5. How obligated are members to each other and to the group as a whole?

6. How are evaluations made about persons who are members of the group?[15]

The answers to these questions indicate where a community lies on a continuum from primary group (familial or supportive in purpose and nature) to formal organization (organized to perform a specific function or task or complex of tasks). The Whiteheads provide an interesting chart of the dimensions that indicate the position of a group on this continuum. It is a chart that I have often handed out to community members to help them describe the reality that they call community. One of the problems constantly associated with this exercise is that the various members of the group come up with such vastly different perceptions of their group that it is often impossible to draw any general conclusion other than how differently people perceive the same reality!

The fact emerges, however, that a communal group may contain some people whose expectations of the group are largely clustered at the familial end of the continuum and others who express few familial-type needs within the community. The latter may seek the kind of professional support necessary for ministry in the group, but find closeness, intimacy and friendship elsewhere, if they seek these at all. There may be still others in the same group who are closer to the center of the continuum, expressing the need for some level of emotional closeness and support while also recognizing the need for cooperation at the level of the *tasks* that belong to their professional life or ministry.

I do not believe that all these differences have to be ironed out and the lowest common denominator agreed upon. However differences need to be made explicit and recognized as part of the pulsing, jostling and sometimes abrasive reality of communal living under the umbrella of a common uniting vision. The *fact* of pluralism in religious life is that such a variety of needs is more admissible now than it once was. Feelings and needs now have a legitimate and recognized place in interaction; formerly the demands of a narrowly defined self-denial and asceticism made them highly suspect.

One unfortunate manner of handling the differences is to regard one's own position as the only right one and to belittle and refuse to meet others. Thus a kind of polarization is possible where people draw up invisible territorial boundaries around their view of the way the social form of community must be shaped. Here are a few common statements to illustrate this:

"I wish they'd stop harping on how we must all love one another around here! It's a bit sick. Anyone would think we were here to nurse each other along. I've no time for all that sentimental garbage. I'm not going to ooze with affection for anybody, and I don't welcome anyone doing it to me, thank you. We ought to stop being sugary and get on with the job."

"There's more to life as a community than work. I wish there was a rule in this place that when we come in from school in the afternoon there can be no talk of the children or the other teachers. We get enough of that all day. I'd just love it if sometimes somebody would notice that I'm feeling tired or discouraged, and *be* with me for a short time."

"I need to belong here. That means that I want people to notice I'm around and *how* I am when I'm around, and I want to offer the same attention to the others. On the other hand, I don't think we ought to sit around discussing and theorizing about ourselves in ways that separate us from the poor and the wounded and the suffering. I'd like to think that the quality of our life together gives us drive and urgency, and that it's safe to reach out because there's a place to reach out from."

If these differences are discussed not only with those of similar opinions, but with those who exemplify a quite different understanding of the aims of community, it may not be possible to arrive at perfect agreement, but the possibility is created of understanding each other's needs in ways that may make for greater attentiveness to them. Mutuality is not necessarily agreement. It *is* a deeply respecting stance before the needs, feelings and total reality of another person. In the examples above, each statement contains a strength—businesslike energy for work, care and the need for care, attentiveness and belonging. When these are shared and received with respect and understanding of where the other is coming from, the likelihood of rivalry and unnecessary competitiveness is minimized or eliminated, and what was potential polarization becomes rich variety that contributes to the sustaining of the whole group.

Where there is little listening, or where disclosures are met with argument, win/lose games, pairing or banding into groups of similar opinions to the exclusion of the rest, there is fair indication of the absence of empathy, and without it mutuality cannot exist. Without mutuality the community has no basically decent human relationships, and if religious community has a counter-cultural witness value, an empathy-impoverished group may witness only to isolation, loneliness and a self-centered struggle for personal survival at any expense. Such a group, far from being counter-cultural, has bought into the competitiveness of a society that says a person's worth is to be found in being better or richer or more talented or more important than the rest. Christianity, on the other hand, establishes our intrinsic worth in the ground of a loving God. We are valuable and value one another because we *are*, and because already we have been loved with an everlasting love.

3. *Awkwardness and Fear in the Area of Feelings*
Vanier's lines at the beginning of this discussion of mutuality speak of "sharing things I love and hate, my hopes, my joys, my fears, my griefs." Clearly it is unnatural and even undesirable to do this uniformly with all people irrespective of the degree of intimacy that has been built with them or of the nature of the relationship (professional, friendship, etc.) However, the difficulty for many religious is not regulating disclosure so much as fear of any disclosure that entails revealing personal feelings of any intensity.

In the training of many religious, hierarchies of feelings were established, some emotions being good and some being bad. In general it was considered good to have loving and charitable feelings, to feel pious, to be concerned for others or well-disposed to everybody. On the other hand, it was bad to have feelings of anger or sexual feelings of arousal or attractedness. This is often confirmed by religious at seminars when we embark on becoming tuned in to the whole range of our emotions. Either directly or indirectly many religious learned that their feelings were a somewhat unworthy part of their humanness, to be disregarded or treated with suspicion as a potential source of sinfulness. Feelings, therefore, were swept into a *moral* category. They were good or bad, right or wrong. Hence to achieve an openness with feelings and to disclose them in the process of building mutuality becomes, in the present, an exceedingly dangerous undertaking. Although many religious clearly reject these old learnings and know that they were the product of past judgments rather than present knowledge, for some, at least, there are lingering traces of guilt and uneasiness when affective statements are made or invited. Among other things, the failure to include affective education in training programs has left some people impoverished even at the level of a vocabulary to describe feelings.

At a workshop recently, I deeply appreciated the risk taken by a man who volunteered this statement in the presence of a large group, following a discussion about feelings:

> "This will probably be laughable to a lot of you, but I came here to learn, and I'm going to ask stupid questions if I need to. The fact is that I hear you all talking about feelings, and I'm afraid I don't know what feelings are."

I am happy to say that nobody laughed. In fact, I suspect that there were some in the group grateful for the comment because they needed the information it evoked. From then until the end of the program we began to amass a language of feelings, to describe them when they occurred and to explore their significance. In answer to the request for information we defined feelings as inner events that delivered a message to the individual about his or her relationship to environment or to self or to somebody else. As such, feelings are to be attended to. They may signify a state of harmony, or point to something happening in a relationship which needs to be dealt with for the sake of the very survival of the relationship. They may indicate that the person is endangered and should take immediate action. They may suggest attraction to another that carries with it the possibility of a loving relationship that will blossom into friendship. They may suggest sexual attraction that requires a decision concerning celibacy, self-control or establishing ways of sustaining intimacy other than genital expression. As such, all of these feelings are real and valuable *if* they are accurately perceived and dealt with.

In developing a vocabulary of feelings, it has been helpful to offer four categories:

MAD

SAD

GLAD

SCARED

and to have people fill in specific feelings under each heading when they come to awareness.[16] Each time a feeling such as *nervous* or *hostile* or *attracted* is written onto the chart, class members are invited to develop the single word into a phrase. So *nervous* becomes "I have butterflies in my stomach," and then perhaps it is extended further into a behavioral statement such as "I'd like to turn invisible so nobody will look at me," or "I feel like turning around and going right out of here and pretending I never came in." The value of this is to allow for some expression of the intensity of the feeling and its unique quality when experienced by this particular person at this particular moment. People begin to be aware that one person can say, "I'm angry with you right now" and mean "I'm mildly irritated with you right now," whereas another might say exactly the same words, "I'm angry with you right now," and mean "I'm feeling murderous and if you don't get out of here quickly I may be violent!" Hence an understanding of the differing weight of emotion carried in a single word begins to be understood.

A number of steps for dealing with feelings may be useful also for those religious who desire mutuality in communal living, but who feel some disquiet about their ability to handle their feelings internally, let alone disclose them in dialogue with another. I believe that one achieves some control over these inner events when they can be named. It is a little like the symbolic naming of the animals by Adam in Genesis. As he stood there on his hilltop and named each passing beast, he symbolically took charge, was king of them all, given dominion over them by a benevolent God. When I can name feelings occurring inside me and say to myself, "I am angry," I immediately establish ownership. The feeling does not own me. I own it. This makes it less likely that I will dump the feelings on someone else, saying, "Now, see what you've done. *You* have made me mad!" Having assumed ownership of the feeling, it may now be appropriate to examine its context, asking what has triggered such a feeling right now. Sometimes this is a little harder than naming the feeling. If I have a history of suppressing anger, a sudden feeling of anger may relate only partly to an immediate incident and may be largely the result of an accumulation of anger from the past. I sometimes have an image of anger (or indeed of many other feelings that may have been suppressed habitually) as carrying a hook on it. When something happens to trigger mild anger, the appropriate amount of anger emerges, but it hooks onto other anger in my inner reservoir and drags it out too. So, poor little Johnny in the classroom makes a mistake in his mathematics, and I am irritated by his carelessness. As I begin to make this known to him, both he and I may be surprised by the vehemence of my feelings, and he may go home that day wondering why it was such a crime not to be able to multiply by seven! Finding the sources of our feelings, then, may involve both present incidents and past accumulations.

In the context of mutuality, the other skill to be learned in relation to dealing appropriately with feelings is the ability to report feelings directly. To say, "Really! You are the most inconsiderate person I've ever had to live with in my whole religious life!" may sound direct enough, but in reality it sadly lacks directness. It dumps my feeling on somebody else and fails to admit honestly that there is a strong feeling in me that requires direct expression. It might have been better reported like this: "When you do . . . , I find myself *being hurt and angry* because I feel as if you don't care about me." Direct reporting involves an "I" statement.

Practicing these skills in workshops where experimental behavior is encouraged is an appropriate way to try out different ways of handling feelings. However, this is not always possible and the communal group itself must be the forum for new and more insightful, though perhaps initially clumsy, behavior.

Old messages about the sinful nature of the emotions are hardly in line with the long tradition of discernment in the church. Even a cursory reading of the Ignatian approach to discernment reveals a prizing of feelings as one of the vectors of significance as we search for signs that indicate the appropriateness and indeed holiness and rightness of a choice. In a religious tradition in which *incarnation* is the way in which the love our God has for humanity is made visible, the mediation of that love, and indeed its re-creation, depends to a large extent on our ability to transmit genuine love, respect and appreciative care to those around us. Learning to expose our feelings simply and directly without burdening others with responsibility for them is one of the key abilities in doing this.

STAGE TWO:
  CHALLENGING TO GREATNESS
  AS THE STORIES UNFOLD

The second stage of mutuality is the exchange of challenge and exploration of the challenge. All of us see ourselves with partial sightedness. Our relationships take place in a limited arena in which we call upon one another's strengths and perceive one another's weaknesses, hopefully enlarging our potential and extending the limits of the arena by bringing to light unused or neglected strengths, and highlighting behavior that is destructive or potentially destructive of relationship. So growth requires challenge as fuel for movement.

Over the years of my religious life, having gone the route of encounter groups and sensitivity training in the 1960s and 1970s, and having run the gamut of gestalt techniques and Fritz Perls, I, like many others, have distorted some of the valuable lessons that these things might have taught. I often wondered why my confrontation or challenge to somebody according to the textbook just didn't work. What resulted quite often was a worse situation than the original one—hurt feelings, angry recriminations, the fracturing or paralysis of relationship. The recipe somehow did not succeed.

Discovery a few years ago of this dynamic model of mutuality shed light on my ignorance, for it highlighted the necessity of preparing the ground for challenge by building the groundwork of a sufficiently elastic relationship that can sustain the stretching that challenge introduces. Hence it becomes clear that challenge that takes place prematurely—before there has been sufficient exchange of self-disclosure and empathy—can be counterproductive. Instead of enhancing and promoting the growth of the relationship, it can be destructive. Honesty can be like hitting someone over the head. This is hardly an invitation to the deeper trust of a more advanced stage of mutuality. Direct and responsible challenge, on the other hand, emerges from and carries forward into stage two the empathy of the earlier stage. The model is a cumulative one, held together by empathy. What was wrong with my honest enough challenges of earlier years was that unwittingly I was irresponsible. I had not taken the responsibility of building a relationship that could support challenge. At early stages, when relationships were still too brittle to be loaded with the extra cargo of challenge, I expected that challenge would be productive and instead found myself shocked by failure.

Appropriate challenge for me now involves getting to know a person well enough to feel relatively safe in offering new pieces of information that may enhance our relationship and enlarge it. In some ways individuals who negotiate early mutuality well get to know each other better than each knows himself or herself. There are some things about us that we do not know, but which may be known to others. To bring those to the other's attention when it is appropriate in the relational context is to invite the other to growth and to urge our relationship also into a new and larger being.

Much has been written elsewhere about the variety of ways in which challenge may be offered—sharing personal experience, giving information, calling on little used or neglected strengths of the other, indicating the effect of a destructive behavior, examining alternative behaviors, etc. I do not intend to examine all these in detail here. What I would like to do is to examine the conditions for good challenge and ways of receiving and exploring the challenge. Also, as I have done with the first level of mutuality, I should like to specify particular issues applying to religious communities in their implementing of this model.

Challenge invites a person to examine his or her behavior more deeply. At this level of building mutuality, the purpose of challenging is the deepening of the relationship. Other motivations are possible. To purse one's lips in judgment and decide to administer a strong dose of confrontation to "straighten out" the other is *not* envisaged here!

The most common form of challenge is confrontation, so common, in fact, that it is often used as a synonym for challenge. Many religious confess that they cannot yet deal satisfactorily with this form of challenge. When I try to speak of constructive confronting, I invariably remember a Pauline expression that couples truth and love.

> If we live by the truth and in love, we shall grow completely into Christ, who is the head by whom the whole Body is fitted and joined together, every joint adding its own strength, for each individual part to work according to its function. So the body grows until it has built itself up in love. . . . *Speak the truth to one another*, since we are all parts of one another (Eph 4:15-16, 25).

Confronting for the sake of our growth together does not mean merely speaking the truth, but speaking it *in love* to persons who are part of us, brothers and sisters bonded already in a common story and a common undertaking. Before I risk the strong medicine of confrontation, then, I need to clarify my own motivation and the conditions that surround the confronting. Is it the truth? Does it emerge out of love? Is it relational?

Over the years I have developed a checklist of questions to evaluate the appropriateness of confronting someone in the group with whom I live and/or work.

(a) *Do I have a good enough relationship with this person to challenge him or her?*   Has there been enough mutual disclosure and empathy for us to call each other brother or sister? If we have not built the substructure for confrontation, it may be destructive, and instead of enlarging our relationship of love it may damage its potential and narrow it.

In religious communities there lingers an unfortunate heritage from the past when "correction" was the prerogative of the superior, and so there is still in some communities an expectation that the person designated as the superior will take all the responsibility for confronting, particularly where the invitation is to examine dysfunctional behavior. Confrontation is confused with the old notion of correction, and it is assigned to a person seen as having particular power in the group. There are several problems associated with this.

The best person to invite another to examine strength or weakness is the person who has best built initial mutuality. It cannot be assumed that the superior is always the one who has done this. Old associations of the superior with punitive and judgmental conduct may make the best-willed superior an inappropriate confronter, carrying as he or she does the inbuilt additional burden of ascribed authority toward which many religious still have unresolved and unspecific anger. Another offshoot of the expectation that the superior will do all the confronting is the likelihood that when others abdicate their responsibility in this regard the superior will indeed begin to accept the expectation and build it into his or her role-definition.

There is yet another false expectation implicit in this. When the superior is required to correct, the confrontation becomes a kind of community vacuum cleaner, tidying up all the untidy and irritating deficiencies of the community's life together. It is another expression of what I sometimes call the religious life hygiene syndrome, a place for everything and everything in its place. Confrontation then becomes something that is engaged in for the sake of harmony of the group at the expense of someone who is "out of line." Mutuality is about establishing, maintaining and extending relationships. Confrontation is for the sake of the relationship, not merely for the sake of tidiness or peace. I make this distinction, which is never entirely popular when I say it at workshops: Confrontation is not for the good of the other, but for the good of the relationship. It seems to me to be supreme arrogance to assume the right to know what is for the good of this other, a unique, sensitive person, whose life path is different from mine. What we do have in common, jointly owned and pursued, is our relationship. In seeking to develop that, we may indirectly change ourselves and each other, without, however, doing so from a position of judgment or assumed superiority.

(b) *Have I won the right to confront this person?*   The best way for me to answer this question in my own relationships is to ask myself if I am willing to accept strong challenge from this person I am about to confront. If the answer is negative, I may need to look again at the extent to which we two have hitherto engaged in the first stage of mutuality. It is easy to be dishonest and a shade righteous about our own motivations. I am in constant need of telling myself the truth, and when I do I often decide that I am confronting another from unworthy and selfish motives rather than from the heart of a relationship that really matters to both of us and is capable of sustaining challenge. It is one thing to enjoy the exchange of self-disclosure and empathy, and to feel the warmth of this. It is a tougher reality to engage more deeply at the level of challenge *mutually* rather than unilaterally.

(c) *Is my proposed confrontation truly appreciative of the other?*   If I look at the way in which I customarily confront others and find that almost invariably my invitation to the other is to examine some negative behavior, the chances are that I am critical rather than appreciative toward the other person. Given the almost universal experience among religious of damaged self-esteem, constant negative challenges may thwart the purpose of challenge by inducing a deeper and deeper sense of inadequacy. Negative challenge will be tolerable and positive in its effects on our relationship only if founded upon a demonstrated valuing of the other. I can illustrate this from personal experience.

Some years ago I was invited to join a group of American psychologists in a visit to England to work with volunteer counsellors. Excited and flattered, I accepted readily enough. But when I compared myself with the rest of the team, I developed fears and hesitations about my own professional ability. My inner malaise grew when, in the context of teaching in pairs, we agreed to supervise and comment upon each other's professional efforts. I suppose I was afraid that in the feedback associated with this, my worst fears would be realized and I might be told that I was inadequate and useless.

What happened, in fact, was one of the best professional experiences of my life. I remember one of the partners with whom I worked writing a sheaf of notes when I was making a presentation to the group. When feedback time arrived I could hardly breathe as I waited in anticipation of judgment! My companion, however, *always* told me first what was the strongest aspect of my teaching and interacting. Sometimes, indeed frequently, he had some criticism to offer. He did not cushion this in any way, but offered it simply and directly. The effect on me felt spectacular. I grew in confidence, became able to offer suggestions, felt creative and found the whole group responding positively to the way I contributed to its discussions. In the context of this good professional relationship (I do not speak of friendship here) my own professionalism grew. Moreover, I lost some of my fear that challenge and rejection are synonymous.

The quality of the positive challenge is important here. It was never a softening up for the heavy negatives! It was spoken first because the speaker is a deeply appreciative and generous person who *sees* positives first. Hence, even through the filter of my own self-doubt, the challenge of being invited to see my strengths was undistorted, held in focus by the complete genuineness of the challenger. In the light of a deeper acceptance of my own abilities, I found it possible to view shortcomings without threat. Always described constructively by my partner, they became for me changeable and challenging in the positive sense that they urged me to try new behavior next time.

There is a thin line between offering appreciative and positive challenge and arrogantly patting someone else on the head. The difference is the presence or absence of genuineness and respect. I would go so far as to say that this is more easily experienced than described, and that it might be a fruitful experience for the reader to try to give examples of both: When did I feel that a positive statement was patronizing or a softening up for something (and therefore utilizing)? When have I experienced challenge that was positive in its tone and outcome?

(d) *Am I as sure as I can be that what I am about to say is true?* My rule of thumb is that if I challenge someone it should be about something *I* have observed, knowing that even then my perception may be skewed and colored by interpretation, or may carry a hidden judgment. I always refuse to confront on someone else's behalf because there is too much danger of my not knowing the facts. I refuse to confront about hearsay, especially when it is negative, since I know painfully how facts can be distorted as they progress along the convent or monastery grapevine accumulating fantasy and innuendo as they go.

I remember once when I was a student, another sister on campus observed a car outside my apartment till late at night (or all night, for all I know) and concluded that the owner of

the car was present with me at that late hour, clearly for im-
moral purposes! When this finally issued in a confrontation by
someone else from miles away who had caught the echoes at
the bishop's dining table, it was discovered that the car be-
longed to a member of the cleaning staff who always parked in
the same spot and who, till this day, 12 years later, remains unknown to me. I can smile about the episode now, but I remember feeling savaged by the incident, belittled by the inaccuracy
and moral judgment, and pained by the fact that the author of
the story stood beside me at the Eucharist each day and held
out her hand to me saying, "The peace of Christ be with you."
It is a salutary story which reminds me not to confront about
hearsay and urges me to be clear about the facts. I have made a
rule never to repeat to anyone damaging comments I have
heard, but to make sure that I do let them know of positive
things said about them in their absence.

In religious life, where some still expect a parental function
from the superior, the superior may be tempted to confront on
hearsay. A more constructive alternative for the superior is to
suggest that the "reporter" take the responsibility for challenging. A second approach for the superior is to offer to facilitate
an exchange between the two persons concerned. It is amazing
how often a reported mountain shrinks back into a molehill
when either of these possibilities is suggested.

(e) *Why am I doing this?*   In the case of a challenge
concerning something deemed negative, I need to check if the
challenge is a loving effort to strengthen our relationship or a
confrontation that empties me of feelings of irritation, blame
and frustration. If it is to relieve my own pent-up feelings, it is
less for the sake of the relationship than it is for my own inner
comfort, and it may therefore be considered inappropriate since
it is basically selfish in its intention.

In the opposite case of challenge concerning a strength, is
it a simple invitation to the other to see, value and use the
strength? Or is it instrumental, calculated to produce reciprocal
praise or obtain some reward of which the other is innocently
unaware?

(f) *Can I stay around?*   When I confront someone,
whether it is about a strength or weakness, do I recognize the
relational nature of the challenge and stay there so that the
other half of the transaction, exploring the challenge, may happen? Confrontation is not a hit-and-run activity, leaving casual-
ties strewn along the way. If it is loving, it bears the responsibility of its aftermath and stays around to clarify, explain,
concretize by specific examples, and to retract if the other per-

son helps us to see his or her behavior in a different light. The confrontee has some rights in this exchange. To deliver a challenge and walk away indicates a closure that is seldom authentic.

Sometimes when I am strongly challenged, I feel a little too stunned to engage in much exchange right then and there. I need time to reflect on what has been said, giving my immediately defensive feelings time to settle and other recognitions to emerge. So, when I indicate the necessity for the confronter to stay around, I am not implying that right there on the spot the exploration of the challenge will happen. Staying around means holding oneself open to the possibility of further exploration, indeed, of inviting this when empathy senses that the time is right.

A responsible invitation may be something like this: "When I said yesterday that you seemed preoccupied and distant at community meetings, you looked upset, and I wonder if what I said sounded unjust or hurtful." If the time is right, this may trigger an exchange that explores the challenge. If I choose to challenge unlovingly, harshly and punitively, I will simply walk away, dusting off my hands and saying to myself, "There! I've said my piece. That's the end of that." Good confrontation is not an end. It is a beginning.

(g) *Am I judging motives or describing behavior?*   I cannot know the motives of others unless they let me into the inner realm of meanings and motives. What I *see* is behavior, which may have a variety of possible intentions behind it. If good confrontation is essentially invitational, then it cannot presume to be judgmental since judgment is not an open invitation to examine a strength or weakness and its relational implications. Judgment presumes already to know these things, and the judge hands the confrontee a closed verdict that has categorized and evaluated a behavior and requires no response.

Because it is never possible to know all that lies behind another person's behavior, confrontation simply describes the behavior and possibly also identifies and describes some of its outcomes within the relationship. The best manner of doing this is with tentativeness born of empathy. Even the sensitive choice of words is important for this. "Am I right when I say . . . ?" or "It seems that . . . ," and a variety of other tentative phrases that are more than facile formulas, ensure the right of the other person to deny, correct or accept what has been said. If approached in a definite, even accusing, manner of confronting, the other person will probably be forced to resort to one of the common reactions to being cornered—fight or flight—neither of which really qualifies as mutually exploring the challenge.

(h) *Am I demanding instant change, or enabling the other to change?*   This question is tied up with the kind of power implicit in the relationship. If I need to dominate, overpower or coerce the other person, then my challenge probably demands instant change. If the spirit of empathy pervades the relationship, I assume that change is difficult and involves a free choice on the part of the person who embraces it. This being so, challenge carries an invitation to examine either a weakness, an unused or too-little-used strength, or a consciously used strength, with a view to change. It invites substituting alternative behavior for what is damaging or inadequate and finding ways of calling strengths into operation in new situations where they are called for.

In addition to these major questions, which safeguard the three qualities of truth, relatedness and love, I add a number of conditions for challenge which are also important.

1)   As far as possible, challenge should be offered as closely as possible in time to the observed behavior that stimulates it. If one is challenged about behavior that happened weeks ago, the impact of the challenge may be lost. This applies to both confrontation of strengths and of weaknesses.

2)   Confrontation should not be cumulative. If I am challenged to examine multiple behaviors, it is likely that I will be overwhelmed and perhaps angered by the size of the challenge. This is a real danger in community confrontations, where one member initiates confrontation of another and the rest add comments related to other behaviors until the individual is psychologically buried under an avalanche of suggestions, challenges and what may be construed as blame. This is often the way in which a simple and quite constructive challenge may develop into scapegoating. Given the propensity of many religious for guilt—sometimes inappropriate and neurotic—it is undesirable to add fuel to the fire. Such immense and often non-specific challenge defies its own purpose. If challenge is for the sake of the relationship and this cumulative challenge backs a person into a corner, a relationship is damaged rather than co-created.

3)   Good challenge is simple, concrete and specific. Generalized statements, vagueness and hints leave the confrontee uncertain as to what is being asked and unable to take action. I remember an occasion when a companion told me I was "too intelligent" for her. After an initial moment of total confusion

coupled with a somewhat irreverent wondering if I was being invited to undergo major brain surgery, I asked her what she meant. It took quite a long time for me to ascertain that I sometimes used abstract language or vocabulary which she did not fully understand. The result was a feeling on her part of inferiority and then, on top of that, anger at feeling inferior. It was a happily resolved confrontation because eventually I discovered that there was indeed a behavior explicit and concrete enough for me to change in order to preserve a comfortable relationship with her. Her inability to handle a direct and specific challenge, however, meant that I had to take a major share of the responsibility for specificity and clarity. Had I not been able to do that, either because I was too threatened or because I had not enough skill to do so, the confrontation might have been less than positive for our relationship. My companion would have departed dissatisfied, and I would have been left mystified.

STAGE THREE:
   EXPLORING THE PRESENT MOMENT
   OF OUR DEVELOPING STORY

The third level of mutuality involves the exchange of immediacy and examination of the relationship. Immediacy is direct mutual talking about what is going on between us in the here and now. As such, it is another form of challenge, this time challenge to us both to examine some particular aspect of our relating that is prominent in the experience of one or the other of us right now.

After learning to offer community members supportive challenge and feedback, we have laid the foundations of a further step into mutuality. This involves more than exploring the impact of a particular behavior. It proceeds into the quality of the relationship itself in the context of the relationship's purpose. For instance, I am living in a community where my ministry is very different from that engaged in by the majority. If because of this I find myself being excluded from communal decisions or uninformed of events that are significant, I may wish to invite all or some of the group to explore with me the impact on my effectiveness, the unsupported feelings that result, and questions about how to remedy the situation. On the other hand, if I am constantly supported in spite of absences or differing timetables which limit our time together, I may wish to draw attention to the support that *is* given and the effect this has on me. The immediacy here is a simple, direct invitation to look together at creative and facilitative behavior.

Immediacy and examination of our relationship are not reserved for close friendship. Community is not necessarily a banding together of close friends. It is a group fired by a common vision and impelled by that vision to various ministries according to talent and capacity. Immediacy in such a group possibly has more to do with exploring together how we support or fail to support one another in the communal effort.

> At a time when one of my close friends was the superior of the house in which I lived, it became necessary at one point to examine together the possible effects of our closeness on the rest of the group. Neither of us was willing to diminish the closeness in any way, but we did need to discuss how much time we would spend together and to agree not to share information she acquired about the community from her position as superior. This was a decision arrived at through exploring together some of the things currently happening in our relationship. Such an undertaking, while it put some small constraints on us, actually enhanced our relationship.

Individuals who misinterpret the scope and purpose of immediacy may make the mistake of overloading a professional or ministerial relationship with inappropriate or excessive disclosure of feelings about it. Immediacy in such a situation calls for the sharing of feelings directly affecting the quality of the working partnership. Too much disclosure may overload the relationship, forcing it toward friendship that is undesirable to one or possibly both and defying the usual pattern of developing friendship gradually over time. It is also important to address only suitably important issues with immediacy and exploration. Squandering valuable time for relating on trivia that both of us can quite well handle is *not* the goal.

Many of the religious with whom I work ask: What is to happen in a group when some of its members value mutuality and others reject it as a value or are too afraid to admit its validity? Does the difference over a key value bring greater difference, emphasizing pluralism and even polarizing the group? I do not have absolute answers, but I do have a belief. Real mutuality will not allow those who embrace it to live in a comfortable enclave of friends, creating a kind of mutuality-valuing ghetto within the group and excluding those who for one rea-

son or another—lack of working knowledge, skills, attitudes—
do not see mutuality as a goal. Empathy will urge those who
value mutuality consistently to engage in gentle, gradual efforts
at mutuality, respecting the capacity and willingness of their
companions and inviting them without pressure to the freedom
of relationship. They will be aware from the more successful efforts at mutuality they have made that freedom may be created,
slowly and almost invisibly, over time. They will recognize that
the invitation to religious life, and indeed to Christianity itself,
has not been addressed to the powerful, the strong and the capable.

> Consider, brothers, how you were called; not many of you are
> wise by human standards, not many influential, not many
> from noble families. No, God chose those who by human
> standards are weak to shame the strong, those who by human
> standards are common and contemptible—indeed those who
> count for nothing—to reduce to nothing all those that do
> count for something, so that no human being might feel boast-
> ful before God (1 Cor 1:26-28).

The fact is that we are a mixture held together by a common vision which is sometimes elusive and sometimes unattractive and
sometimes frightening. We learn at different rates, carry different impedimenta from the past, have different degrees of readiness for risk-taking. Those who *do* have some freedom to begin
to model and build mutuality in the community are the poets,
whose empathy readily recognizes fear and timidity or rigidity
in others without judgment or condemnation; the prophets,
who proclaim the value of mutuality in action, challenging to
more vital and equal interaction; and the pragmatists, who
model mutual relating as an appropriate model of community
solidarity.

Jesus hand-picked his own community and passed on to
them the common vision that was to bind them together, making known to them all he had learned from the Father. In the final crisis the leader denied even knowing him, one of them
sold him for 30 silver coins, and most of the rest deserted him.
Communities, even those fired by a divinely inspired vision,
have a way of remaining distinctly human and fallible. Mutuality
does not guarantee that it will be otherwise. It merely offers
greater possibility that the differences necessarily present and
integral to any human group may be held in pulsing equilibrium
and challenged to creative, rather than destructively polarizing
expression. Mutuality is one of the ways of translating the
founding vision into living reality among us now.

A Communal Experience of Mutuality

Over a number of years I have been privileged to work as a consultant to a province of brothers who serve the poor and deprived in a variety of ministries. My initial contact with them came precisely because they asked me to discuss with them and then to conduct workshops for them about mutuality in community living. As time went on, I had the opportunity of getting to know all of them individually as well as of seeing them in action as a group. The mutuality that developed between them and myself has deepened into friendship. The vision that binds them together as an order has become part of my story also. I prize my contacts with them, not only because of their belief in my professional contribution to them, but also because relationship with them has been and continues to be transforming in my own life.[17]

Some time ago, one of the local sub-groups of the province, a communal group of six, invited me to visit them for a week and to assist them with some evaluation of their life together. They were willing to sacrifice quite a lot of time for this, carrying on their usual ministries but rearranging schedules and giving up all their free time to reflect on their present reality. This fact alone gave me a clue as to the importance of these days for them.

As a way of beginning the reflection I presented them with two questions:

1) What is the best thing that being in this community group has done for you so far?
2) What are the toughest issues still needing to be addressed here?

The two questions, it seemed to me, offered an opportunity for each of the six to enter the exchange, no matter what level of mutuality he felt comfortable with. The questions allowed for simple comments about external events and/or reflections on the meaning of those events in the lives of individuals and of the group as a whole. They also provided scope for challenge as well as self-disclosure.

It emerged almost immediately that this was a group that was already at home with mutual exchanges of self-disclosure and empathy. Beginning with the first of the two questions, they made comments about the level of acceptance they found in the group, the tolerance for their shortcomings, and the willingness to share responsibility for mission. From the beginning several of the men challenged strengths in one another and acknowledged how those strengths affected their own lives and the atmosphere of the house. This was not just generalization; individuals were faced and addressed.

"I find you doing a lot to create this atmosphere, Paul. You have a way of listening to everybody. You always seem to have the time to stop and hear what we are saying. Last Tuesday when you were in a hurry to get to the board meeting, you gave me precious time to talk about what had just happened in the workshop."

"I'm much more conscious of the prayer life of the community since living alongside you, Larry. It's clearly so important to you that I catch a bit of your enthusiasm. You don't mind sharing at the level of faith either, and I rarely experience that sort of openness."

As the first question continued to be addressed, a sense of brotherhood and mutual valuing became more and more explicit. Partly this state had already existed, but I had the impression that in the very telling, new recognition and a new excitement about being together was created. It overflowed into the community prayer that day and on following days. And it was expressed also in the unspoken need to remain near one another, people leaving the room reluctantly when their apostolate demanded it.

Eventually, we began to take up the second question, and it quickly became apparent that there were issues that members wanted to address. I shall not list these here because a single confrontation soon became the focus of the group's energy, and it remains in my memory as the best example of communal confrontation I have ever had the privilege of witnessing. I believe it was a challenge for which the group required the safety of a facilitator, and it largely explained my presence there.

One member of the group, Carl, was giving every indication of being an alcoholic, but until now only one person had attempted to address this with him directly. What I know of that encounter, which preceded my visit by only a few days, is that it took courage and honesty and directness, and that it was offered with unmistakable care. The groundwork for a communal confrontation had been prepared by this, and Carl referred to it himself many times. Richard, who had been the confronter, demonstrated a sense of integrity in his care not to reveal details of the encounter that might have been regarded as private disclosures in the context of the one-to-one relationship between himself and Carl, and in the exchange that took place in the common room his relationship with Carl was clearly supportive without being in any way soft or conciliatory.

The communal confrontation was initiated by Larry, a sensitive and gentle person. With his face pale and voice trembling, he looked directly at Carl and said quietly, "Carl, you can probably tell from my shaking voice how scared I feel about saying this, but I feel as though I have let you down recently. I'm worried about how much you are drinking. The other night when there were several members of our lay staff present you got drunk. I was embarrassed and awkward, and I didn't have the guts to say something to you at the time. I'm glad Richard did, but I'm not too proud of myself. Anyway, I've been sitting here thinking now's my opportunity to speak to you. The fact is, Carl, you're my brother, I love you, and I cannot sit by and see you destroying yourself without saying something."

There was silence for a while, and everybody waited for a response from Carl. He looked directly across at Larry and nodded, then, looking around at each other person in turn, he gave a great sigh and said, "I'm really relieved that it's out in the open at last. I know I have been drinking heavily, but I wasn't aware how visible it was. I think that I could easily become an alcoholic."

Immediately, Larry replied, "Carl, I think you may already be an alcoholic."

Other members of the community described other examples of Carl's periodic drinking to support this, with Carl insisting that because he could control his drinking he could not possibly be an alcoholic.

At this point there was no arguing. Nobody set out to prove anything, but each brother with warmth and gentleness insisted that the facts spoke for themselves, while at the same time recognizing Carl's fear and doubt. Carl himself began to tell the story of how he began to drink while he was on an isolated mission, sometimes in danger and most of the time lonely. The rest of us listened as he told the story, hearing the history of the drinking problem, even feeling a little guilty that a man should be left so isolated.

The evening drew to a close with the community standing firm in its concern that Carl was already an alcoholic, and Carl denying this but admitting to having a problem. At this point I ventured the opinion that when there is an alcoholic in a family or a community, it is likely that the whole group shares in the problem by ancillary behavior—ignoring the drinking, attempting to keep it hidden, laughing at the drunken antics, complaining about the drinking but never confronting directly. I invited the whole community to examine the ways in which they were part of Carl's alcoholism. I obtained a copy of James Gill's article, "The Religious Alcoholic,"[18] and had it distributed for each person to read in preparation for further consideration the following day. Carl and the rest of the brothers had explicitly commented that the issue was unfinished and that they wanted to continue with it the next morning.

Early on the following day Carl approached me and admitted that he was more than "nearly an alcoholic" as he had previously described himself. Pointing to Gill's article, Carl said simply, "I *am* an alcoholic." As the import of this admission sank in he asked in alarm, "What am I to do? What will become of me?"

I suggested that there were several options, but that first perhaps he should tell the rest of the community what he had decided about himself. When the community assembled, he initiated discussion without invitation and asked for suggestions about getting help, insisting, however, that he was unwilling to move away from this group who had offered him such support. He suggested seeking psychiatric help from a doctor in the city and carrying on with his usual apostolate. He pleaded with the community, "I beg and implore you do not send me away from here."

A very clear and caring statement followed this. Larry said, "Carl, there's no way we'll send you away. We want you here, but we also want whatever is best for you. It seems that some kind of residential group treatment works best with alcoholism, so we should perhaps take a look at what is available. If we can find something suitable, what we'd want is that you simply take some leave, still belonging to us, and when you've been taught how to manage your drinking, we want to be a part of helping you and supporting you in that."

Carl registered great fear of this, but understood its caring nature immediately. He was able to disclose his fears, and the community could hear them without being blackmailed emotionally by them. Once again there was no argument or coercion, but a steady, direct exchange that was mutually respecting. Carl finally decided to apply for inclusion in a residential program that began the following month. He took primary responsibility for telling the provincial what had transpired, and undertook, with the community's help, to deny himself alcohol totally in the interim. The community, aware of previously turning a blind eye to Carl's excessive drinking, also undertook to confront him if they saw evidence that he had broken his pledge to quit drinking. They spontaneously offered to inform the provincial of their desire to have Carl reappointed to their group when he returned, and they also planned to remain in close contact with Carl by letter and telephone during the treatment period.

There was a final touching moment. Carl turned to the group and with quiet delicacy thanked them for their courage in confronting him, recognizing the difficulty of offering such a challenge with care. When he had finished speaking and the group prepared to disband at the end of this morning session, I noticed that Richard was sitting quietly on the opposite side of the room with tears streaming down his face. I asked if he needed to say anything more, and he said "No, I'm just moved by all this."

Turning to Carl, I said, "Take a look at those tears, Carl, because I think they are saying something to you."

There was a hush. Then Carl said, "I want you fellows to know that I have never felt so *loved* in my whole life as I do right now."

I have omitted many of the details of this story. Other members of the group contributed in creative and enabling ways to what happened. Paul, the prior, in an effort to clarify some of the difficulties in his relationship with Carl, was a key person in stimulating and modelling self-disclosure. Michael, a senior member of the group who was still mourning his departure from a previous community where he had been very happy was able to offer the wisdom of his experience and the fruit of his years entirely without condescension or advice-giving. Indeed, the exchange with Carl made it possible for him to disclose how he felt about the group he had left and a dawning need to belong to the present group more actively. There was a visible letting go of his clinging to the previous group. The junior member of the group, Gerry, demonstrated the sense of equality present in the group by his confidence to intervene whenever he felt it appropriate, knowing his disclosures and challenges would be met with respect and acceptance. The provincial, informed by Carl of the love of the local community, assured him of the love and support of the entire province, a love borne out in the frequency of their contact with Carl during his absence.

I cannot say that the story has a happy ending since the story is not ended! I can, however, claim that the outcome so far is a happy one. Carl is back, actively contributing to the life and ministry of the group, and he has so far confidently controlled his drinking.

I am reluctant to analyze all that happened. Suffice it to say that the group dared to be appropriately self-disclosing over time, at different levels with different individuals according to their readiness. As a result of this, when the time was right, confrontation—a deeper mutuality—was accomplished with visibly positive results both for the individual confronted and for the rest of the group, but most of all for the bondedness and relationality of the whole community. They continue to be able to speak with immediacy to one another that preserves a sense of brotherhood visible to all who are involved with them. Their efforts at mutuality, sometimes clumsy, at times abrasive and faltering, almost invariably warm and loving, witness powerfully to the value of communal life. This creates a safe place for the custody and expansion of the founder's original vision. Their sense of fragility and yet strength recalls the Pauline reminder:

> We hold this treasure in pots of earthenware, so that the immensity of the power is God's and not our own (2 Cor 4:7).

For community consideration

A.   Reflect together on the following questions:[19]

   1. What is the major focus of this group?
   2. How fully is the individual member expected to be involved with this group?
   3. How appropriate is it for the members of this group to share with one another on an emotional level?
   4. How is behavior regulated in this group?
   5. How obligated are members to each other and to the group as a whole?
   6. How are evaluations made about persons who are members of the group?

As you reflect on these questions, remember the model of mutuality. Listen as individuals share their opinions and do not argue. Try to receive their experience with respect as an indication of their frame of reference, which is not and does not have to be the same as yours. Offer your opinion only when you are satisfied that you have heard the previous speaker clearly.

B.   Share with one another your reflections on these two questions, allowing time for quiet and refusing to proceed from the first question to the second until everyone has a chance to speak:

1.   What is the best thing that being in this community group has done for you so far this year? Communicate this concretely and specifically.

2.   What, in your opinion, are the toughest issues that this group needs to confront together as this year goes on? What strengths are present in the group for accomplishing this?

C.   Are you able to identify together factors that are perceived as uniting the group?

Are there any identifiable separators that can be changed by communal efforts? What are they? How might they be changed?

For individual consideration

A.   After a period of time spent in centering, recall to awareness the best relationship you have or have had. Picture yourself interacting in this relationship. Allow its texture and feeling-tone to become present to you. What is good about this relationship? What does it evoke from you that is a strength for relating?

List and describe a few of the strengths you would like to mobilize in your relationships with others in the community.

B.   Now recall in the same way a relationship where you are often at your relational worst. Again, allow your memory to make the relationship present to you.

List and describe a few of the dysfunctional things you do in this relationship. What would you like to change? How does the information in this chapter about mutuality enlighten you about mistakes in this relationship? Can you challenge yourself to make one small but concrete and measurable change in your behavior that might improve the relationship?

C. From the awareness you have of these two relationships, and from all those other relationships between the two extremes, what stages of mutuality do you think you handle best? Where do you need to do some remedial learning?

D. What obstacles do you perceive, if any, to developing greater mutuality within your present community group?

E. Which feelings do you find it easy to recognize and express? Which ones are usually harder to identify, own and express? Why? (You may care to remember back to the early chapters of your family and religious life history as you try to answer this, possibly finding there the origins of both freedoms and fears and the people from whom you learned them.)

F. Call to mind, as in the earlier exercise, an occasion when you were confronted or challenged in a way that was experienced as positive and helpful. Who challenged you? About what? What was the effect on you? Can you describe what was helpful in the manner of the other person's challenge? What was the effect on the relationship?

G. Now call to mind a negative example where you felt damaged or at least unhelped by another person's challenge. Why was this felt to be unhelpful? What impeded you from growing as a result of the challenge—either in your own receptivity to the challenge or in the other person's offering of it?

H. What can you learn about effective challenge from these two experiences? What skills do you have for challenge? What do you need to learn?

I. How deeply do you listen—at table, during informal conversations, at team or community meetings?

What filters operate in you to diminish your capacity to listen at times? How habitual is deep listening for you, or on the contrary, how much is it a professional skill to be switched on and off at will?

J. What are the deepest beliefs you have that are the foundation-stones of a life characterized by the constant growth of mutuality?

Notes

1. I do not use the word *experience* in the colloquial sense of "what my senses tell me," but in terms of the definition Shea derives from Alfred North Whitehead: "Human experience is the reciprocal flow between the self and its environments." John Shea, *Stories of God: An Unauthorized Biography* (Chicago, Illinois: The Thomas More Press, 1978), pp. 15, 16.

2. William James, Address to the Yale Philosophical Club, 1891.

3. Jean Vanier, *Community and Growth* (Sydney: St. Paul Publications, 1979), p. 35.

4. George A. Aschenbrenner, "Religious Community: That the World May Believe," *Human Development*, 3:2 (Summer, 1982), p. 16.

5. Johannes B. Metz, *Followers of Christ: The Religious Life and the Church*, trans. Thomas Linton (London: Burns & Oates, 1978), p. 12

6. Ibid. p. 15.

7. John Paul II, *Redemptionis Donum*, No. 15.

8. Jean Vanier, *Tears of Silence* (London: Darton, Longman & Todd, 1973), p. 82.

9. Andrew M. Greeley, *The Friendship Game* (New York: Image Books, 1971), p. 46.

10. Ibid. p. 44.

11. Gerard Egan and Michael A. Cowan, *People in Systems: A Model for Development in the Human-Service Professions and Education* (Monterey, California: Brooks/Cole, 1979), pp. 180-202.

12. Matthew Fox, *Meditations with Meister Eckhart* (Santa Fe, New Mexico: Bear & Co., Inc., 1982), p. 125.

13. The best treatment of this subject that I know of is to be found in Gerard Egan, *Interpersonal Living: A Skills Contract Approach to Human Relations Training in Groups* (Monterey, California: Brooks/Cole, 1976), pp. 38-63. Egan appends a useful reading list on self-disclosure on p. 63.

14. Greeley, op. cit. p. 47.

15. Evelyn Eaton Whitehead and James D. Whitehead, *Com-

munity of Faith: Models and Strategies for Developing Christian Communities (New York: Seabury Press, 1982), p. 34.

16. I am grateful to Dr. Jim Bryer and Dr. Michael Cowan for this tactic.

17. The story told here is a delicate one. Before writing it for publication I submitted a rough draft of it to the community members who figure in it. With their permission and approval, it is presented here. Some details have been changed to safeguard their privacy and anonymity, but the account is as faithful a rendering of their story as my memory and theirs can recall. I am grateful to the brothers who allow it to be told.

18. James J. Gill, "The Religious Alcoholic," *Human development*, 1:4 (Winter, 1980), pp. 27-38.

19. Whitehead, op. cit.

3
A SPIRITUALITY
NAMED EMPATHY:

The Life Blood of the Community Story

In a discussion with a friend and colleague recently, a priest who was seeking counselling became the focus of our common concern and we spoke of making an appropriate referral. The priest had already telephoned me and asked for an appointment, but after some deliberation we had decided together that distance was a difficulty that might become a real obstacle to continuity and that a therapist geographically closer to his place of residence and ministry might be more suitable. I promised to investigate the matter and make a referral. When I mentioned this to my friend he commented casually, "It's probably just as well. If you refer him to . . . he'll be unlikely to get away with much. He plays a lot of games, and he may think he can put it over on you. He needs more than empathy."

When my anger at the insouciant chauvinism of this statement subsided a little I became aware that it contained a misunderstanding that I had often heard in different guises before. I have heard therapists ask, "After empathy, what?" and I have heard community members lament that "warm fuzzies" or "soft" relationships were phony and not the stuff of which real community experience is made. The assumption is that empathy is something one does, a sort of low-level helping skill which, when one learns to help more strongly, is subordinated to other more confrontative and even coercive skills. A second assumption is that empathy is a weak tactic that smooths over difficulties, masks hostility, agrees with people and generates a sort of warm, blanketed cosiness that lacks genuineness.

Empathy is much more than this. It is a spirituality. I do not deny that there is a level of skill involved in responding to another with accuracy and understanding, but there is more, much more, to it than that. It is not just a therapeutic tool for psychotherapists but a stance toward life that can bond vastly different people. Neither is it simply an attitude toward other persons. I regard it as a valuing of the whole of life, touching nature, oneself, God and prayer, the environment and other people. It is a lively and appreciative recognition that "there lives the dearest freshness deep down things" and that the whole of reality is charged with a grandeur of divine origin, over which the Holy Spirit "broods with warm breast and with ah! bright wings."[1]

Spirituality

Spirituality is a movement of the spirit, a stance of the person toward reality, toward life. I regard personhood as holistic; there is no area of life untouched by spirituality. It is an orientation of the spirit-person which emanates in congruent action. All too often religious confuse spiritual exercises with spirituality, and for many the result is an unfortunate dichotomy in which prayer, liturgy, meditation and reflection are placed in a holy or religious box and the rest of life in another. But for the person who sees, nothing is profane.

Spirituality is a way of seeing that results in a way of being and behaving. To be a just person and to act justly, for example, are not two separate realities. One is the necessary extension of the other. To value life and one another is truthful only when my actions reveal my inner belief, only when I respond with empathy to the world. The process is not a linear one. My inner attitude requires action, but the action feeds the inner attitude. It is a symbiotic relationship of vision and action, each promoting and enlarging the other, each drawing sustenance from the other. So, if I understand life to be good, and I understand myself to be a relating and co-creative part of that goodness, I will not retreat from but engage with my world, my neighborhood, God, the environment, people. My spirituality is authenticated by the congruence between belief and action. For this very reason, I believe it is inauthentic to make a clear distinction between the communal vision (charism) and ministry, since ministry is the acting out of the fundamental gospel insight that fires the community into existence.

Inspired by the Ignatian concern to unite contemplation and action, Teilhard de Chardin saw mysticism as extending into homes and factories, cities and institutions. Specifically, he regarded Christianity as the illumination of the existing world, forging bonds between inner faith and faithful work.

> . . . by virtue of the Creation and, still more, of the Incarnation, *nothing* here below *is profane* for those who know how to see. On the contrary, everything is sacred to the men who can distinguish that portion of chosen being which is subject to Christ's drawing power in the process of consummation. Try, with God's help, to perceive the connection—even physical and natural—which binds your labor with the building of the kingdom of heaven. . . . For what is sanctity in a creature if not to adhere to God with the maximum of his strength?— and what does that maximum adherence to God mean if not the fulfillment—in the world organized around Christ—of the exact function, be it lowly or eminent, to which that creature is destined both by natural endowment and by supernatural gift?[2]

It is my belief that this habitual recognition of the sacredness of life and of work springs from empathy. When life is deeply embedded in empathy as a way of being-in-the-world, there is born the possibility that the differences existing in a pluralist community will not merely co-exist as uneasy bed-partners, but that a genuine unity of vision will create an appreciation of the differences and their potential richness will be accepted and maximized.

Such spirituality is not a kind of divine steam-roller that will iron flat the paradoxes of pluralistic communal living. The tensions will remain:

diversity and commonality

uniqueness and sameness

separateness and bondedness

conflict and harmony

sensitivity and insensitivity

differences of meanings, hopes, fears, understandings.

A spirituality of empathy recognizes the possibility of creation in all of these rich differences. This issues in "collaboration trembling with love" whose "roots and elemental sap lie in the discovery and the love of everything that is true and beautiful in creation."[3]

Empathy

St. Paul declares that we must put on the mind of Christ, being in our minds the *same* as Christ Jesus. Immediately following this injunction he launches into the magnificent hymn celebrating the humanity of Jesus:

> Who, being in the form of God,
> did not count equality with God
> something to be grasped.

> But he emptied himself,
> taking the form of a slave,
> becoming as human beings are;

> and being in every way like a human being,
> he was humbler yet,
> even to accepting death, death on a cross.

> And for this God raised him high,
> and gave him the name
> which is above all other names;

so that *all* beings
in the heavens, on earth and in the underworld,
should bend the knee at the name of Jesus

and that *every tongue should acknowledge*
Jesus Christ as Lord,
to the glory of God the Father (Phil 2:6-11).

This hymn always comes to mind when I reflect on the meaning of empathy as a spirituality, for it is a poem about the incarnation of God's empathy for the human race. It involves not a God who observes from a great height, not a kindly God bestowing largesse on creation, but a God who enters totally into the human condition in the person of Jesus, who is completely open to being broken in upon by our humanity. At times the incarnation is spoken of as God's inbreaking into human life. Perhaps the opposite is true and that God is broken in upon by creation! This hymn is a celebration of the humility of the Messiah. What greater self-forgetfulness is there than to be totally receptive of the human condition even to the point of death? Empathy is self-forgetful receptivity before the reality of another.

Religious are taught from the novitiate onward to engage in ministry, to be self-denying for the sake of the kingdom, for those to whom they minister. They become the church's professional *givers*. I do not wish to deny the desirablity of actively trying to bring the Word of God alive in the life-situation of those to whom we minister, but what is to stop this giving becoming a kind of unconsciously condescending do-gooding? The answer for me lies in the *receptivity* of empathy. This is not a grasping, selfish desire to receive, but a willingness to leave the clamor of my own needs in order to enter deeply into the life experience of another, to taste the quality of this experience, and to respond to the other as a person rather than to offer "help" out of the treasury of gifts I think he or she "ought" to be given. An incarnational spirituality implies a desire to become as all people are in the sense of entering their lives with an openness to their stories, encouraging the living out and completion of those stories, indicating sometimes that there are new directions possible, walking along new pathways with them, encountering the same difficulties in the landscape.

When the risen Jesus walked along with the disciples on the way to Emmaus, he did not lift them out of their despairing sadness and sense of let-down by revealing himself immediately. Instead, he listened to their story, encouraging its telling and hearing its quality—the loss, the pain, the crashing disappoint-

ment, the breakdown of their hopes and plans and expectations. Then he began to locate their little mundane story within
the larger story of the prophets, inviting them to examine the
roots from which their present story had sprung, drawing them
gently into their sacred story, preparing them for the revelation
yet to come. His empathic presence to them was neither the
passionless presence of a holy-card Jesus nor the overpowering
presence of one who stands outside their experience and claims
to have the whole truth. First Jesus joins them on the journey,
goes at their pace, listens to them, receives their story with respect and asks the occasional question to extend their awareness:

> "What are all these things that you are discussing as you walk
> along?"
> "You must be the only person staying in Jerusalem who
> does not know the things that have been happening there
> these last few days."
> "What things?" (Lk 24:17-19).

The receptivity of Jesus here includes walking with and listening to, in a manner that is simple, uncoercive and conveys a
sense of equality.

The willingness to live like this is far deeper than skill. The
willingness is a movement of the spirit, or if you prefer, a movement of the Spirit. The kind of listening here is listening that
goes beyond merely hearing the words or even hearing the
meaning of the words and the feelings conveyed. It is a listening
that tunes in to the spirit of the other. It is a meeting of spirits
and a partnering of stories. One translator renders the line, "In
your minds you must be the same as Christ Jesus" as "Let your
bearing toward one another be shaped by what you really are in
Christ Jesus."[4] Because we are already *in Christ Jesus* we are ex-
horted to *be* what we really are in Christ Jesus, living our lives
with the same authenticity and reverence toward those who,
along with us, are restored to true humanity by a Christ who
has healed our humanity from within. Paul sees Jesus as the
new and final Adam, the founder of a new humanity. For Paul,
Adam was someone who symbolized and gathered together humanity as sinful. The new Adam gathers us together in the
bondedness of a newly created unity, a common unity, community. A spirituality of empathy is the life-blood of such unity.

It is from this that a hunger and thirst after justice is born.
Open, sometimes painfully open to the life experience of all
whom the gospel bids us call brother or sister, we cannot be at

peace with the inequalities of haves and have-nots, with oppression or exploitation or destructiveness. As a result, religious cannot be comfortable with dichotomous thinking that places community on center stage and sees ministry as another and separate reality. Empathy born and nourished within the local communal group overflows its boundaries and seeks every corner of human existence that resounds with the cry of the poor.

To listen to the cry of the poor, to the quality of another's experience, means learning the abnegation of silence. It means learning a wordless silence. There is no place here for pious reassurance or social bandaging. We must allow ourselves to be seared and singed by the other's reality before any action may be discerned as appropriate. This begins in the close-up relationships, with colleagues and partners in the apostolate, with members of the immediate communal sub-group, widening, like the ripples from a stone thrown into a pond, to those about us whom we meet and serve.

At times I am appalled by the level of chatter and empty small talk in religious communities and by the substitution of television-watching for real conversation. I am equally appalled by the ready remedies applied with facility by religious to the pain or brokenness they encounter in one another or in those to whom they minister. I am sure my own experience is not unique when I recall the times of silent, companionable, listening presence offered to me by another or others—a presence redolent with wisdom that needs no words and would, indeed, be ruined by words. I remember also, by contrast, the well-intentioned but useless flood of words, usually religious, poured over me by self-appointed helpers at difficult times in my life. In particular, I remember someone saying to me just before I underwent surgery I was afraid of, "Evelyn, I'm sure God has sent you this illness to slow you down because you've been working far too hard." I understand the concern that prompted the remark. At the time, however, when fear was my dominant feeling, I found myself being angry and wanting to declare that I had never met such a God! The person who helped me the most at that time was a friend who gained entry to my hospital room after I had received my pre-surgery injection and simply sat there in a silence that somehow recognized the tumult of feelings in me and did not add to them by words. Empathy is built upon such a silence.

Many people are looking for an ear that will listen. They do not find it among Christians because these Christians are talking whereas they should be listening. But he who can no longer listen to his brother will soon be no longer listening to God either. He will be doing nothing but prattling in the service of God too. This is the beginning of the death of the spiritual life and in the end there is nothing left but spiritual chatter and clerical condescension arrayed in pious words.[5]

To deny myself the quick and knowing response is part of the asceticism of empathy. I cannot respond genuinely until I have heard what it is I am responding to, and it is a mistake to think that every response has to be with words. At times the clearest response is quiet presence, a touch, a tear or a smile. At other times, a sensitively worded response does transmit the empathy. Advice is never an empathic response. Advice comes from what *I* think, from my opinion. Empathy is a focus on the world of experience that pulses right now in this other person.

I remember a day when I was feeling the isolation of coming home after counselling other religious and could not speak of what had happened in my office in the way the other people in my group could discuss the happenings of the day in their respective classrooms. I sat at the dining table and listened to the stories of their day with a little echo of loneliness in me. As we were washing the dishes after the meal one of the sisters in the group said to me quietly, "It must be hard for you to hear us all going on about what we've done and not be able to say some of the things that you've been through in a day. I hope you know there's a lot of real appreciation around here for you, and that we don't ask questions because we respect the confidentiality of your work." She so accurately perceived my lonely and slightly left-out feeling that I felt the prick of tears behind my eyes. Although I said nothing about how I had been feeling, she had been able to feel her way into my experience with gentle but sharp accuracy.

The word empathy is Greek in origin, derived from *pathos* meaning a strong or deep feeling, with overtones of suffering, and prefixed by "in." Thus, literally, *empathy* means "to feel into." It is often used instead of the word *sympathy*, "to feel with." The distinction is unfortunate but necessary since although the basic meaning of sympathy accurately describes what I mean by empathy, it has gathered a colloquial sense of pity, a meaning that I do not see as germane to empathy. In fact, pity somehow denies the very entering into which is the essence of this exchange. I pity someone from the outside and from a "better off" position in relation to him or her. I empathize by entering in, by becoming as this person is. Psychologists have a great deal to say about the value of objectivity and of preserving a sense of separateness. I cannot see, however, how we can enter into the experience of another without at least momentarily losing our separateness. Even if immediately thereafter we recover a sense of separateness, something has changed in *both* of us because of the current of empathy that has passed between us. Jung speaks of the exchange as being like the contact of two chemical substances, each transformed by the other, and claims "You can exert no influence if you are not susceptible to influence. . . ."[6]

Many times in the last few years I have read and re-read the final homily given by Francois Marty, Cardinal Archbishop of Paris, on the occasion of his retirement. The statement breathes with the spirit of a man alive with empathy. He speaks of his receptivity to the sights and sounds and spirit of Paris and his people, and he tells of how he was influenced and educated there.

> For me man is not an abstraction; man is not an idea to be defended. I have met many; I have listened to many. . . .They have all taught me about life. They have all taught me about Jesus. They have all passed on the gospel to me. In each one, in what he told me of his life and aspirations, I was able to receive the echo of the God whom I serve. You are my prayer.

He urges Parisians not to deafen themselves to the sights and sounds and cries of appeal rising from the streets they pass through, exhorting them to talk to one another and listen to one another and refuse to be isolated from one another. And he confides to a questioner the secret of his faith:

> Love man. For my faith in God is a wonder before the faith which God places in man. And God saw that man was good. I would like to convince you of this.

Cardinal Marty's homily concludes with an anecdote that images for me the kind of vision that is born of empathy, for it is indeed possible to define empathy as a way of seeing.

> Recently an old Aveyron friend was operated on for cataract. A few weeks later he returns home. On his arrival at the house, he catches sight of his grandson. He sees him with new eyes. And he exclaims: "Oh, my little Jean, I never knew you were so beautiful!"

> Blessed be the Lord who, in the evening of my life, gives me a
> fleeting insight into man's heart as it really is: I never knew it
> was so beautiful![7]

Is it too daring to suggest that the incarnation gives God an ex-
clamatory insight into the beauty and originality of humanity? I
certainly risk the assertion that empathy removes the cataracts
of self-absorption and prejudice from our eyes and allows a new
vision that is not merely a seeing from a distance but a savoring
of the value of another.

I do not believe that empathy is reserved for people. It has
its beginnings in an appreciative manner of seeing that takes in
sunrises and acorns, gentle breezes and raging hurricanes, rock
and surf and flying sand, taste and texture, littleness and greatness, joy and delight. I find myself wishing that we all had that
same appreciation of the complexity, beauty, possibility and fluidity of one another's being-in-process, an appreciation that is
far deeper than mere external admiration, springing as it does
from touching one another's experience from within.

One heresy in religious life, in my observation, is that empathy is about pleasing everybody all the time, about generating
a false harmony that seems untouched by any breath of disagreement or conflict and which issues in universal liking for
everyone. This is nonsense. Empathy is a tough reality that allows me to stand respectfully within the reality of another person's anger or hostility toward me in the knowledge that this is
the other person's truth at this moment, a truth that is uncomfortable and even frightening to me. Empathy is also a tough reality which, when directed toward me, leaves me vulnerable
and exposed. At times when someone to whom I am not particularly attracted enters my experience with the very gentlest of
empathy, I have some feeling for the fellow in the ditch, robbed
and assaulted, who suddenly finds himself being ministered to
by a Samaritan, an alien, not one of the chosen of Israel. I
would often rather be the Samaritan than the one to whom the
Samaritan ministers! Empathy from such a one is a raw reality.

There are some factors about the Samaritan's ministering
that are worthy of attention. His is the simple action of a person
who recognizes in the other a fellow human being whose
whole situation calls out for contact. The Samaritan does what
is necessary without words, pays the inn-keeper and then goes
off about his other business. He does not hang about waiting for
gratitude, posturing and grandstanding. It is almost as if he takes
it for granted that this is everyday behavior that ought not surprise anyone. It seems to be ordinary, humdrum helpfulness

that is part of the pattern of his life. It is sensitive in its ordinariness. I would like to be with and for others like that. I would like others to be with and for me like that.

When empathy is absent from or breaks down within a group or a one-to-one relationship, hope decays. In the isolation of an affective desert it is hard to maintain belief in ourselves or our world. Where worth is not regularly reinforced by the transmitted respect of others, belief and hope in our own value dry up. When empathy is lost, all is lost. Then one lives godlessly.

Compassion

Empathy as spirituality is more frequently spoken of under other guises. The word *compassion* is often the name given to behavior issuing from an empathic understanding of reality. Like many other words used frequently, particularly in a religious context, it has suffered a weakening and softening with usage that is unfortunate. The similarity between compassion and empathy is clear. Literally meaning "to suffer with," compassion is grounded in empathy; it is impossible to share the life experience of anybody unless we are capable of the receptive listening of empathy. In a sense, then, compassion is half of empathy. It is the active entry into the life of another that follows the initial empathic stance of attentiveness and self-emptied focus on the reality of this other.

John V. Taylor concludes his book *The Go-Between God* with a story that epitomizes this aspect of empathy. He recounts the grief of a West Indian woman upon hearing of the sudden tragic death of her husband in a London traffic accident. Plunged into an almost catatonic state by her loss, she sat silent and immovable, untouched by the sympathy of well-wishers who came and went from her flat that day. Finally her son's schoolteacher arrived and, unlike the rest of the callers, simply sat beside the woman and put an arm around her, holding her tightly. As the current of the grieving woman's pain reached her, the teacher's grasp grew tighter still, and she began to cry with the transmitted pain of the other woman, her tears falling onto their clasped hands. After some time, a sob broke from the West Indian woman, and she too felt the release of tears, her rigidity melted by the nearness, the "within-ness" of her visitor. No word was spoken. The two women wept together for some time till the immediate force of the grief was spent, and then quietly and gently the schoolteacher disengaged her hand from that of the other and left the room, leaving behind her a gift to assist the family's needs.

At the moment when the schoolteacher felt the pain of the other woman, actually registered in her own being the sharpness of the loss, the agony and the unfairness of the tragedy, compassion was born in her. Such an encounter has no kinship with facile consolation or even words of faith and hope, for in such a crisis mere words cannot be heard. There is only the present—a biting, burning moment. What broke through to the woman in this story was the quality of presence offered by the teacher, not a clinical, objective presence, not a professional helping presence, but the simple engagement of one human being in the suffering of another. This presence in some ways sharpens the pain and cannot take it away, but takes the risk of walking in there. The meaning of incarnation becomes a little clearer to me when I contemplate a story like this one. And the meaning of incarnational spirituality makes a little more sense, for this is how life, love and hope are mediated, not with words or promises or skills from afar, but from entering in at close hand and risking being burned in the same fire. This

> is the embrace of God, his kiss of life . . . the embrace of his mission, and of our intercession. And the Holy Spirit is the force in the straining muscles of an arm, the film of sweat between pressed cheeks, the mingled wetness on the backs of clasped hands. He is as close and as unobtrusive as that, and as irresistibly strong.[8]

So, to appreciate the reality of another involves a *vision* and a *poverty*. It is a vision that is unclouded by the need to use or to change the other by instrumental means. Transformation may indeed happen, but not because I set out to change you, or vice versa. If transformation happens, it is because, in the context of our relationship a creative event is happening and meanings are coming together in a new configuration that is richer and more integrated than before. I am not alone any more. Your world of meanings interpenetrates mine and we are both richer and larger in spirit. Your entry into my world of experience opens windows in my frame of reference, stretches the limits of my experience, dignifies it and gives me a new connection with the world, with events, with you. I am larger. I have you for my brother or sister. This may not mean that I *feel* better. In fact, your presence may enlarge my contact with whatever it is that is going on in me. My condition of lostness or loneliness, of grief or abandonment may be more acutely felt, but it is felt in connection with a larger world. It may awaken in me a sense of and quest for a good that is not my own.

Curiously, a reverse process also begins. Enlarged by your entry into my world of meanings and feelings, I begin to be drawn into yours. New interrelatedness brings a new sense of community with you in your world. New horizons—new connectedness along with new restlessness and new hunger—are born. Compassion is a creative event when this takes place.

I cannot offer you compassion if I am locked into the small world of self-preoccupation. The eyes of compassion are opened when the darkness of egocentricy is taken away. Paradoxically, however, when this does happen, I am returned to myself enlarged and enriched with sensitized vision. This is not usually a sudden and blinding revelation. It is the faithful stretching and reaching beyond myself toward larger and greater reality. I am often struck by the depths of Mark's account of the man born blind. This story has layer upon layer of significance for me. First of all, it is the faith of the community, the *vision* of this compassionate little group, that brought the blind man to Jesus in the first place. They ask Jesus to touch him. The blind man stands there saying nothing. And then there is the multiple anointing of his eyes, first resulting in entire confusion. The old way of perceiving was with his other senses, an incomplete way of seeing to be sure, but a familiar one. When this is changed, the result is an entire reorganization. The man no longer senses human presence through hearing and smell and touch, but sees people like trees walking about. In a way, this intermediate stage of his new vision is more painful than blindness. It is all so new. So many other ways of being have to be surrendered now that the light is dawning. Final healing comes only after this stage is negotiated. New seeing means letting go of old seeing. There is an extraordinary vulnerability about this man. He is led by others where he did not ask to go. With simple docility, he allows himself to be led by Jesus outside the town, submits to the anointing and the questioning, describes the confusion of his half-light, sees for the first time and then goes quietly home as bidden.

Reflecting on the story, I am always impressed that when full light invaded his sight, the once blind man looked first on the face of incarnated compassion:

> From the blind eyes a little darkness falls
> and men, as yet unseen, become
> Dim movement, trees that strangely walk—

> Until
> A little light mothers a little more,
> And suspicion,
> Guess,
> Half-awareness,
> Deepen, expand into sight.
> Touched eyes, new lit,
> See the grace of men,
> See the grace,
> See Grace.

I have said that the vision that is compassionate is coupled with poverty. I am speaking of the poverty of spirit of the beatitudes, the unclutteredness and openness of heart that already possesses the kingdom because there is room for it there. The poor have no armor against the sharp experience of the human condition. They cannot take refuge in the distractions of affluence or the masks of professionalism. They are naked to the world. What is happening there registers. The genuinely poor have a way of being present in the world that has much to teach those of us who are rich, hands full of the goodies that religious life has bestowed on us and taught us to regard as ours—prestige, security, companionship, the luxury of spiritual nourishment for which we simply open our beaks like birds in a nest! So often as religious we are urged to serve the poor, to give to the poor. I would like to declare a moratorium on giving and suggest a time of receiving from the poor, of being ministered to by them, for the poor have privileged access to the meaning of the gospel.

Compassion is counter-cultural. At least in western cultural patterns, personal worth is frequently defined in terms of differences. If we are richer, more accomplished, more intelligent and, above all, more successful than others, we have value and worth. If our awareness of differences and our commitment to competition is at the heart of our relating, we are blind to each other's experience and world of meanings. Compassion has no home in such relating, for compassion is born of the knowledge that we are made of the *same* clay, that we hold our humanness as a common gift for whose co-creation we are mutually responsible. We do not cling to any sense of superiority, but become as all people are. In the shared incompleteness of our common humanity we recognize in one another the need for meaning, for growth, for re-creation, for healing. We do this out of the sameness that bonds us rather than out of differences that separate us. This presupposes the capacity to be in touch with our own brokenness and experience of life and to be impelled by it toward the parallel experience of the other. If the teacher who sat wordlessly beside the grieving West Indian woman did not know pain in her own depths, she could not have known instinctively how to draw near. It does not mean that I must have the same experience as you in order to approach you with compassion, but merely that I am in touch with whatever experience gives me kinship with you. In fact, respect for the uniqueness as well as the sameness of your experience will keep me from yielding to the temptation of being certain that I know exactly how you feel. I will, however, be drawn into how you feel in a way that creates a common experience and generates a temporary indwelling that has lasting effects.

When I can see you with this kind of vision, I have the option of moving toward and into your experience. There are other options. I can walk away from what I see. Or I can approach your experience with clinical detachment and offer professional solace. To do so, however, takes the passion out of compassion and reduces it to an abstraction and an absurdity. To walk by choice into the inner world of another person's experience is no such bloodless and dispassionate discipline. Compassion bleeds. It comes not from Platonic or Aristotelian reasoning, but from the guts!

Sometimes I hear religious communal groups speaking of a member who is currently experiencing more than the usual share of problems or pain. Too often this is a discussion at a level of abstraction and analysis that seeks solutions rather than truly hears the quality of the experience. It is often a discussion that takes place in the absence of the person concerned. Causes are named and remedies suggested, but nobody makes a real approach. At least nobody makes an approach empty of advice-giving and suggestions about available help. In this regard, the ready referral to professional helpers is a way of avoiding entering the other's inner world. As I sit in my counselling room with the many religious who come here, I am aware, time after time, that had there been enough simple warm attentiveness to this individual at home, and even one brother or sister willing to walk into his or her life, my services might have been rendered redundant. I am impatient with the excuse, "We simply don't have the skill." Compassion is not a matter of skill. It is a matter of passionate risk-taking. Unless we understand this, we cannot hope even to begin to know what hunger and thirst after justice is all about, and we thus take refuge in righteous-sounding words *about* justice, rather than "justice-ing."

I remember with shame an episode that happened some years ago:

> A member of a group with whom I lived had fallen in love with a man in the neighborhood, and her behavior increasingly demonstrated this. She was more and more often absent from communal gatherings and her demeanor bespoke the tension of the double commitment she was trying to sustain. We noticed all of this and talked about it in her absence. We discussed the pain of the situation, judged the possible scandal that might be created by it, uttered pronouncements about how it should all be handled—and did absolutely nothing. I do not know of any person in the group, including myself, who dared the risk of walking into the loneliness and tension, the fears and hopes, pain and joy of the complex situation this woman was experiencing. We "tut-tutted" from our ivory tower and *called* ourselves her sisters. She made the lonely decision to leave the community. Indeed, there was little encouragement for her to do otherwise. The man she loved had other commitments that he continued to pursue, so no marriage ever took place. She now lives alone.

We hated her. I am sure the members of the group, reading this, may be outraged at such a statement. However, it has been pointed out that the word *hatred* in the Bible means lack of compassion,[9] "an apathy, a coldness, an abstractedness that prevents love of neighbor or is indifferent to it."[10] We hated her. We isolated her. Passionate caring through interaction was absent even though there was probably not one of us who had not at some stage struggled with the tension between celibate living and vibrant intimacy. The stuff of compassion was there, but we gathered up the hem of our garments and kept ourselves pure by avoiding contamination. We hated her. With pharisaical propriety we kept ourselves ritually clean. But the person of compassion gets dirt under his or her fingernails.

The compassion of which I speak is not mere altruism. It is a way of being that is grounded in a passionate God, for the God of our deep story is a God who woos his people, is angry and jealous, loves tenderly, wreaks havoc on the enemy, cares deeply. The incarnation of the story, Jesus, is a man who lives and loves, weeps over Jerusalem, mixes with tax-collectors and prostitutes, befriends a motley group of fishermen and is eventually betrayed or abandoned by almost all of them, dying for what he believes. Those who profess that their immediate story is grounded in the deep story of Jesus, whose deep story is in turn enmeshed in the deep story of Israel, profess discipleship. This does not imply a slavish imitation of Jesus but the radical following which Bonhoeffer calls spontaneous obedience. It begins in fascination with the person of Jesus and his place in the web of the Christian story to which we belong. It is sustained by contemplation of his humanity, so totally open to the in-breaking of God that he can claim "I and the Father are one." It blossoms in an expansion of the spirit that responds to life authentically. Ultimately, the gospel assures us, our discipleship is manifest in our way of loving one another. We have a passionately variable God, a gregarious and risk-taking Christ. Obedience requires that we find our own authentic thrust toward life that mirrors that reality in the unique setting of our time, our capacity and our culture, aware that

> the living spirit grows and even outgrows its earlier forms of expressions; it freely chooses the men [women] in whom it lives and who proclaim it. This living spirit is eternally renewed and pursues its goal in manifold and inconceivable ways throughout the history of mankind.[11]

Care

The expression of empathy or compassion is sometimes named care. Empathy and compassion are far more than feelings or the luxury of sentimental tears. They reach out to ensure the right of the other person to connectedness. The reaching out is care.

I hear religious speaking of care in a variety of ways, usually in terms of their own need for it or their concern that others be cared for. It always has a connection with being at home or belonging. When a person says, "Nobody cares about me," there is usually contained in the complaint a homelessness and non-belonging that nothing but care can assuage. When ecology and environment-conscious persons say they care about their surroundings, about keeping the neighborhood and the country and indeed the world free of pollution or protected from rapists who would denude the forests and undermine world-wonders, they are speaking of keeping and protecting the world as *home*, something to be appreciated rather than instrumentally ravaged. They are keenly conscious of the relationship between humanity and the rest of nature. It is not only other people who are part of our web, but rivers and trees and wild animals, power and grandeur and beauty and mystery. To care for all this is to fight to sustain the bondedness. When a person who is truly generative (that is, committed to making the world a better place for future generations) says "I care," he or she authenticates the statement by working for peace, justice, equality, better working conditions, and so forth. To care is to do; it is personally undertaking the doing, and not mere arm-chair theorizing about what ought to be done by someone else.

Some years ago, during the evacuation of refugees from Vietnam, I was driving along listening to the local radio station. The usual program was interrupted by an appeal from the district medical superintendent who asked medical and paramedical people to go to South Vietnam and help with the evacuation of those incapacitated by injury, illness and starvation. It was an invitation not merely to send medical supplies, necessary as these undoubtedly were, but to make a much greater personal investment, to go where these deprived persons were, to walk into their life situation, in proximity to their dangers and diseases, and to offer them new possibility of life. Real care is always about the enlargement of life.

In an instrumentally inclined society, it is easy to confuse care with a kind of psychological and social tidiness that cleans up the things we are ashamed of, gets rid of what is unsightly, removes suffering to a less conspicuous place if we cannot cure it, sends the unproductive to nicely appointed and government-funded Siberias. (Are there echoes of this in the way we move troublesome sisters or brothers from one communal group to another to take the pressure off the others who have to live with them?) In a predominantly instrumental society it is all too easy to confuse care and cure. The word *care* originates in the Gothic *kara* meaning "to lament, to grieve, to experience sorrow, to cry out with." It is interesting to note also that the Gaelic word for friend is *cara*, and in the Romance languages the same word is used as an expression of affection, "dear" or "beloved." This is a far cry from an antiseptic and objective assessment and treatment of symptoms sometimes referred to as cure. Care enters in; cure is clinically objective. Care hugs lepers; cure scrubs against infection. Care embraces the whole person; cure attends to "the gall bladder in Room 315." Care is from equal to equal; cure is often from haves to have-nots, clean to unclean, professional to lay person.

The gospel is full of references to the healings accomplished by Jesus. In his message to John in prison, he himself cited the teaching, healing and life-giving aspects of his ministry as signs to be assessed in answer to the question, "Are you he who is to come?" For years I have read the gospel and the accounts of miracles with a superficial credulousness that borders on the naive. They have somehow remained in the realm of mystery, discounted as a kind of divine sleight of hand to be wondered at but not imitated. Yet, tucked away in any of the stories are clues that are easily overlooked. In the story of the multiplication of the loaves, for instance, the first thing Jesus does is call for what food is already there. "Give me what you have," he says. He holds out his own empty hands and first receives, knowing his own poverty and admitting it. It is a child who gives to him. People are fed not out of the largesse of a rich person but out of the poverty of one who shares their hungers.

When, outside the gates of Naim, Jesus saw a widow accompanying the body of her dead son toward his burial place, the gospel of Luke describes his approach to her and notes that he grieved with her. There is first an entering in. The entering in is transforming. The transformation is mutual. The Jesus who gives the young man back to his mother is not the same now as he was when standing talking outside the gates a few minutes before. He is a person inextricably related to this widow and her son, all of them marked by the encounter.

Once again, as with empathy and compassion, care does not consist primarily of isolated services to others, acts that are engaged in from time to time or even habitually. It is, rather, a permanent stance toward the world, a way of seeing and a w of being that impels to action. It is a congruence between ini valuing and outer service, attentiveness and responsiveness.

My own view of care and compassion as the heart of m istry and, indeed, of appreciatively relating, has a eucharis connection. Jesus takes bread into his hands, blesses it, breaks and offers it to those around him with the words, "This is r body which will be given for you." In the same moment as tl deeply symbolic gesture of relationality, breaking and sharii the bread, he says to them, "Here I am for you. Take, brea eat." When I care for another, I say the same words implicitl Here I am for you; here I am with you. Take, break, eat. *Hei* . . . in this moment and in this place and in this commitmer . . . *I am* . . . with my presence, awareness, gifts and limitation . . . *for you and with you* . . . focused on you as you are, not a I would have you be, connected with you right here and now knowing that in large or small ways something transforming i: possible for both of us. There can be no discontinuity betweer the sacrament of Eucharist, ritual enactment of unity, and a life that extends the sacrament beyond ritual into the daily gestures of care. For Eucharist and eucharist are a single sacrament.

Hospitality

> Avoid what is evil; stick to what is good. In brotherly love let your feelings of deep affection for one another come to expression and regard others as more important than yourself. In the service of the Lord, work not halfheartedly but with conscientiousness and an eager spirit. Be joyful in hope, persevere in hardship; keep praying regularly; share with any of God's holy people who are in need; look for opportunities to be hospitable (Rom 12:9-13).

Reflecting on this text of scripture with the Hospitaller Brothers of St. John of God who see their charism as hospitality has forged some connections for me in understanding empathy as spirituality.

It is abundantly clear that the scriptural notion of hospitality enshrined in the quotation given above is relational. St. Paul juxtaposes hospitality with love, generosity, hope and prayer. Thus it is impossible to accept the conventionally superficial image of hospitality as tea, polite conversation and cucumber sandwiches. Neither is it good enough to regard hospitality as welcoming selected (and respectable) individuals into our home. If hospitality is relating in some way, then it has more to do with hospitality of heart than with hospitality of house, though the two are not mutually exclusive. Hospitality offers "friendship without binding the guest and freedom without leaving him alone."[12]

Friendship and freedom imply a concern for the belonging needs of a person as well as for his or her need to be a separate but related individual. The practice of hospitality is demanding because it involves a constant going out to the other without possessing him or her and demanding a return in kind. This is not to say that the host is closed to the influence of the guest. This could not be further from the truth. The outreaching of hospitality is an expression of compassion, and as such it is an opening up of the giver (host) to growth and challenge and newness.

So the engagement with life involved in hospitality enlarges both the host and the guest. There is a co-creativeness in the encounter when it is real and not just a mere external formality. It involves holding open the doors of our life to others and welcoming them into the wholeness of our being, at the same time leaving ourselves vulnerable to their influence. The process is two-way. It is giving, but it is also receptivity.

The parable of the Good Samaritan defines hospitality and compassion as key qualities of neighborliness. But I believe that to read a parable merely as a holy story with a powerful moral message is to miss the strength of the literary form and to avoid the deep disturbance of the challenge that it offers.

> Parable is always a somewhat unnerving experience. You can usually recognize a parable because your immediate reaction will be self-contradictory: "I don't know what you mean by that story but I'm certain I don't like it."[13]

Crossan speaks of parable as story that attacks and undermines the hearer's expectations. It is shocking. This is precisely the impact of the parable of the Good Samaritan. Those who pass by are Jews ("one of us"). They are the ones whom the Jewish hearers would have expected to help the wounded man. It is the enemy, the person of no account, the one *not* expected to help who manifests tenderness and compassion. In this lies the radical impact of the story.

What, then, does the parable say to us? It points most clearly to the boundlessness of love and the inclusiveness of the kingdom in which there is room for Samaritan as well as Jew. It demands that love reach out to the poor and despised, the helpless and insignificant, not as our instrumental society would define the probable recipients of welfare aid, but in terms of the innate poverty of a sinfully damaged humanity which creates hierarchies and harbors enmity and prejudice. It is yet another statement from Jesus about the centrality of relationship. Indeed, in the accounts of the final judgment it is only the way we have related to and welcomed Jesus in the persons of the poor, the lonely, the outcasts and the needy—*all* our fellow human beings—that determines our reward. Nothing else, just the quality of our relatedness. Guilt in this context, then, may not be the commission of gross sins, but the omission of service and hospitality to our brother or sister.

Loomer[14] points out that the kingdom that Jesus preaches may be viewed in terms of the web of relationships that shapes and creates us. He interprets the parable of the laborers in the vineyard not as a statement about justice and injustice, but about the magnanimity of God in his relationships with all of us. God loves prodigally, and not merely according to the measure of what we do. The fullness of the kingdom is available to us whenever we accept it, at any time of the day, whenever we arrived. Perhaps it is true that our hospitality to one another, all of us poor, is an image of this, an image of the kingdom's availability to all who truly seek. Justice is radically redefined.

In this light, the parable of the Good Samaritan becomes a parable about our bondedness to one another. If we have understood the message of the kingdom, to bind up the wounds of our neighbor is to save not only him or her but ourselves as well since our bondedness is at the core of our own salvation. To pass by our neighbor is to pass ourselves by. Our neighbor's diminishment diminishes us. His or her gain is our salvation. Jesus is the one who saw most profoundly that this is the elemental covenant, and the radicality of the message is underlined when we recognize that he taught it to a people whose national and personal pride rested on a covenantal sense of their special relationship with God. Jesus undermined with this parable the very structure of Jewish expectations. Religious leaders in every age have taken up the challenge again when Christian people have begun to sink into apathy or to surround themselves with the security of the ghetto of the chosen ones.

Francis de Castro describes St. John of God as

> so inebriated with charity as never to refuse anyone who asked for something for the love of God, even to giving away the poor clothes from his back, which happened several times when he had nothing else to give.[15]

In the tradition of this hospitality of heart which is John of God's special insight into the gospel we are challenged to that magnitude of spirit that places no limits on the value of the human person and excludes nobody. We are prompted to a stature of spirit that tries to provide conditions in the hospital, the school, the monastery, the neighborhood, in which others may grow in stature of soul. The emphasis, therefore, can never be merely on cure, on external service, on efficiency at the expense of compassion. Hospitality demands largeness of heart.

Escape Routes

Commitment to compassion expressed through hospitality has a high personal cost. It is a call to suffer. Almost inevitably, then, ways of escaping are invented. These are often well-disguised rationalizations clad in common sense. I invite the reader to pause at this stage and consider personal strategies for escaping the burden of hospitality. Having compiled a personal check list, you may now care to peruse mine!

Competitiveness: If I constantly vie with others for status and importance, or choose only the important and influential to serve, it is possible that I am escaping from the contact that genuine solidarity engenders, and that I am creating distance that is not consonant with opening my life not merely to the presence, but also to the influence, of another.

Bland superficiality: This can be hidden under a geniality that offers kind and encouraging words, cheerful greeting and smiles, but no real engagement with the other. It may give the impression of a good bedside manner, but it has more in common with dispensing psychological largesse than with the genuine opening up of myself to another.

Privacy: It is possible to argue very cogently that our hospitality has to be limited in order to preserve privacy. I believe quite strongly that human beings require aloneness and private space. Jesus often demanded time to go up the mountain alone and to spend time with friends away from the hubbub of daily ministry. But to place privacy above hospitality as a pattern of living is to lose sight of the fact that at times when Jesus was on his way to the lonely place, the crowds pressed on him and he yielded to the pressure. When we use privacy as an argument for a kind of closure, we are using it as an escape.

Anesthetic activities: Work itself, busyness, can anesthetize and dull our sensitivity to the needs of another, or deaden our responsibility to respond. It is easy to excuse ourselves from engagement on the plea of needing to study or even to pray. Observation suggests that there is real guilt experienced by religious and clergy when they are not seen to be busily working. To spend time with another, to be faithfully present to the pain of another without necessarily being able to alleviate it, does not seem to them sufficient justification of their existence as busy spiritual leaders or ministers of the good news. Thus that which is the core of service may be set aside for a cheap substitute aimed at shoring up a need for personal recognition.

Avoidance of strong feeling: Compassion and hospitality imply relationship. Only a utopian relationship is devoid of abrasiveness, conflict and other strong feelings such as anger. If we cannot allow ourselves to feel and have to deal with these feelings within the context of relating then there is no other way of living except distantly. We cannot offer compassion or hospitality from a distance. Neither can we be re-created by another person if we never approach that person.

Exclusive friendships: It is possible to obtain almost all of our primary need for loving and being loved within the context of exclusive relationships and to thumb our nose at the other creative possibilities that life, especially a ministerial life, constantly offers. Besides being an anti-celibate stance, this is also another form of closure which makes the reckless loving of the disciple of Jesus an impossibility. Within the richness of open and empowering friendship there is to be found a creativity and a sending out which increases rather than diminishes the extent to which we can touch with healing the timid poor. Once a relationship begins to exclude others, however, it becomes a form of personal impoverishment and the decay of hospitality of heart begins.

The list is almost inexhaustible, and it is pointless to go on adding one example to another. It is clear, however, that commitment to hospitable love has a high price. There is nothing romantic, sweet or easy about it. Perhaps that is why a founder with a passion for hospitality also knew deeply the meaning of the passion of Jesus.

The example of Jesus leaves no doubt that anyone who would be a follower and thus enter into a life of discipleship cannot avoid the pain of the world; in fact, he or she accepts a challenge to enter into its very center. The passion and the dying involved in this may not be spectacular nor even visible to any except the most discerning, but it is indeed a dying. Sanctity in our day looks different. Once the language of sanctity referred to miracles, levitations and heroic deeds of a magnitude that would discourage the fainthearted. It involved prayer that produced the perfume of sanctity and a quality of living that inspired the sonnet writers! In the here and now the language has changed. Key words in the new language of sanctity are *brotherhood* and *sisterhood*. Another is *service*. I believe it is true to say that real sanctity today consists of the many small daily martyrdoms of tiny, inconspicuous and often unrecognized and unthanked services to all those we call brother or sister. There is death in this, not the big death that places the halo of canonization around our heads, but constant little deaths to self that enlarge the spirit and put us in contact with the meaning of the death of Jesus.

I search for the core of my Christian vision in Jesus Christ, crucified. And I see that this Jesus demands of me a personal appropriation of the central dynamic of his life: that this dynamic has to do with the free acceptance of death; not just the Big Death, physical death—often unexpected, pointless, or grindingly inhuman—but the slow, lonely little deaths of self; the deaths that come with the erosion of pretensions and illusions of heroism, with the patient, effortful living out of love—not self-inflating romantic love, but love that shows itself in the continual, undramatic, persistent, shrewdly resourceful, often unrecognized, forgiving caring for all those whom Jesus calls my neighbor; and finally that I believe that immersed in the often cruel, seemingly meaningless moments of my life is a God who bids me, through Jesus, call him Father, and who, I must trust, without any guarantee of miraculous vindication in this life, will bring new life out of all these deaths.[16]

Clearly, then, for anyone who hears the call to be a Samaritan in today's world there is also a call to reflect upon and internalize the meaning of the passion of Jesus, a direct outcome of the kind of universal loving that he proposed. Conversely, anyone who wishes to make the passion of Jesus central to his or her spirituality must recognize the blazing dedication to active and practical loving of neighbor exemplified in the compassion of the Samaritan.

Practical Outcomes

None of these things come easily. It is one thing to speak the ideals in words. It is another far more complex reality to realize them in practice. A number of practical options are offered here as a stimulus to further exploration.

1. Formation means education to love. It should emphasize, therefore, the values and skills of relating appropriate to the developmental stage an individual has reached.

2. It is possible to hold values hinging on an apostolate of compassion and hospitality without having the companion skills to express the values.

3. Ongoing education should give attention to the development of the values themselves in the form of a spirituality grounded in the passion of Jesus and expressed through the discipleship of the Samaritan.

4. Education in the skills of mutuality, in awareness of feelings and ways of expressing them seems necessary since culturally these have been somewhat de-emphasized.

5. It may be appropriate to examine the rules of our settings, our local communities, to see what impediments may have grown up to counteract basic values.

6. Our responsibility for our own formation demands that we examine our own ways of escaping the invitation to live out our values in daily practice.

7. Forms of community prayer require frequent reappraisal to see whether they nourish the inherited vision the community holds from its founder and ultimately from Jesus himself.

The hospitality discussed here is a moving outward which at the same time, often invisibly, has a profound effect on the identity of the host. It is a part of the spiritual adventure of becoming deeply human, part of the growth in wisdom, age and grace before both God and humanity that characterized the growth of Jesus from birth to death. It is a voluntary walking into our own passion and an embracing of the poverty that Jesus experienced totally.

> Have we really understood the impoverishment that Christ endured? Everything was taken from him during the passion, even the love that drove him to the cross. No longer did he savor his own love, no longer did he feel any spark of enthusiasm. His heart gave out and a feeling of utter helplessness came over him. Truly he emptied himself. God's merciful hand no longer sustained him. His countenance was hidden during the passion, and Christ gaped into the darkness of nothingness and abandonment where God was no longer present. The Son of Man reached his destiny, stretched taut between a despising earth that had rejected him and a faceless heaven thundering God's "no" to sinful mankind. Jesus paid the price of futility. He became utterly poor.[17]

Hospitality demands a fidelity, an obedience to the history that has shaped us, but a flexibility that allows us to reshape its expression to meet the needs of our own culture and our own time. While external manifestations of the work of hospitality may change, obedience to the relational core of Samaritanism remains.

Hospitality seems to me to demand from us a renunciation of exclusive relationship, but never of passion. It means a celibacy that is far more positive than the mere renunciation of genital gratification. Indeed, it shares with the vocation of marriage a central imperative to loving which requires education to self-awareness, responsiveness, forgiveness, adaptability and self-giving. Far from reducing celibate loving to a cold and distant concern for the welfare of others, it urges to a passionate involvement with them costing not less than everything.

Affirmation—the Product of an Empathic Spirituality

Whenever the much used and abused word *affirmation* comes to mind, I remember immediately a counsellee who taught me by his story and his struggle something of its real meaning. With his customary generosity and openness, he has given permission for me to write his story here.

Mark came to me through a referral by his provincial. A lay brother (for as long as the category existed, and in practice for a long time after that) in a clerical religious order, Mark was described as "having some difficulties and needing to talk them over with someone, preferably a woman." The provincial's referral was warmly caring of Mark in its tone, but non-specific in content, so, as I usually do, I asked him to get Mark to phone and make an appointment for himself. When Mark did so, his voice trembled and he professed himself amazed that he was actually taking this action of seeking help. Hearing in the voice the nervousness and fear of the unknown, I said something like, "I can hear that you feel a bit shaky about this, Mark. I recognize the feeling from how I feel myself when I need to ask for help."

At the other end of the line there was a stunned silence followed by, "Do *you* have to ask others for help sometimes, too?"

When I admitted this, the voice became stronger and more resolute and the next words were, "How soon can I come? Today?"

When Mark arrived, he was sweating and shaking and spoke in short bursts. He was so nervous that he conducted the whole interview himself, asking the questions he expected me to ask and then answering them. I sat rather helplessly by and occasionally interjected a signal that I was listening! Gathering confidence, he told a story of a lonely and grindingly laborious life. He had spent the many years of his religious life cooking meals, scrubbing floors, cutting down trees, putting up fences, cleaning toilets, painting walls. He had no complaint about this but kept lamenting the lack of simple recognition of the worth of his labors.

The crux of the story was that in his isolation and loneliness he had developed a relationship with a woman in his locality, and the friendship had recently become overtly sexual in its expression. A fracturing sense of guilt and infidelity plagued him, and so he went with utter simplicity to his local superior and confessed what he had done. The superior, as Mark recounted it, told him that if that was the way he intended to live his religious life, he should think seriously about leaving for there was no place for traitors in the community. Mark was shattered. Believing that the superior possessed some special infused wisdom, he nevertheless kept asking, "Must I really leave? The only thing I've ever wanted to do with my life is love God and be a religious in this congregation."

This became a kind of theme song, uttered with tangible innocence and directness whenever the horror of what the superior had said dawned on him. He wept and spoke of his need for warmth and comfort and his guilt at seeking it in a sexual encounter. I remember feeling silently grateful that there had been some solace for him somewhere in his life. As I tried to gather up some kind of appropriate response to Mark, he looked at his watch, stood up and said, "Well, my hour is up and you'll be telling me it's time to go. Thanks very much for all your help. I feel much better."

Still stunned by his assumption of total responsibility, even for time-keeping, I watched him walk to the door. With his hand on the doorknob he turned and said, "Sister, I'd love to know what you are thinking."

I said slowly exactly what was in my mind at that moment: "Mark, I'm remembering a story from the gospel. Jesus prayed, 'I bless you, Father, Lord of heaven and earth, for hiding these things from the learned and the clever and revealing them to mere children.' I think you are one of the little ones who instinctively know what the gospel is about. I know you can't read or write so you probably haven't studied the gospel that way, but somehow you know about being direct and simple and honest and uncomplicated. I think you are precious."

Mark burst into tears, not the controlled and quiet tears of an adult, but the noisy sobs of a child. I took him by the hand and brought him back to his chair, sat opposite and waited till some calm returned, and then I said, "Somehow I seem to have hurt you with what I said."

He looked at me, tears starting again, and said, "Yes and no. It's just that when you spoke I suddenly realized that only two good things have ever been said to me in my whole life and you just said the second one."

I wept too. My tears were partly for the utter desolation of his experience, and partly tears of anger that any communal group could leave a person so completely unaffirmed.

Affirmation is a way of being, not a series of behaviors to be implemented. Mark was unaffirmed probably for a variety of reasons, but essentially because he lived in the midst of a group of people whose stance in the face of life seems to have been unappreciative. Basically what was important for him was not that more and more people would say good things to him and increase the list he could remember from two to two thousand. Rather, the quality of his life and his belonging to life might have been enhanced by the simple and mostly wordless recognition from those around him that he was good and valuable and worth prizing. This appreciation has myriad subtle expressions and creates a climate that is in the air we breathe rather than solely in the words we say.

For too many religious, recent teaching and writing in the area of the emotional life of the community and of affirmation places emphasis on doing. Thus the question becomes, What do we *do* to be affirmers of one another? In reality, the question is more complex and may be restated, What values and attitudes and ways of seeing must permeate my perception, not just of you, but of the whole of reality, so as to transmit acceptance and valuing? Affirmation does not mean pushing the affirmation button and producing a kind or praising statement, though a kind and praising statement that issues from a genuinely appreciative person has a dimension of credibility that distinguishes it in quality from a more superficial and tritely bland "charity." Affirmation never merely pats people on the head for a job well done. Affirmation is deeply about the worth of the person, and the worth of a person does not rely solely on deeds and performance. This person is valuable because he or she *is*. Only those with eyes that can see can know and respond to this. They alone are the ones with spirits saturated with an affirmative vision of the world. They alone, therefore, can transform their world.

The pragmatists will inevitably ask, "How can I get to be like that?" Without any claim to have a complete answer to the question, I do have a few suggestions. In a world dominated by left-brain awareness and instrumentalism, a re-education of the right brain, the appreciative, imaginative faculty, is needed. To arrest the rush from one task or problem to the next in order to savor the present moment may be a simple beginning. In many a religious house I am appalled by the way the sacramentality of a meal together is ignored or insulted. Food is ingested in haste with scant attention to hospitality to one's neighbor or even to basic good manners at times. The purpose of the exercise seems to be to stoke the nutritional fires and rush off to the next task. I am tempted at times to ask what the food tasted like, and I would be willing to wager that many could not answer the question. They eat without appreciation. To extend the example of the meal, I draw attention also to the simple ways it is made attractive, the preparation of the table, the color, the delicacy of serving. I abhor the extension of work discussion at table when it overlays the enjoyment and sense of unity with organization perspectives. If the eucharistic extension of sacramental agape is contained here in this celebration of sisterhood and brotherhood, it is often well camouflaged.

What assists the growth of appreciation, then? First of all, the desire for it. Then *time* is needed, a slowing down of the ministerial rush, a gradual appropriation of a sabbath mentality that recognizes the need to loiter. My advice to clients sometimes is to take longer over a meal, to eat less but to focus on taste and texture, deliberately enjoying and distinguishing flavors, holding them on the tongue the way a mouthful of wine is allowed to register its delight upon the palate. The instrumentally oriented person says of many things, "I've been there, done that, what's new? How can the flavor of tarragon today be any different from the taste it had yesterday? Why would I read a poem twice or go to see a movie again and again?" For the appreciative person life has inexhaustible riches to be savored again and again, each re-experiencing being a new experience, each new experience carving out space for more.

Religious have been effectively trained to deny their senses gratification in the name of asceticism and sanctity. An unfortunate by-product of this has been an association linking enjoyment with sinfulness. The model they follow cannot be the Jesus who picked and crumbled ears of corn, admired the lilies of the field, spoke tenderly of the birds of the air, ached with the grief of the widow and enjoyed himself in the company of his women friends. An emphasis on willpower, decision-making and logical thought, good in itself, has nevertheless been dissociated in our education from genuine valuing of feeling. What we desperately need to recover is the proper reconnecting of intellect and affectivity.

To do this, there has to be more standing and feeling the wind in our hair and the sun on our skin, more sensing of the rhythms of life around us, more yes-saying to the life inside us and around us. Then, perhaps, we will have eyes to see the loneliness in the eyes of the person across the table, the beauty and intrinsic worth of another human being. Seeing it with the eyes of the spirit, maybe then we shall communicate it with the freedom of the Spirit.

How do I recognize unaffirmedness in myself and others? It is a well-documented fact that our story holds the secrets about our inability to affirm and to be affirmed. If at the heart of the story is an early life experience of non-affirmation, it is clear that we stand in need of re-education. If, as most religious have been, we are taught that the emotions are suspect or even bad, then we cannot risk being in touch with the very building materials of affirmation. If, as most religious have been, we are taught that our present self is inadequate and that we ought constantly be reaching for a perfected and just-out-of-reach idealized self, then the seeds of self-dislike have been sown.

The behavioral effects of lack of affirmation are multiple. Not every unaffirmed person has all the characteristics in the following list, but lack of affirmation produces many of them:

- egocentrism—it is unsafe to move out to anybody else, and there is a chasm of deprivation inside that clamors for attention

- fear of getting under other people's feet, of being in the way, of being a nuisance—apologizing for existence

- self-consciousness—concern about what others may be thinking, a shrinking need to stay out of sight

- inability to ask a favor of anyone, since refusal may accentuate the already strong sense of worthlessness

- inability to say no to anybody, since to do so may reinforce worthlessness in his or her eyes

- hoarding and attachment to things as a substitute for attachment to people—displacing affection onto inanimate objects which are "safer"

- fear of being abandoned and not seen as deserving of the fidelity of others (common among women)
- feeling intellectually inferior or even stupid, and therefore being reluctant to express opinions
- loneliness and a sense of abandonment
- oversensitivity and more than average susceptibility to being hurt
- a long memory for hurts, storing them up and replaying them as evidence of worthlessness
- a propensity to read criticism into a look or an innocent remark
- inability to distinguish between seriousness and jest (exacerbated by the tendency of others to use humor sometimes to convey criticism, a severely immature form of humor)
- need to please, to win or buy affection, a need that often has unfortunate counter-results
- feelings of insecurity, uncertainty and dependency
- high levels of fear
- scruples
- hesitancy, and the need for reassurance, especially in the area of interpersonal relating.

In some ways the unaffirmed person does not develop; he or she grows to adulthood feeling like a child. It will be clear that many of the above manifestations of an unaffirmed story bear this out. The only healing that I can see for this in communal groups is the faithful presence of those few who know affirmation as a way of being open with the heart. Unfortunately, a complication in many religious communities is that *most* of the members are largely unaffirmed and the process of transformation is more tentative and slow.

Not all unaffirmed behavior is as naked as the list above might suggest. Various forms of camouflage are used to deny or escape the experience. Among these the following may be seen among religious:

- accumulating a lot of acquaintances who are called friends, thus giving the illusion of being widely esteemed—these acquaintances are often drawn from people other than the communal group with whom one lives

- generating the image of generous service, always being at the beck and call of others—an attempt to buy popularity and love

- aggressive bullying or boasting which covers up feelings of hesitancy and nervousness

- premature invalidism which invites service from others and creates the illusion of being loved and cherished—this invalidism may be physical or psychological in its symptoms

- compulsive or addicted behavior such as overeating, over-garrulousness, alcoholism or drug-addiction—among many religious, the addiction is to analgesics, sleeping pills or valium

- flight into false spirituality, which is divorced from reality—hearing the call to give up the active ministry and to dedicate oneself to a life of contemplative prayer

- becoming a professional student or a pathological seminar-goer to avoid real involvement and to project a sense of respectability because of accumulated knowledge

- a form of bragging that uses the language acquired at such seminars to explain and analyze every event

- rigidity that resists change and claims to have found a permanently satisfactory way of being.

Those of us who have a few or many of the characteristics I have listed know that we shall not be healed by having affirmation practiced upon us. That is condescension, which exacerbates the inner loneliness. The healing, the unlearning and new learning, indeed the *conversion* required to change our unaffirmed emptiness is a long-term drinking-in of the spirit of affirming others. They offer us much more than the pseudo-affirmation of do-gooders, who must walk softly around our propensity for hurt, so as not to offend or challenge us. Affirmation is not about avoidance of hurt. It is about loving. Love gets to know us, to know what we can and cannot bear, risks stretching our capacity for relationship, challenges us to enlarged being. It loves, but it is not soft.

Perhaps I might return to Mark's story briefly. We engaged in therapy together after the initial encounter for a period of about three years. Often he would look around the little room where our meetings took place and say: "This is the one place in my world that is not scary. I'm not afraid when I'm here. It's not hostile." I would like to think that he felt affirmed there. Over the time I knew him, a remarkable process began to unfold. His story was eventually told, chapter by chapter. He did not immediately surrender the genital dimension of the relationship that caused him so much guilt, though he worked at transforming it and eventually succeeded. What did appear to be happening was a gradual integration. He began to have the confidence to offer a suggestion or give an opinion without first apologizing. His image of God changed from an angry, monitoring and punitive God (alarmingly like the superior who had condemned him) to a God who deeply understood him. His favorite text became, "See I have carved you on the palm of my hand." Once, when he had disappointed himself morally by a further sexual transgression, he recounted the incident and then looked at me in silence a moment as if mentally gauging my response. Then he said slowly, "You may think I'm a heretic when I say this, but every night before I go to bed I kneel down and thank my God that I am such a sinner." He paused and looked at me as if waiting for an incredulous response.

I said, "How do you mean, Mark?"

He replied, "Well, I must be one of the richest people on earth. If I weren't such a sinner I wouldn't know how loving God is. I know how much he forgives me, because I know how far I fall."

Along with this recognition was a kind of inner reconciliation that had more peace, a sense of being unfinished but hopeful. When eventually he moved to another place, he was in a group of men who valued him, gave him the same attention as they paid to their professional members, treated him as an equal and sought his assistance in their projects. He blossomed. He no longer saw his companions as potential sources of hurt but as fellows, brothers to whom and with whom he could risk himself. As I tell his story I am aware of how much this simple man taught me and how, in the reality of encounter, *I* grew.

Mark taught me that the kind of contemplation needed to transform the unaffirmed wasteland is not a locked-in pseudomonastic separation from the world but simple seeing and appreciating in the midst of a world of action, opening the senses to touch, taste and be aware. It is a singing contemplation that plays and celebrates.

The words poured out to describe the reality of affirmation may be learned and even obscure at times. I believe that the reality is simple. It means to love life. It is not blind to the reality of evil or the shortcomings of those close to us, but when it is

appropriate to challenge these aspects of reality affirmation preserves its sense of goodness. It is a wheat-and-cockle vision. It
never does violence to goodness in its efforts to eradicate evil.
It, like love, is

> always patient and kind; . . . never jealous; . . . never boastful
> or conceited; it is never rude and never seeks its own advan-
> tage, it does not take offence or store up grievances. Love [af-
> firmation] does not rejoice at wrongdoing, but finds its joy in
> the truth. It is always ready to make allowances, to trust, to
> hope and to endure whatever comes (1 Cor 13:4-7).

Affirmation is a resounding yes to life. It issues in a thirst
for justice, not the world's kind of justice, which imprisons and
punishes, but justice that seeks freedom for all.

For community consideration

A. In what ways does the life of your communal group manifest a lived spirituality of empathy?

B. Who gets left out in your community? Why?

How much loneliness exists in your community? Do you
have any suggestions for alleviating this?

C. Who models empathy and compassion for you in community life—not just sympathetic words, but empathy that is
tangible and non-manipulative? Give some examples of
this.

D. How are strong feelings dealt with in your community?
Think of times when you or someone else has been angry
or frustrated or grief-stricken. Who could stay alongside
this without taking it away? How do you feel about letting
others in the community know that you have strong feelings? What are the feelings hardest to express within the
community?

E. As a communal group, consider together your hopes for
the community's outreach this year as a ministering group.
How well does listening happen during the discussion?
Who clarifies? Who makes suggestions? How prevalent are
interruption, argument, contradiction?

For individual consideration

A. How habitual is an approach of empathy for you in your
ministerial and communal relationships?

B.   Can you remember a time when you were listened to deeply? What was the effect on you?

C.   Recall a relationship in which you felt enlarged and freed and empowered. What did the other person do to create this growth?

D.   Consider your own interpersonal style. Write down five adjectives to describe it. Now take each of these adjectives and flesh it out with an example from your interpersonal encounters. As you complete this exercise, what do you appreciate about your interpersonal style? What would you like to change? Plan one small, conscious change in your behavior for the next week.

E.   How is a spirituality of empathy reflected in your life of prayer? What text(s) of scripture are of particular relevance?

F.   Let your mind touch each member of the community. Think of each by name. How well do you think you understand the way each person experiences his or her world? How well acquainted with the broad outlines of each person's story are you? If people seem to guard themselves against you, are there any identifiable attitudes or behaviors that may send them a message to keep out?

G.   Reflect on the proverb, Help thy brother's boat across, and, Lo! thine own has reached the shore.

Notes

1.   Gerard Manley Hopkins, "God's Grandeur," *Gerard Manley Hopkins: Poems and Prose*, selected and edited by W.H. Gardner (Harmondsworth, Middlesex: Penguin, 1953), p. 27.

2.   Teilhard de Chardin, *Le Milieu Divin* (London: Fontana, 1957), p. 6.

3.   Ibid. p. 97.

4.   Brendan Byrne, S.J., in an unpublished lecture to the Brothers of John of God, Sydney, January 1982.

5.   Dietrich Bonhoeffer, *Life Together* (London: SCM Press, 1954), pp. 75-76.

6. C. G. Jung, *Modern Man in Search of a Soul* (London: Routledge & Kegan Paul, 1933), p. 57.

7. Francois Marty, farewell homily delivered in the Cathedral of Nôtre Dame, February 18, 1981.

8. John V. Taylor, *The Go-Between God: The Holy Spirit and the Christian Mission* (London: SCM Press, 1972), p. 243.

9. Jose Miranda, *Marx and the Bible* (New York: Maryknoll, 1974), p. 128.

10. Matthew Fox, *A Spirituality Named Compassion and the Healing of the Global Village, Humpty Dumpty and Us* (Minneapolis: Winston Press, 1979), p. 21.

11. Jung, op. cit. p. 282.

12. Henri J.M. Nouwen, *Reaching Out: Three Movements of the Spiritual Life* (Garden City, New York: Doubleday, 1975), pp. 50-51.

13. John Dominic Crossan, *The Dark Interval: Towards a Theology of Story* (Niles, Illinois: Argus, 1975), p. 56.

14. Bernard M. Loomer, during informal discussion, St. John's University, Collegeville, Minnesota, July 1981. Much of the following discussion is derived from listening to Loomer on this occasion.

15. Francis de Castro, *The Life of St. John of God*, trans. Benignus Callan, OH (Christchurch New Zealand Foundation, Silver Jubilee Edition, 1980), p. 30.

16. Gerard V. Egan, "Group Insearch: Propaedeutic for a Contemporary Spirituality," *Listening* (Spring 1972), pp. 10-11.

17. Johannes Baptist Metz, *Poverty of Spirit*, trans. John Drury (Paramus, New Jersey: Paulist Press, 1968), p. 18.

4
CONFLICT:

The Tangle of Our Stories

Images

Sometimes, to save my sanity when the many stories told in my consulting room press in upon me, I engage in the leisure activity of collecting, polishing and setting stones. Along the miles of beaches near my office lie pieces of petrified wood half-buried in the sand along with gray, black and brown pebbles overgrown with weed or crusted with sand and salt. Occasionally the children collecting sea shells look at me with eyes that seem to say, "Why gather dun-colored chips of rock when she could be picking up shells that glow with color and echo with strange tales of the sea?" An eccentric among them, I go on my way, filling an old paper bag with my treasure. At home, I tip them out onto the bench, a pile of dull, oddly shaped rocks, some sharp and jagged, recently fallen from the cliffs to the ground above the line of the tide, some rounded and smoothed by the constant caress of the ocean, others pitted and scarred by who knows what events and traumas. I select them, large and small, wash them and place them in the small tumbler where for a whole month they will toss about in water, scoured by abrasive material, and jostled against one another. Three times I take them out of the container, wash them, discarding a few that are too pitted to polish, and replace them in finer abrasive powder and clean water. On the first two occasions the stones are slightly smoother versions of their former selves. But the third time, after a week of polishing in tin oxide, they emerge transformed. Translucent, veined with color, unique in grain and shape and beauty, they yield up their inner magnificence. What was a brown pebble now reveals the ringed markings of ancient wood held now in the permanence of stone. A gray rock becomes a glowing quartz that changes color against the light. I do not know the names of all the stones. This is an aesthetic rather than a scientific project. But I do begin to get hints of their eons-old and hidden stories told now in line and shape and color.

This is a special moment, nothing less than a moment of ecstasy. It is a moment when I always choose to be alone, not wanting the instant of revelation fractured by conversation. It is a moment when the "Ahhh!" of novelty and re-creation is often spoken aloud. It is a time when I know with biblical knowledge the truth of Hopkin's words, "The world is charged with the grandeur of God." I spend a long time touching, looking, holding up to the light and exclaiming aloud at the surprise of what has been revealed. It is *always* a surprise, for each new batch of stones contains new and unique beauty, richness, strength, fragility.

At times I reflect that the experience with the stones is paralleled by what I know of human growth. When I look back over my own life and recall the many stories with which I have been entrusted by countless religious over the years since I began counselling, I know that recognizable growth and personal revelation have emerged from conflict. Abraded over time by the jostling of conflicting events, beliefs, relationships, we emerge different. When I am privileged to accompany another person on the re-storying of his or her life, I am struck with the same sense of miracle that I feel when the stones pour out of the tumbler. The analogy is by no means perfect, but it is a strong one. When I see communities of religious struggling to resolve conflicts among them, or an individual agonizing over personal conflict, I hear a call to new life. As a result I cannot look upon conflict, painful though the experience may be, as an intrinsically evil process. I know from the stones that hidden beauties may be uncovered precisely because of the conflict.

I have two memories that date back long before my interest in collecting and polishing pebbles ever developed.

Some years ago I was working with a group of religious at a workshop in which we were engaged in exercises in self-awareness, and I had set the class the task of finding, each person for himself or herself, a symbol that described or represented a personal quality or characteristic. I remember advising them to walk around the spacious grounds of the conference center until some object said "This is me!" People came back after some time carrying a variety of objects, animate and inanimate, and we settled down quietly to tell stories about them. Trite little analogies, touching memories, streams of consciousness, tales of joy, success, failure and trauma filled the air as the objects were placed on the floor in the center of the circle.

One sister sat silently clutching something in her closed fist. She did not volunteer to speak and had to be asked about her symbol by another member of the group. She remained silent for a moment and then, with tears in her eyes, held out her open palm. On it lay a small flat piece of gray slate. "This," she said, "is me. It has been formed under great pressure, and it's small and gray and ugly." She then painfully shared with the group the pressure and difficulty that she was currently undergoing, ending the story with doubts about her own worth and drawing a parallel between the drab ugliness of the slate and her perception of herself. The group members' perception of her was in contradiction to her own, and in a variety of ways they told her this, but nobody seemed able to convince her. Against the weight of opinion and appreciation in the group she placed the rest of her life experience, and it weighed much more heavily in the scales of her own judgment. The next day, however, there was a change in her. She came into the room smiling and wearing around her neck a piece of the slate she had found on the day before. She had pierced it and threaded a chain through it and wore it like a necklace. Asked about it, she replied, "Well, last night, after the group sessions finished for the day, Marguerite took me back to her school and in her geology laboratory she cut a thin slice through my piece of rock and put it under a microscope for me to see. I found that what I thought was ugly was really exquisitely beautiful and that I hadn't been able to see it, *really* see it, before. Maybe there's some hope for me, too. Maybe under the microscope of this group and with your insights, I'll discover that I'm not so shabby either."

The event loses some of its depth and emotional impact in the telling, but the stone began the process for her of the re-storying of old conflicts, of seeing them in new ways with new meanings, of finding that, far from being destroyed by them, she had been abraded and pared and sculpted into a person of beauty and promise. I believe that this is the positive side of conflict.

Years ago, a pebble imaged for me meanings I had been struggling to come to terms with. It was 1974. I was in another country suffering what in retrospect was probably culture shock. In addition, I was working on a team where I felt inferior and useless, where the intimacy I had expected to find was not present, where conflict with one of the team members was not overtly faced except with angry outbursts, and where the disintegration of my hopes opened up other awarenesses about my life, its past pathways and present pain. When the team leader asked our class to write a story, an allegory, about our own perception of our life pathways, this is what I wrote in my journal:

Once there was a small pebble. Formed in the fire at the heart of a mountain it first came to recognize its existence in

the green grass beside a stream. It was only a small pebble—
small and black and rough from the mountain fire that it
could not remember. For a few years it lay in the warm grass
where the mountain had thrown it. It saw the sky and felt
the earth, was loved by the sun and bathed by the rain, and
knew no other world. Then one day a traveller passing by
idly picked up the pebble, fondled its roughness for a moment and then tossed it into the shallow water at the edge
of a stream.

The last ripples echoed into lonely silence across the
stream. And there the pebble began another phase of its life.
It looked up and saw the sky, less clearly now, felt the sun,
less clearly, and the wash of the stream's ebb and flow.
Slowly, imperceptibly, the pebble began to change. The
roughness inherited from its fire-birth grew smooth and the
blackness became polished, glistening like ebony.

In time new currents in the stream washed the pebble up
onto its bank and into the once-familiar grass again, where it
lay in the sun and rain until someone came by and built a
fireplace there, gathering stones to make a bed for the fire.
And in the heart of the fire the pebble began to recognize
the dimly stirring memory of its beginning life in the womb
of the mountain-fire. And it lost its sheen and grew rough-
ened and ugly, and it even cracked a little here and there.

In the time that followed, generations of travellers kin-
dled their fires on this spot, extinguished them with water
from the stream and walked away not knowing. And the
pebble lay there—on fire, then mercifully cooled by the water, and it learned to dance in the fire and to wait for water's
relief, and as it did, it sang this song:

"I love, I hate,
I burn, I wait,
I die but do not die.

I drown, I rise,
I agonize,
In a death that does not die.

I am lost and found,
I am freed and bound,
Dying, I cannot die.

In sun and rain,
In love and pain,
I die but cannot die.

I dance, I sing,
But questioning
A death that does not die,

I ask, 'Why birth?
Why tears, why mirth,
If dying I cannot die?

Why love, why hate?
Why burning wait
For a death I do not die?'

In the dance, in the song,
In the fire life-long,
Is there death that I dare not die?"
(With profound apologies to St. John of the Cross!)

This little allegory served as a way of "storying" the conflict I was feeling, the paradox of hope and disappointment, the invitation into the little death of self-transcendence which I could not embrace because of the painful self-preoccupation that I was caught in. The story was my way of putting together tentatively an account of what was happening as I sought to discover its meaning.

I often find myself saying to groups of religious that I would rather be invited to work with a community in conflict than with one which is either superficially joyful or which exhibits signs of apathy. At least conflict indicates a group that is alive, and the invitation to work with them manifests a willingness on their part to examine what is happening.

I do not claim that conflict in and of itself is good. It is a fact of life. Total harmony has not been a quality of our existence since the symbolic expulsion from the garden! When conflict is dealt with constructively it may open up new avenues of growth and meaning for individuals and for groups. In the rest of this chapter I want to take a look at some of the sources of conflict for religious and discuss some constructive ways of resolving it.

Sources

Usually, human life, is a tangle of stories. Our conscious lives, at different depths, are divided by contrary impulses. . . .

Meanwhile our inner lives are theaters of conflict. We are inhabited by many stories at once: by cover stories, by stories to which we only aspire, by stories that would seduce us, and by stories that others have learned through living with us to find reliable, even though we have not put them into words.[1]

When I listen to clients who seek counselling, or fellow community members, or members of client communities, they often mention "personality clashes" or say such things as: "They just don't understand me"; "I'm caught in the system"; "We disagree on what community is and what we're looking for"; or "I just don't understand what he/she is making all the fuss about." They are talking about the enmeshing and sometimes clashing of stories, sometimes multiple stories in one person, sometimes the stories of individuals who see worlds of meaning that are not mutually understood, sometimes the stories of systems with gargantuan appetites for gobbling up the smaller personal stories of individual members. I believe that conflict in religious life, as indeed everywhere else, is

(a) intrapersonal

(b) interpersonal

(c) between person and system

(d) between system and system

At the level of intrapersonally generated conflict, I believe that a low, inadequate, impoverished and often static self-image is by far the strongest source of inner conflict among religious. At the heart of much inner conflict lies the individual's manner of perceiving himself or herself and the world which that illusory self inhabits. I deliberately use the word *illusory* because to try to pin down and describe our "self" is like trying to hold a handful of water or stop time. The I that I was a moment ago is already in the past. If I "slow down the movie" and examine its individual and static frames, I may learn some facts, but I will never taste the quality of the moving, shifting, constantly refocusing process of being a person, a baffling composite of past, present and not yet. Bonhoeffer's reflection in prison is probably a familiar one to each of us, wrestling with questions and doubts about the source of our own worth.

WHO AM I?

Who am I? They often tell me
I would step from my cell's confinement
calmly, cheerfully, firmly,
like a squire from his country house.

Who am I? They often tell me
I would talk to my warders
freely and friendly and clearly,
as though it were mine to command.

Who am I? They also tell me
I would bear the days of misfortune
equably, smilingly, proudly,
like one accustomed to win.

Am I then really all that which other men tell of?
Or am I only what I know of myself,
restless and longing and sick, like a bird in a cage,
struggling for breath, as though hands were compressing
    my throat,
yearning for colors, for flowers, for the voices of birds,
thirsting for words of kindness, for neighborliness, trembling
with anger at despotisms and petty humiliation,
tossing in expectation of great events,
powerlessly trembling for friends at an infinite distance,
weary and empty at praying, at thinking, at making,
faint, and ready to say farewell to it all?

Who am I? This or the other?
Am I one person today and tomorrow another?
Am I both at once? A hypocrite before others,
and before myself a contemptibly woebegone weakling?
Or is something within me still like a beaten army,
fleeing in disorder from victory already achieved?

Who am I? They mock me, these lonely questions of mine.
Whoever I am, thou knowest, O God, I am thine.[2]

When one begins to unravel the tangle of stories the first
that emerges is the story of birth and family. The huge impact
of significant others in the early years of childhood is well doc-
umented. Immersed in the formative story of our infancy and
childhood we begin to read the larger story of our world and to
learn attitudes, values and modes of behavior that color all our
perceptions. What is good and what is bad becomes largely established. Whether *we* are good or bad is transmitted to us in a
variety of ways, both verbal and non-verbal. Patterns of seeing
are set up and motivations for life are born. Filters through
which we see, judge and interact with our world are fitted to
our eyes like contact lenses that we seldom think of taking off.
Through these lenses we see our unfolding future as a set of
static and similar moments strung like identical beads on a
thread, accumulating rather than qualitatively changing. This
fixed and seemingly permanent state is often expressed in my
counselling room: "Well, with my background, what more can
you expect?"; "I've been so damaged by my past"; "That's the
way I was brought up to behave, and I'm not about to do vio-

lence to myself now." Therapy for some of these individuals consists of gradually learning that they have power over their present moment, a moment that may be qualitatively different from those that have slid by into the past. Learning to let go is a slow and frequently painful business.

Although the pattern may be changing now, many religious have moved successively from Catholic family to Catholic school to Catholic novitiate. The passage has often been from a morally monitoring family to a school where the teaching of religion was sometimes, indeed all too often, equated with the teaching of morality, to a novitiate where patterns of monitoring even stricter than those of the home were imposed. Here models—saints and "good" religious—were held up for imitation at a time of transition when models of adulthood are grasped at. In all of this process approval, disapproval and punishment were the order of the day for many as they were socialized to the system. Appreciative caring was spoken about, but simple human warmth from companions was often lacking. One religious of my acquaintance recalls:

> I remember a day when we were novices and the novice mistress caught us having a conversation during a period of silence time. She didn't say anything much at the time, just let us know she'd seen us, so I had a sleepless night wondering if this was the last straw and if tomorrow I'd be sent home.
>
> Next day each of us was called up—there were three of us—and because I was the junior I was last on her list of criminals. We were all standing there as she berated each one in turn. Ahead of me the other two were given fairly humiliating public penances, and I waited for my turn to come thinking I'd probably merit similar treatment. But when she finally came to me, the novice mistress looked down at me kneeling there at her feet, and I don't know if she ran out of ideas or if there was some other reason, but she said, "Oh, get out of my sight. You aren't even worth punishing." The good news was that I escaped; the bad news was that I believed her. I know stronger people got through their time in the novitiate and somehow laughed off things like that. But I didn't. For years I carried those words inside me: "You're not worth punishing." How small can you feel?

Asked how she finally came to reject such a deep and lasting learning, the sister reported various new relationships in which she felt loved and free to love in return. She half-laughingly, half-sadly referred to these as "delayed intimacy."

Added to the injustice of all of this—and I use the word *injustice* not to judge conscious motives but to describe an objective state of affairs in which dehumanizing happened—I believe that a spirituality that emphasized seeking after perfection created further difficulties related to healthy self-valuing. An oft-quoted scriptural maxim, "Be ye perfect as your heavenly Father is perfect," was interpreted as "Be ye perfect *now*, or else!" When people assessed their growth or progress (another crucifying image) in terms of this injunction, they always found themselves short of perfect. When they tried to speak of their growth to anyone else, they always had to report in terms of their failure, in negatives. Particular examen as a spiritual exercise counted and listed failures, transgressions and imperfections.

The one condition that might have alleviated and stood against such accumulations of negativity about self, virtue, life and others was prohibited. Particular friendships where an individual might have felt loved and cared about for himself or herself were forbidden. Feelings were dismissed as trivial and of no significance when placed beside the desirability of asceticism and self-denial. Intimacy was seen as sexual and sexuality was seen uni-dimensionally as sex, so any closeness had to be seen as a potential violation of celibate commitment. This was rarely said explicitly, but it was present in definitions of celibacy, attitudes to marriage, touch, friendship and self-disclosure likely to lead to closeness. Love was most frequently presented as service and as speaking only good of others (charitable). A strict hierarchy in terms of seniority and official position made mutuality difficult if not impossible. A theology of redemption meant constant preoccupation with sin and temptation. Is it any wonder, then, that many religious are still struggling out of the belly of the paradox of a past "You are worthless" and a present "You are God's work of art"? Worse still is a suspicion I harbor that for some there is neither a painful appreciation of the paradox nor intimations of a future struggle, but a deeply internalized belief in what was taught and an inability to take possession of a new and fluid self, created and re-created moment by moment.

In this conflict between past and present I recognize a number of directions in which religious are being invited to move. Once, in a wild and beautiful part of Scotland I watched salmon leaping and swimming up a waterfall. In a way the invitation out of a frozen past into a future of creativity and novelty and freedom is an invitation to do just that, to defy the gravity of the past and recognize the creative potential of the now. I see this creative dynamic for many beckoning them

- from static understanding of perfection to an openness to creation and recreation moment by moment in the context of co-creative relationship

- from emotional suppression to healthy and appropriate recognition, valuing and expression of feelings

- from images of God as static and judging (and always male) to a God who calls us beyond each now, lures to harmony and pilgrims along with us; a God who, far from being the Ultimate Chauvinist, is Animus and Anima; a God about whom we continue to tell stories as we try, always inadequately, to encompass and understand the divine reality

- from self-depreciation to self-valuing

- from infantile dependency to adult interdependence

- from comparison and competition to mutuality

- from ignorance to understanding in the area of growth and personal development

- from acceptance of oppression to a passion for justice

- from comfortable middle-class security and certainty to fringe-dwelling insecurity and ambiguity

- from asexual celibacy which avoids and eschews closeness to warmly loving, closely relating celibacy

- from self-doubting submission to assertiveness

- from self-protectiveness to radical risk-taking

- from prison to possibility

But hasn't all this been happening? I think we must yet make the journey from rhetoric to practice, and that while the poets have been saying all this for some time we now need prophets with ringing voices to challenge us more strongly—perhaps by modelling rather than verbalizing the challenge—and pragmatists who will show us how.

One thing I feel sure of is that the face of ministry will change when religious change in the directions outlined above. As we re-story the injunction to be perfect as God is perfect, we will revise our understanding of obedience. It will cease to be dependence on "parental" authority from within or without. It will cease to be the relinquishing of responsibility.

> Obedience is not conformity. Indeed we must refuse to conform in order that we may obey. Conformity means accepting a direction or destiny that belongs to someone else; obedience is the actualization of our own destiny.[3]

As we seize responsibility for our own destiny, poverty can no longer mean concern about small economic scruples while we live in middle-class security. It will impel us to voluntary displacement and uncomfortable sharing of goods, space, time, energy and privacy, to be fringe-dwellers with the fringe-dwellers. Celibacy will cease to be a cautious drawing around ourselves of the mantle of religious life in order to preserve "safe" distance. It will fling us in the direction of reckless universal loving that risks involvement, is not afraid to feel and to share the feelings of others, and is generous enough to demand no return.

As the past becomes the past and not a giant magnet drawing us back into old patterns of seeing the world and stylized, stereotyped ways of being in that world, we will carry into the future that we are co-creating the appropriate lessons we learned from the past married to the insights and challenges of the present. We might then become what we once were in the history of religious life, "the institutionalized form of a *dangerous memory* within the Church,"[4] radical to the core, challenging institutional complacency even within the church, quietly repudiating temptations to establish ourselves comfortably on the "middle ground where everything is nicely balanced and moderate . . . adapted to and tamed by the institutional Church."[5]

Expressions and Symptoms of Conflict

As I reflected on the various ways in which conflict is manifested in religious communities, I enlisted the help of members of two communities with whom I have been working over a period of time and among whom there is overt conflict that is being confronted creatively. One community is female, the other male. I asked them to list (in the random manner of brainstorming) the things that revealed conflict in their communities. Although the men more often noted the use of humor as a hostile communication and the women placed more emphasis on the tendency to judge each other's motives, few differences emerged between the two lists.

CAUSES AND BEHAVIORAL EXPRESSIONS OF CONFLICT: ✓

1) not really hearing what the other person has to say

2) hearing words but not meanings

3) making jokes to cover up discomfort

4) sniping at another member of the community in such a general way that the person isn't sure it's personal

5) seeing what someone does and making a judgment about the motives behind the behavior

6) wanting everyone to be the same all the time

7) being afraid to confront someone and not really knowing how to do it

8) being deaf to the validity of another's opinion because of personal dislike

9) strife and differences of attitude among various age-groups

10) sub-grouping and pressure groups

11) overwork and cranky, tired feelings

12) feeling lonely and wanting someone to notice, but no one does

13) having decisions made for me and imposed on me

14) different views of religious life

15) needing different things from community: some people need it as a refuge when they come in from work; others need closeness and warmth and even a bit of mothering

16) communication difficulties

17) differences of values: some see the value of close relationships and friendships inside and outside the community; others see heterosexual friendship as dangerous to celibacy

18) secrecy about things that are going on, when the information isn't really private

19) rivalry

20) not admitting that conflict exists when we're all really hating each other

21) exaggerating small differences and mannerisms so they become major incidents

22) friendliness that's sweet and sickly and based on "charity," making you feel that the other person is practicing his or her virtue in relating to you

23) an unspoken rule that everybody must know all about everybody else, often called "openness"

24) lots of holy words

25) manipulation by one or a few who always get their own way

26) not allowing people to change, holding images that they set up years ago against them now

27) keeping people locked in roles such as the community's comedian

28) the "let's all be friends" expectation

29) constant harping and criticizing

30) not enough affirmation

31) affirmation that's superficial and even artificial

32) carrying tales about community members to people outside the community

33) a need to keep the community closed and not let anyone else in

34) not knowing how to heal old hurts between people

35) either not enough willingness to forgive small daily offenses or premature forgiveness when we really need to take a look at what has divided us

36) people in the community who can't let you have a good fight without trying to pour oil on the troubled waters

37) expecting that there won't be any conflict and that it is bad when it does happen

38) glaring differences between our lifestyle and the lifestyle of those we serve

39) carping about small domestic details and not addressing larger and more important issues

40) controlling the group by silence

41) appealing to authority to resolve differences, or the superior seeing this as part of the role

42) being treated (or treating others) as children

43) being smothered

44) using honesty as a weapon to hit someone else over the head

45) insensitivity

46) awkwardness that comes across as hostility

47) shyness that comes across as aggressiveness

48) limited definitions of maleness (e.g., football and locker-room conversation) and femaleness (e.g., slightly fluffy, conforming and lacking assertiveness)

49) not understanding what it's like to be old, or, for that matter, what it's like to be at any stage other than the person's current one.

Earlier I used the analogy of polishing the pebbles to underscore my belief that conflict can lead to happy and creative outcomes. Unfortunately this is not always and invariably so. I have met some communities whose members have subsisted for years sustaining a level of superficial friendliness that masked seething hostilities. Others have lived in a destructive and self-perpetuating cycle of blame and counter-blame, using up survival energy that might have been channeled into lively and productive relationship within the community and in ministry elsewhere. Huge energy, it seems has been devoted to preserving distance and keeping each other at bay. It is clear that conflict may be either constructive or destructive. This is true of all relationships. There is no such thing as a neutral relationship. Either we create possibilities for growth or we limit them for one another. Conflict itself may open new avenues for discovering human potential or it may build escape-proof prisons.

> A conflict among group members is a moment of truth in group effectiveness, a test of the group's health, a crisis that can weaken or strengthen the group, a critical event that may bring creative insight and closer relationships among members—or lasting resentment, smoldering hostility and psychological scars. Conflicts can push members away from one another or pull them into closer and more cooperative relationships. Conflicts may contain the seeds of group destruction or the seeds of a more unified and cooperative unit. Conflicts may bring aggression or mutual understanding. They have the potential for producing both highly constructive and highly destructive consequences for group functioning.[6]

As I experience my own religious life and as I engage in helping communities to navigate the choppy waters of their own differences, I do not see ill-will, indifference or unwillingness as major ingredients in failure to resolve conflict. Failure appears, rather, to be a product of fear, previous failure, lack of working understanding of the conflict and insufficient skill.

Failure to deal constructively with conflict may also emerge out of differing values that are deeply held. For instance, many religious have carried from past to present a deeply ingrained willingness to embrace suffering, which leads them to try to live peacefully, if somewhat passively, in the midst of conflict. They invoke texts like "He must increase, I must decrease" as the source of their motivation for this. Others in the community, with different history and training, tend to deal with the pain of the conflict by wanting to confront it, discern its source and, if possible, eradicate it. Each group might regard the other as engaging in something dysfunctional. As I often tell groups I work with, I personally am not into suffering in a big way! I mean that I believe we are entitled to a measure of human satisfaction and harmony and happiness, and that misery is not a necessary sign of, nor requisite for, virtue. I also believe, however, that no constructive relationship deepens and grows without the partners both losing and gaining through the encounter. The losing requires genuine and sometimes painful surrendering of cherished insularity of life-stances that exclude the other. The gain is in the new selves that are co-created in the relationship. It may well be that neither group has to let go of real values; the problem may arise because the values are never explicated to the other. The behavior arising from the values is expected to be clear enough evidence of the position held, but it is a well-known and well-documented fact that non-verbal behavior is highly ambiguous and open to myriad interpretations. Conflict often arises from the interpretations rather than from the values themselves. Hence, taking the risk of communicating without the need to make converts seems an appropriate starting-point for dealing with such conflicts. Simple self-disclosure may build sufficient mutual respect for the differences either to remain or to be resolved. I have found at times that such disclosure has led me to re-examine what I had been calling a personal value and to recognize there a stubbornly defended prejudice.

Advice From a Pragmatist

Much of the persistence of conflict comes from ignorance about its source and about appropriate ways of negotiating its resolution. I would therefore like to turn now to an examination of some basic working knowledge and skills. In doing this, I shall take up again the concept of models, that is, tidy ways of talking about and organizing our perception of untidy human realities. I think it is unwise to "canonize" any single model since knowledge and understanding grow and develop. Old models may be supplanted, hopefully by new and better ones. Furthermore, to canonize a model is to give it control over the user, and my view is that a model is as good as the person who employs it, and not vice versa. I shall draw on several contemporary models applicable to conflict-handling in religious life with the proviso that they are not the only ones available and certainly not the last word on the subject. They may, however, provide some road maps for individuals and groups attempting to face their own conflicted reality with insight and honesty and an effort to change. I shall begin with two people's account of a conflict that has developed between them over a considerable period of time.

Diary of a Conflict

Brother Martin: When I came to this community three years ago, I was feeling new and raw and a bit lonely at transferring from the school and community where I had been for the previous four years. One of the things that made it possible for me to say yes when the provincial suggested the transfer was Colin's presence in the new community. We had been at school together, went through the novitiate together, studied and trained together, and although neither of us had corresponded much over the previous four years, I looked forward to taking up where we had left off. The thought of a relationship with a person I knew so well excited me. Col's a fun person—bright, witty, full of life. At the same time he can be serious and share some deeper stuff when he wants to.

But it hasn't worked. He hasn't had as much time for me as I've needed, and when I've said that, he's just told me he's busier now than he used to be and has some new interests that occupy him. He says we're still friends like we used to be, but it doesn't *feel* the same to me. When I start to talk about things that matter, he seems to get restless and often looks at the clock and says he has to go. I feel kind of hurt on the inside, but shrug and say OK. He often says we'll talk later, but it doesn't often happen. I sit around waiting for him to come home, but when he does he seldom knocks on my door, so I go to bed that night with lousy feelings, mad with him and unsure about me.

Brother Colin: If I'm really honest I've got to say I'm a bit
disappointed with old Marty. When I knew he was coming
here I wrote to welcome him, thinking we'd get on the way
we used to. But hell! He really leans on me. He never used
to do that. He was an independent sort of guy, good at
sports, liked by everyone, got on well with women, a good
staff-member popular with colleagues and kids.

Now he seems to cringe and crawl a bit. Always wanting
deep and meaningful conversations. I sometimes feel as if
he tries to keep hold of me by starting sort of counselling-
type conversations, and I get uncomfortable. I want a
friend, not a client! But I'd probably hurt him too much if I
said that.

I don't want to be his personal property. I thought I'd be
happy to be his friend, but I'm not even sure of that now.
The price might be too high. He seems jealous of my other
friends and acts as if we were married!

Martin and Colin come to this new encounter in their relationship with a set of expectations about each other generated
at an earlier fact-finding stage of their relational history. This is
how all relationships begin, whether these are friendships, community acquaintances or working partnerships. Each person
surveys the other and directly and indirectly amasses a fund of
information about the other person. This information is frequently an amalgam of the things they have in common that attract them to one another, qualities that enrich each other, differences that need to be accepted. It is rather like a jigsaw
which, when assembled, makes a predictable and stable picture.
It is often tacitly assumed that the pieces don't make a picture if
put together in any other way, that this is the one and only way
they will ever go together. After all, if a person hates spinach,
he'll always hate spinach! Out of this knowledge comes expectations. (If she doesn't like spinach, I'd better not serve it to her!)
We avoid doing things we know embarrass or discomfort the
other. We do not write down a set of rules, but the rules are
there all right, and it is usually easy enough to know when either of us has broken one.

In marriage the partners are physically present to one another for a great proportion of their lives, yet as divorce figures
indicate, it is difficult to negotiate the changes in expectations
that inevitably happen, more or less subtly, over time. In celibate communities where we cannot commit ourselves to physical presence to our friends for life, the shifts and subtle changes

can be even more startling when a new encounter brings us in touch with them.[7] New influences, relationships and events along with the changes brought by increasing age all work their subtle changes, but we try to take up our relationship right where it was years ago.

Martin's and Colin's friendship encountered difficulties because (a) they carried over unchanged expectations and applied them to changed persons (b) without communicating or renegotiating them (c) assuming that neither person had changed significantly and (d) going on in the relationship without directly addressing new elements, feelings of anxiety and discomfort or confusion. The relationship was allowed to go on as if it were a past without a present.

This is where many relationships begin to founder, and I shall offer here a model that explains the progress of the deterioration and offers suggestions for arresting the process, not only rescuing the relationship but potentially deepening it. Failed relationships are frequently the cause of crisis among religious who find their sense of belonging in and derive energy for ministry from the supportive relationships in their community. The breakdown constitutes a crisis when the individuals (or indeed the whole community who witness the breakdown in relationship) face a new situation without the appropriate coping skills either because the protagonists do not have adequate coping skills or because old ones now prove ineffective.

Of Pinches and Crunches[8]

When the interaction between Martin and Colin is examined, it reveals a series of stages in which they try unsuccessfully to restore their relationship as they once knew it.

1) Old expectations, valid in their time, are transferred into the new situation and into this new stage of the friendship. *He used to be like this. . . . Why isn't he like that now?*

2) Implicit in this is a more or less total denial of the changes brought by the passage of time or, at least, a blindness to new elements in the other person's way of seeing his world. *I guess it'll take time. We need to pick up the threads, work back into the ways we used to enjoy life together. If I'm patient enough and wait around, it'll all get back to normal again.*

3) Personal discomfort follows, uneasiness with the lack of fit between expectations from the past and the quality of the

present interaction. *I'm starting to feel a bit ticked off by his behavior. What the hell's wrong with him? Is he mad at me about something? Is it my fault or his?*

4) Inappropriate ways of addressing the problem exacerbate it. The partners may ignore the problem hoping it will disappear; they may deal with it indirectly by silence or punitive behavior; they may temporarily resolve it by premature apology and acceptance of the apology. *Sorry to put pressure on you, but once I get settled here we'll be OK.*

As soon as either or both of the partners sense that all is not going well in the relationship, a "pinch" has developed. This is a hunch that something is wrong. It is not yet a serious disruption of the relationship, but it signals the need to renegotiate the relationship or some element of it. In the relationship under discussion here, Martin is uneasy that things are not what they used to be, and Colin is uneasy because demands are being made on him that feel uncomfortable and unacceptable. Each is likely to project the problem onto the other.

For example, Martin may say: "He's a bit off-putting and casual. He never used to be like that and now he's acting coolly and not as close as we used to be. If he were a bit more generous with his time and company we'd be old pals again."

And Colin might complain: "He wants me to be around almost all the time and doesn't seem to want me to have other friends. He's as dependent as an infant, but I don't want to be trapped into being his father, thank you."

Much earlier in their relationship, Martin and Colin, without being fully conscious of the process taking place, gathered information about each other from observation and mutual self-disclosure, and on the basis of the accumulated knowledge chose to continue their relationship, to attach the word *friend* to it, and to establish patterns of interaction where each was more or less sure of the other's responses in specific situations. The mutual roles were relatively clear. They learned what could be said and not said, what demands they could and could not make on each other, likes and dislikes, and because the relationship deepened, they knew many of each other's hopes, beliefs, goals and aspirations. They therefore progressed from sharing appropriate information and setting up acceptable expectations to a pattern of give-and-take, of bondedness with one another that was apparently stable. Later, when the tenuous nature of this stability became evident and was not directly addressed, a pinch occurred.

There is new information in the relationship now. A heightened need for companionship at a time of loneliness on the part of Martin (not made explicit) and interpretation of this by Colin as uncomfortable dependency inappropriate to a relationship previously characterized by independence and equality. Expectations have changed and also the predictable roles. Both the partners have new roles that characterize a change in the style of their commitment to one another. Colin now perceives himself to have been assigned a parental role in the duo, and Martin has adopted a dependent stance which he assumes is understood. No doubt both of them also bring to this changed pattern the freight of their early family experiences of dependence and independence. This has its own strong but not necessarily conscious effects on the way they act and react to each other now.

The result of the composite pattern of change is the threatening of the old stability and the need to renegotiate the relationship or at least some of its roles and expectations. The fact is that stability in any relationship is a mirage. To insist on it is to ask that the relationship be placed under glass. To expect it to remain the same as it was at any previous time is to halt the fluid process of growth and development which is the nature of all relationships. This is a piece of working knowledge that many religious lack. To *expect* change will not purge relational growth of all pain, of the stretching of new demands, of new give-and-take, but it may at least build in reasonable expectation of change that can help people recognize what is happening when pinches occur.

This is not enough. When a pinch occurs, the partners may do what Martin and Colin did initially, that is, try to maintain the status quo. This is a little like pedalling an exercise bike: It uses a great deal of energy but goes nowhere. Attempts to maintain the status quo may be briefly successful, but the energy generated by each new pinch eventually makes them aware that the relationship is in trouble. Often the irritation or uneasiness associated with the early pinches escalates into anger and hostility which, even if not spoken directly will begin to make itself felt through non-verbal signals.

In religious life a number of factors exacerbate the problem experienced at this state. Many religious have been trained to ignore or devalue their feelings. Their ears still ringing with injunctions to asceticism, which involved suspicion of emotions, they have little skill at naming their own feelings, owning them and directly reporting them. False definitions of forgiveness lead to heroic efforts to "get over" what is happening without really discussing it. Because some internalized such lessons more than others, an imbalance in their willingness or capacity to engage in immediacy may occur. One partner may begin haltingly to name what he or she sees happening, while the other reacts with denial, internally threatened by the greater freedom of the other. When both intimacy and anger have been discouraged, it is exceedingly difficult to renegotiate pinches, even when the old learnings have been repudiated.

But if the relationship is to continue creatively, renegotiation must be planned and this involves a number of key skills. An attitude of wanting to heal the small breaches created by successive pinches is a start, but it is not enough. It may be painfully frustrating to *want* without knowing how to *act*. Many religious, having been exposed to education programs on communication, have learned some of the skills without learning the sequence of the skills. As a result, with the best will in the world they plunge into challenging and confronting without preparing the ground for this by adequate self-disclosure and empathy. This often creates a sadly unnecessary breaking-point. In healthily renegotiating a pinch or series of pinches, the partners need the skill of self-disclosure and a receptivity to the other often spoken of as the skill of empathy. Appropriate and timely self-disclosure is based upon the capacity to recognize, name and directly report feelings without "dumping" them upon the other.

Where successful renegotiation is achieved, the partners look at new information, work out revised expectations and arrive at altered roles in the relationship. It may be that in order to do this they have to agree to relinquish some old and cherished pictures of each other. Where this letting-go has happened successfully in my own life—and usually for me it takes a deal of time and energy—the ensuing stage of the relationship is marked by greater trust and confidence and an increase of intimacy because we have succeeded in weathering a storm together. Where it has not happened successfully, the relationship has either continued in a kind of smiling limbo, where neither of us takes the risk of anything but a distant amicability, or it has erupted into the exchange of hostilities that has brought avoidance and termination of the relationship. My own personal experience of this is the carrying of a wound that never quite goes away, and of guilt because at a time long gone there were opportunities I might have taken, but let slip through my fingers, to our mutual loss.

There is one other possibility at the early stages, when pinches are recognized and felt. In the process of mutually addressing the changes in our relationship, we may discover that our lives have gone in such different directions and taken on such new hues that we cannot see ways of continuing our relationship, and so we plan its termination. If there is consensus about this, it may be that the friendship becomes acquaintance and is maintained at a different level, or that we agree to treat each other with the same respect and depth of communication as we extend to others in the community whom we do not regard as personal friends. In other words, we may sustain our relationship at the level of working mutuality that does not carry the old emotional closeness.

The story does not end with the way we handle the inevitable pinches of a lively relationship. Unaddressed or improperly addressed pinches develop into "crunches." If we do not renegotiate satisfactorily at the pinch points what happens is the shattering of our shared expectations, accompanied by hurt, anger, pain and blame. The confusion and ambivalence felt at first deepens into accusation and resentful bargaining fuelled by our anxiety concerning the immediate future of the relationship. At this stage, in a futile effort to arrest the downward slide of the relationship, the partners deal with the serious disruption of their expectations of one another by contradictory insistence on them. Positions harden. They embark on a roundabout of accusation and repudiation of blame, and now healing and recovery become less and less likely. The detachment required to discern the source of the conflict may be impossible because each person is mired in the anguish of it and all they have energy for is the repetitive pattern of recrimination.

With Martin and Colin, if their relationship is allowed to proceed to a crunch, their discussion may sound somewhat like this:

Brother Martin: You never have time for me anymore. I keep getting the message that you wish I hadn't come to this community. I'm not asking all that much, just a bit of your precious time! It's available to everyone *except* me these days.

Brother Colin: If you didn't damn well cling so much, I might give it to you, but you hang on as if you were helpless or something. I do give time to others. It's freely given, because *they* don't demand it. Damn it, Marty, you don't own me.

Brother Martin: Well, I *have* to insist, because if I didn't you'd ignore me totally. I have to jump up and down and beg for attention or I'll not be noticed. You keep running away from me. Even when we've agreed to spend some time together you're late or you find some lame excuse to be with someone else.

Brother Colin: Can't you see, you dummy, that's just the point! If you weren't so clingy, I would want to be there.

Once people become embroiled in this cyclic pattern it generates its own energy and is self-perpetuating. It produces a form of tunnel vision painfully difficult to break out of. The only way that any further repair of the relationship may take place, however, is for the persons involved to break out of it, or to be helped to break out of it. Genuine self-giving love requires dying.

Martin and Colin now have a number of options, not all of which are equally easy or possible. If the pain and resentment are intolerably high, the most likely next step is resentful termination. This is an avoidance step that releases the partners from the immediate pain of their embattled state. As such, it is an attractive possibility. It is made even more likely if either of the partners uses avoidance habitually as a way of dealing with anxiety. A second alternative is to forgive each other and return to "the way things used to be." Because this embodies a falsehood it is usually a short-lived solution. In fact, things are *not* as they used to be, and it will probably not be long before the pinches gradually begin to accumulate again, or before a small incident in the partnership leads to a crunch in which angry cycling around the blame track begins again.

There is a third possibility: renegotiation under stress. However, it should be pointed out that it is far more difficult to renegotiate a crunch than a pinch. When the level of hurt is high, the basic instinct for self-preservation can unseat and supplant empathy and care for the other. There can be so much pain that there is an experience of "no love left to lose," and the best form of defense becomes attack or total withdrawal. In most instances renegotiation under stress is rarely achieved without help from someone else. The same skills of self-disclosure and empathy are required of the couple, but it is far harder to call on them when one is endangered. So, at this stage, a third person who can model other possibilities, help to exorcise the ghosts of past learnings, call upon neglected skills, and perhaps teach new ones, may be required. For this person the task is daunting because the difficulty of helping the embattled partners to hear each other is massive.

For many religious it is at the stage of crunches occurring that their problem in relating begins to be apparent to the rest of the community. The community becomes the arena in which some of the interaction happens, and a variety of interventions are typical of communities at this juncture. For those threatened by conflict of any kind, the typical strategy is to refuse to see what is happening, to suggest that they remove themselves to their own rooms if they want to fight, or to appeal to authority.

There are more positive attempts to help that unfortunately may be equally ineffective:

1) good advice: take a holiday, talk it over, go out and have a meal together, see a movie.

2) suggesting that one of the persons move to a new community. This is dysfunctional for the obvious reason that a relationship is not a geographically determined thing but a process and bondedness that can exist over space and time. In addition, if the persons move apart without resolving their crisis, it will

   a) remain and express itself in stress or other symptoms,

   b) never become a source of growth and meaning and positive learning for either of them, and so they both risk the possibility of repeating the pattern in other relationships.

3) the use of religious language or pious exhortation. To say, "I'll pray for you," and indeed to suit the promise to the deed, contains an element of hypocrisy unless it is accompanied by a behavioral effort to answer the prayer.

> Irresponsibility is inevitable, given an understanding of the prayer of petition which permits the substitution of prayer for active concern. Hence, the importance of emphasizing that the normal mode of God's response is through the Christian community. To pray is a grace, but the grace is not in the words, but in the insight into the need which prompts the petition.[9]

I believe that the real miracles of transformation that do happen are effected by tough love, by the power of empathy and by the willingness of loving people to involve themselves constructively in the pain of others. To pour the oil of religious language over the troubled waters of a turbulent relationship is at worst an invitation to a new form of denial, translating a gritty human reality that requires hard work, asceticism and no escapes into some sort of heavenly illusion of peace.

4) pairing and siding with one individual against another. The community thus becomes somewhat like the in-laws of a married couple whose relationship is in jeopardy. Such pairing and partisan behavior in the community is inevitably marked by blame and injustice. Far from helping resolve the conflict, new conflict now arises between opposing groups.

5) playing amateur psychiatrist, analyzing and offering ready-made solutions.

There are, on the other hand, some ways in which a community can offer realistic and faithful support not to one or the other but to the relationship itself. I list these with an invitation to the reader to try to add to the list.

1) A basic stance toward both persons of affirmation and valuing. This is best when it avoids over-solicitous or gushy encouragement, but offers brief statements of concern and small services that demonstrate the awareness of how difficult life may be for the persons in conflict right now.

2) Where a person concerned wants to talk to another member of the community, listening with warmth and respect is helpful provided that the listener does not become caught in the blame-cycle. Listening and judgment are poles apart. In a community there may be difficulties involved with this listening, such as blame from the other person, who resents being talked about when absent. Privacy and confidentiality are supremely important. Unfortunately, many religious communities of both sexes are renowned for their grape-vine systems. At times, the mistake is to tell the story (with elaborate confidentiality, of course!) to a major superior who may, if unwise, react with unilateral power.

3) Modelling non-judgmental care for both in simple, direct ways. Those community members who are closer to the pair than others may be able to challenge gently when it seems likely that the challenge will be heard, but the best challenge of all is relating normally to each person in the most constructive and receptive ways available.

4) It may also be a helpful and challenging suggestion to remind the pair of the availability of professional help, even to assist with a referral, where this is possible.

5) The genuine, unsentimental love of the community is the

richest environment in which the pair may find hope and draw energy to transform conflict into a painfully renewed appreciation of one another. This love is demonstrated in faithful presence and few words. The pair in conflict often requires an oasis in the midst of the lonely desert. The climate of a good community provides exactly that.

6) Affirming strengths rather than pointing out weaknesses. In the heat of their embattled state, people often overlook strengths that might be employed in the present crisis. Offering concrete examples of how such strengths have been used previously constitutes useful and positive challenges to new forms of action that are within the range of possibility. The usual rules for appropriate challenge apply here (see Chapter 2).

Group Conflict

Not all conflict occurring in religious communities is one-to-one. Conflict happens between groups and often appears just to be there without being clearly located. It is a diffuse conflict that produces malaise, criticism and defensiveness among group members without an immediately recognizable source. Or it is recognizable as a division over an issue or value or course of action.

Once again, such conflict requires cognitive and behavioral approaches to resolve it. Community members must ask, *Do we understand how conflict may be resolved?* (working knowledge) and *What steps must we take in order to resolve it?* (behavioral skills). This may involve additional questions such as *What skills do we have available in this group and who has them? What other skills do we need to co-opt or learn?*

Observation suggests that in most communities there is a variety of approaches to conflict, many of which stem from individual and group experience of what has worked in the past. Not every approach that has worked in terms of assuaging the anxiety attached to conflict is constructive in the long term, though it may relieve the immediate pressure of stressful feelings, competitiveness and anger attached to whatever issue is at the heart of the conflict. Often anxiety-avoiding patterns of handling conflict have their origins in people's early childhood; for example, "You do not get mad in this family," or "Go outside and count to 10 and calm down!"

Avoidance of conflict is one common way of managing its effects in communities. This manifests itself in any one of the following behaviors:

- absenting oneself from community gatherings where the conflict is most likely to surface
- absenting oneself psychologically by having nothing to say or by smilingly agreeing with everyone and adopting no clear position
- denying that conflict exists and finding other ways of describing it
- if conflict is of an enduring nature, asking for a transfer out of the community
- dissociating oneself from the conflict by pointing out that it is really the concern of the superior or the principal of the school or some other community member.

Such ways of dealing with the inner fear generated by conflict are not dismissed by facile exhortations to courage and risk-taking. Help to change requires empathy, time, support, gentleness and respect. It is well-known that avoidance reinforces avoidance. I remember when I first moved into post-graduate studies at a local university, I was invited by the faculty to attend their informal gatherings, to take morning tea with them and to be present at meetings for the presentation of thesis defenses. I felt shy, gauche and a little obvious as the only religious in the group, attired at that time in a medieval habit that made conversation die (at least that's how I perceived it!) when I entered the room. Rather than subject myself to the anxiety of these entrances, I found many ingenious excuses to be somewhere else at the appropriate times, thus relieving myself of the anxiety attached to being there. I remember the enormous sigh of relief as I sat in the library the first time I retreated from a staff meeting! After that it became easier and easier to find excuses to absent myself. Simultaneously it became harder and harder even to picture myself walking into the faculty lounge and to try to imagine doing so generated immediate anxiety. I would never have gone back had not an understanding faculty member sought me out and gently invited me, accompanying me and covering my entry with small-talk and conversation that drew me quietly into a sub-group. Eventually, in fact in a surprisingly short time, my phantoms departed and I began to regret the fears that had led me to miss pleasant opportunities for befriending and learning. Some of my most enduring relationships were born in that group.

Another set of behaviors that conflict may evoke are *defusion tactics*. When tension is fairly high from trying to resolve a disagreement or make an unpopular decision and the community is nearing real confrontation, someone may crack a joke. This interrupts the process in a way that requires considerable back-tracking to resume it again. Often the person has this behavior reinforced by others in the community who feel the tension of heightened and intense feelings and do not want to deal with them. The humorist destroys the intensity and "saves" the situation from potentially explosive interchanges. It is easy to continue to do this because the behavior is reinforced by the approval of some of the others and often not confronted for its destructive properties. The clown role in the community may harden into a set of expectations that severely limit the clown-person's future contributions; it is difficult to make serious or self-disclosing statements in a gathering that consistently expects to be entertained by what you say. On several occasions when I have been facilitating a community's interaction, the pain of this for the stereotyped individual has become apparent and, where there is enough awareness and sensitivity on the part of others, the injustice of limiting a person to a single function has been admitted and the destructiveness of this recognized.

A second common defusion strategy is unnecessary or premature harmonizing. When disagreements surface, arguments are engaged in or feelings run high, it is common for someone to intervene with comments such as, "Well, I don't see your difference as so great, because I can see the things you have in common. You both agree that . . ." Such a statement attempts to shift the focus from the core of the conflict to peripheral commonalities. Another harmonizing statement may go something like this: "We're all a bit hot under the collar right now, so why don't we leave the whole thing till everyone has had a chance to cool down?" A further defusion technique is the proposal of prayer or discernment as a way of dealing with a thorny issue. I hasten to say that prayer and discernment are priorities for me, but I do not believe God zaps us with sudden solutions or circumvents the usual painful human process of coming to terms with our own earthy reality using the natural gifts of communication, compassion, intelligence and relationality. When prayer is *substituted* for human effort and responsibility, I believe it is illusion. When it is understood as the faithful living out of the deep invitation to be true to our own humanity, to cry yes to the authentic demands of that humanity in the knowledge that there is a God who constantly, subtly and invisibly lures us to harmony, *then* I believe we are for real.

I do not claim for a moment that there is anything sinister in the intentions of those who employ avoidance or defusion methods of dealing with conflict. I do claim, however, that such methods do little to deal permanently and constructively with the fear and anxiety experienced by those who habitually instigate such behavior. While they may be temporarily effective in substituting harmony for conflict, it is harmony at a price. One likelihood is that a simple disagreement or conflict of interest is submerged and, still active below the surface of the community's interaction, it generates angers and resentments and competitiveness out of proportion to its importance. Sadly, conflict may then become polarization; a community pinch has become a large-scale crunch.

A third approach to conflict is to face it head-on, to confront it. Not all confronting of conflict is constructive, however. Enough has already been said about unilateral power to make it clear that overpowering approaches to people diminish then, rob them of respect and often immobilize their capacity to act freely. Threats and blandishments, inappropriate recourse to authority figures, punitive ways of dealing with dissidents such as ostracism or the withholding of information, emotional blackmail, win/lose tactics, even democratic vote-taking on important issues, may all be manifestations of negotiating conflict by using a destructive kind of power. One camouflaged version of unilateral power in religious communities is the easy assumption on the part of vocal and educated sub-groups that once they have clearly stated their position on an issue and the rest have not immediately responded, the matter is settled. The loud, strong voice of a few may so overawe others that their fearful silence may be interpreted as consensus. Things are accomplished, but at what a price!

The power of mutuality emerges as the most constructive approach of which I am aware. Where it is valued in a community, conflict negotiation will be seen as a joint enterprise to which each person will bring his or her unique abilities. Win/lose expectations and relational power are incompatible, and an honest search for consensus where nobody wins and nobody loses is the ideal approach. The one and the many, ideally, stand shoulder to shoulder to contemplate a question and determine a course of action. They do not stand against one another, power ranged against power.

Learning and practicing the skills of negotiation will include:

1. *Determining the nature and source of the conflict*

If this is difficult between two individuals, it is exceedingly complex in groups where hidden agendas and unconscious motivations are multiplied. If the conflict is about a profound difference in *values*, it will be a more delicate, difficult and long-range task to resolve it or to find ways of living with it. If it is about *behavior*—furnishing the house, planning the budget, organizing a community function—it may boil up quite a quantity of steam, but remain essentially manageable in the short term.

2. *Using confrontation skills with sustained empathy*

The conditions for confrontation given in Chapter 2 are relevant here, remembering that to confront is to "speak the truth to one's brother or sister in love." In particular, it is important to initiate negotiation of conflict by describing its occurrence rather than launching into blame or accusation and unnecessarily provoking defensiveness and counterattack.

3. *Valuing and understanding feelings*

If the community values empathy not merely as a skill, but as an appreciative way of seeing the world, then, even in the sometimes heated conflicts that inevitably emerge, members will deeply respect each other's feelings with strength, generosity and unsentimental acceptance.

4. *Dying to defensiveness*

Tension and conflict automatically trigger feelings of defensiveness. To hold these in conscious awareness as part of our present reality, but to try to withhold using them to win, attack or compete is a form of asceticism that indicates largeness of spirit.

5. *Listening deeply without prejudice*

The emergence of the conflict situation, whether one-on-one or within a larger group, triggers argument. Part of our defensiveness is often to pour out words to illustrate and prove our own point of view. If we are talking all the time, or planning what we will say at the earliest opportunity, how can we even hear what the other is saying let alone feel the pull of his or her way of seeing and understanding? Deep listening does not necessarily mean that we will arrive at instant agreement, but it does protect mutual respect. After we truly hear each other our disagreement or criticism cannot be a put-down or a belittling of the other.

6. *Employing problem-solving skills*[10]

   a)   Clarifying: What is the issue and where do we stand on it?

   b)   Specifying: In what *specific* ways does this issue affect us?

   c)   Involving: Does everyone understand? Has everyone been heard? Who wants to be heard?

   d)   Brain-storming: What possible behaviors will help deal with the issue. Create a list without yet debating or discussing the items on the list. Can we be as creative as possible with proposals?

   e)   Ranking: Reorganize the list we have produced by our brainstorming into order of probable effectiveness. This requires more time than the other steps since this is where disagreement will most likely surface.

   f)   Deciding: Choose the solution(s) most acceptable to the whole group by consensus rather than vote-taking. Consensus has been arrived at not when there is total and unanimous agreement, but when there is large agreement, with those who do not fully agree expressing willingness to support and participate in the proposed solution.

   g)   Planning Action: How will the solution be implemented? When? Where? By whom? Time limits? Ways of keeping everyone informed?

   h)   Evaluating: When will we get together to share our perception of the success or failure of what we planned? What are our criteria for judging this?

   i)   Renegotiating: If successful, are there further goals to be turned to now? If so, decide, plan and evaluate the new goals. If not, look again at our brainstorming list, add to or subtract from it in the light of our current experience, and begin again. The joint experience of failure can be as unifying as success!

   After all this has been said it must be added that not every conflict occurring in a community may be taken away by even the most faithful and skilled application of the principles suggested. Profound differences stemming from a pluralism of potentially polarizing views of religious life, church and even God, may mean that we must search sensitively and appreciatively for ways of living with the differences, hearing and understanding them as fully and respectfully as we can, and holding them in dynamic and sometimes uncomfortable equilibrium.

It may be that within a single religious congregation many *forms* of community need to be set up to provide a home for the varying understandings of religious life. My own fear is that this can become a system of ghettos separated by differences that might have mutually enriched us had we had the courage to live alongside each other more closely, a costly but valuable risk. I am afraid also of the possibility that separate community structures to house different stances may also create closure and eliminate that abrasive jostling and tumbling which creates and unveils beauty. I am aware also that if polarization becomes so unbridgeable as to consume the whole energy of a group and destroy its capacity for ministry, then perhaps such a separation may be a last-ditch stand to resolve otherwise insoluble difficulties.

Previously I made a distinction between the essence of community and its various forms. I am personally in favor of a rich diversity of forms while we retain the essence of community's relational bonds, but I see the shape of new and different forms emerging not from internal conflicts but from the demands of ministry.

Diminishing Behavior

From the myriad other things that might be said in relation to conflict, I elect finally to present two case histories that image for me the way that people may become imprisoned and conflict may become perpetuated. I do this, gratefully acknowledging the permission of those involved to tell part of their stories. The first is the story of an individual and the second is the story of a group. It is clear that I do not know all that might be told, because the people concerned do not yet know themselves all that might be told, but at least the main outlines may be presented.

SISTER MAUREEN'S PRISON

Sister Maureen is 70 years old. She has long since given up active duties as a nurse but has steadfastly refused invitations to take up residence in her congregation's retirement home. She prefers to remain in one of the local small communities with a group of younger sisters and one other retired sister. Other members of this small community tell of the reaction when Maureen's name appeared on the appointment list for the year as a member of their group. There was a kind of community shudder. One member describes her thoughts something like this:

I was scared and angry when I saw her name on the list. Nobody asked me if I wanted to live with her, and I sure didn't.
Everybody in the congregation knows she's an old battle-axe.
The only way she ever relates to anyone, especially younger
people, is by criticizing, disagreeing, judging and being an old
bitch! Nobody stood a chance with her and she knew it. I'd
heard that from other communities and even though I had
never been at close quarters with her, I knew I didn't want her
around. You can't teach an old dog new tricks. I knew she'd
dish out more of the same to us. Thanks for nothing!

Both Maureen and the rest of the group remember vividly
the day she arrived and the cautious and cool welcome she received. Acting on reports and evaluations from previous communities where Maureen had been briefly a member (briefly because either she requested a transfer or the community did) this
new group did not assign her a task and often excluded her
from common decision-making by waiting till she had gone to
bed at night before holding meetings. In such a milieu Maureen
was true to previous form—angry, hostile, difficult and resentful. The tension in the community ran high, but nobody said
anything directly to Maureen until one day one community
member observed Maureen sitting in the chapel covertly weep-
ing. She recalls walking outside and anxiously summoning the
courage to say something gentle (an approach often scorned by
Maureen as "weak"). When Maureen did not come out, the sister went in, sat beside her and without words simply stroked
her arm and looked at her. Maureen sobbed and said some inco-
herent things in which the word lonely was repeated several
times. Months later, after a series of further events, Maureen was
able to describe the release that happened inside her when the
touch of the other sister let her know of someone's presence to
her. She had one really insightful comment. "At last," she said,
"somebody was alongside me as I am *now*, and not as what I
was *then*."

At about this time, I was engaged to work with the communities of the province. As a result I became a frequent visitor
to the community in which Maureen lived. No major observable
changes had happened after the incident in the chapel except
that there was a bond between Maureen and the other sister
which was expressed occasionally in a glance of understanding
or a tentative smile.

On a weekend when we were deliberating on the quality
of their religious life, I asked the members of the community to
say what they thought they each offered to the community that

was potentially or actually enriching. One person commented that she was a willing listener and was happy to hear how things went for others during the day. Someone else prepared good meals and enjoyed offering that form of service. Another with gifts for liturgical creativity took on preparing the community's special celebrations. Then Maureen gruffly said, "I don't have anything that is good for the community." There was an embarrassed silence, and then someone else rushed in with a statement totally unrelated to Maureen's. There was no response to her at all. In my own mind I was on the horns of a dilemma. I wanted to encourage a response to Maureen, and I wanted to confront the community with a description of what had just taken place. I did neither, deciding that a simple genuine response that I could honestly make to Maureen might model what the community had failed to do.

Turning to Maureen, I said quietly, "Maureen, you may not know it, but often when I arrive here on Friday afternoon to begin a weekend of work in this community, you are the only person home. When I walk into the common room you light up, even though I'm aware that my coming means fairly scary group work that maybe you'd rather avoid. You make me feel welcome. You drop whatever you are doing. I love it, and I always enjoy that little bit of private time we have before the others come in from work. Yesterday, you said the words, 'Oh, Evelyn, I'm glad to see you,' and I knew you meant it."

Maureen sat there for a few moments looking down at her hands, and then tentatively she began to speak, gathering confidence as she went on. She spoke of knowing that she had a reputation as a cranky, stubborn and useless old lady, and that she craved to get rid of it but could not do it alone. She spoke of community after community who expected her to be like that because of information passed on from a previous community. When she knew that, as she put it, "I'd been ratted on," her anger reached a new intensity and before she knew it she was reinforcing the old image, putting herself back in its prison by living up to it once again.

Perhaps encouraged by our silent attentiveness, perhaps energized by a story half-told and needing completion, Maureen began to speak of her early years in religious life and, before that, of her family and of the accumulated bitterness stemming from it all. She remembered a family so poor that the children had to be sent out to relatives and the family broken up for survival. She herself, youngest in a family of 12, was sent to her ancient grandparents who were, by her account, excessively strict and repressive. As the story unfolded she remembered later cruel incidents. As a novice, she was not permitted to attend her mother's funeral. During her mother's final illness she was allowed only to stand outside the family home and call to her mother through the bedroom window. Incident after bitter incident was relived in the common room that day, almost as if we were not there. Eventually Maureen looked up at each one of us and said quite gently, "So you see, when I'm angry at you, it's not really at you. It's just so hard to let go of all that. Harder if you don't help me."

Co-creation began in the community that day. For Maureen, prison doors opened a little, and the supportive understanding she created within her hearers became a beckoning influence that permitted the surrender of some of the anger and the emergence and expression of her warmer qualities. Some of these qualities no doubt had been there, masked, and some may have been born that day. Something creative happened for the community too. They began to understand that their expectations had been bars on the prison doors. They also understood that the only way that Maureen till then had been able to relate to her world was with anger.

In the months that followed there were many occasions when Maureen produced her angry behavior again, though less violently and less often. The rest of the community, still threatened at times by the anger, have learned to affirm strengths in Maureen rather than fasten attention on lapses. With a little help they have avoided being seduced into false sympathy by the cruelty of the story, and from time to time they challenge Maureen to be her whole self and not merely a bundle of sad memories. They still criticize at times, but one significant event has been of immense reassurance to both Maureen and the entire group. About a year and a half ago, the provincial visited the house and suggested that Maureen transfer either to the retirement home or to another local community. Maureen was able to say at this meeting that she found her present community a place where she could spend her last active years peacefully without stagnating, and the community banded together in a unanimous request to the provincial not to move Maureen.

As communities and individuals we can tighten the stranglehold of the past or call each other to new and miraculously freeing ways of being in our world. To place one person in bondage may in fact ensnare and cripple us all.

THE BROTHERS' STORY

For the past eighteen months I have acted as a consultant to a community of brothers who, prompted and encouraged by their provincial, invited me to intervene in a continuing state of conflict among them. I understand that I have joined a long procession of consultants who came and went, many deciding that their intervention had borne so little fruit that they were wasting their time. The group has described the hurt of this abandonment even while recognizing the frustrations of the helpers when they saw their best efforts aborted.

Unwittingly, therefore, I walked into a situation loaded with suspicion that I would live up to the image of the other helpers. Punctiliously polite to me at all times, the community masked its skepticism and cynicism with an apparent willingness to spend time working at discovering the sources of their conflict. I began, as I customarily do, by asking them to tell as much of their collective story as they were willing to tell. Reluctance was in the air, and only superficial facts were given. People did not look at each other but made veiled references to one another without addressing them directly to any particular person. Anger and defensiveness against each other's anger characterized almost every exchange. Their defensiveness carried over into the apostolate. The community ran a boarding school for boys, and each brother had carved out a patch of territory that was exclusively his. Nobody crossed boundaries.

In spite of my early resolution not to repeat the "desertion" behavior of other helpers in this situation, I felt the frustration that they must have felt. The only openly expressed feeling that I could touch with empathy was anger, and this was very much the cyclic pattern of blame and denial that happens in a crunch. In fact, for this community every pinch seemed to translate immediately into a crunch. A few crumbs left on the diningroom table could start an international incident! The challenge for them and for me was to find ways of breaking through that pattern and shaping new ways of being in relationship, a daunting task.

As I grasped, almost with desperation, for insight into what was going on, two hunches were uppermost. The first was that there must indeed be a dreadful story behind what was happening and that the story was not yet being told but merely hinted at. My second hunch was that the anger so evident among them hid something that was beginning to feel to me like shame. So the first task seemed to be to trigger the telling of the story.

Since for me modelling is the best form of education, I began to tell bits of my own story, deliberately choosing to let them know of some of the injustices of my early training as a novice and some of the personal needs and expectations that preceded this and were inherited from my family. Along with this I tried to build on the one thing they had in common, a faith commitment. In our prayer and reflection sessions together I proposed that we consider the theme of the Word of God, spoken through the scriptures, spoken in the incarnation and spoken in our lives. We enthroned the scriptures in the room, chose texts that described the Word as both sweet as honey and sharp as a two-edged sword, and in an atmosphere of prayer tried to spell out how that paradoxical experience made itself felt in our individual and group life.

Something a little gentler began to happen. Tentatively a few of the seven men began to be a little more specific about their stories, and tales of incredible injustice began to emerge. I think I was right about their sense of shame. When I mentioned it, some corroboration was given. Those who could not yet freely tell their stories at least began to describe the pain of the untold stories. Eventually most of them have shared at least a part of their history.

What emerges from all these partial stories is a script that has enormous power to govern present attitudes, expectations and behavior. Almost brainwashed in a system where law superseded love, they had been encouraged to report on one another to authority figures, bringing down punishment on one another and creating an atmosphere in which nobody was ever safe. In addition they saw some individuals favored and privileged by the authority figures. They have carried resentment toward those favored ones into the present even though the remembered events took place at least 16 years ago.

Gradually we put together the pieces of the script:

- Trust nobody. Eventually people let you down.

- We are all irreparably damaged so nobody can really help us.

- Our story is so wildly improbable that nobody will believe it anyway.

- Even if it's true, it's so much worse than any other religious order's history that we dare not tell it. It's shameful.

- We can't change our story or escape from it.

- The effects of it are on us and we'll carry them to the grave.

- Each of us must be responsible for his own survival at any cost. If you don't make sure you're a winner, you'll be a loser, and who wants to get hurt all over again?

In the light of all this—which I listed in precisely this way for them—we are now in the process of asking:

1) Are there any ways out of the grip of the past?

2) What new learnings are needed?

3) What would we like to change?

In addition, I am asking for a mandate which the community rather than the provincial shapes. This in itself is a reversal of part of the old pattern of autocratic rule and submission to imposed directives.

The way out of all this conflict is, I believe, going to be slow and difficult. Layer upon layer of the story must be attended to. In accompanying the community on this journey, now painfully embarked upon, I have a number of expectations of myself, some of which I have made known to the group, some of which are still dawning on me. I know that the telling and re-living of the story is of paramount importance, and that as I walk through it with them I must not be caught in its tentacles myself if I am to help find new ways of understanding it and growing out of it.

I regard empathy as a tough virtue and not merely a kind of warm fuzzy. That conviction is deepened by my contact with this community, where I want to empathize deeply with the pain without joining in the common belief that there is no way out of it. Part of my task is to challenge them to find ways out of it.

With tough empathy I know the need to be patient with the inch-by-inch, advance-and-withdraw progress of our joint enterprise. Respect and fidelity are so important to sustain the will to work at it that if I go the way of other helpers I have a suspicion that there may be no further efforts. Any disrespect or belittling of the story will reinforce their shame. I am conscious that gentleness is not weakness and that strong gentleness may create enough safety to touch what has until now been too dangerous, too explosive and too potentially destructive to touch.

For community consideration

A.   At a community meeting at which interpersonal disagreement is voiced, what are the common responses in
the group? List these responses—arguing, silence, appeals to authority, taking a vote, sarcasm, clarifying,
and so forth.

When you have produced a list, try to agree on a ranking of the listed behaviors, placing the most constructive ones at the top of the list and the least helpful at
the end. As you go, discuss *why* particular responses are
constructive or otherwise.

As you do this, note that some interventions are at
times helpful and at other times blocking.

B.   Complete the following sentences and share them with
the group.

1.   When conflict arises in the community between me
and someone else, I . . .

a)   Try to find what we have in common and place
the emphasis on finding ways of establishing
some common ground for mutual cooperation

b)   try to win

2.   When a group in the community conflicts with me,
I . . .

a)   use all my power and capacity for persuasion to
get my own way

b)   respect not only my own opinion but the frame
of reference of everybody else and try to find
ways of establishing consensus or arriving at a
creative solution that we can all live with

3.   Ways in which I use my resources in a win/lose game
are . . .

4.   Ways in which I try to preserve mutuality and cooperative efforts are . . .

For individual consideration

A.   What scares you most when conflict arises between you
and somebody else in the community?

What scares you most when conflict arises in the community between others?

B.   Are there any perceptible echoes in your answers to the above two questions of earlier parts of your personal story? How was conflict handled in your family? Who taught you to handle conflict? How? What other learnings may be important for you now in order to balance past learnings?

How were you expected to handle conflict and strong feelings during initial formation? Is there anything there that needs to be unlearned?

C.   What are your *gifts* in situations of conflict? Can you illustrate this? How thoroughly do you use these gifts in daily life?

D.   Conflict resolution happens best when an atmosphere of trust is developed in the community. How high is the level of trust in your community? What are the signs of this? How do you and others in the community contribute to the building of trust?

E.   What skills do you need to practice or learn in order to handle conflict better?

F.   Can you identify any pinches that you presently experience in community life or work. What can you do about them? Rehearse the confrontation in your imagination. Try it in direct encounter.

Notes

1.   Michael Novak, *Ascent of the Mountain, Flight of the Dove* (New York: Harper & Row, 1978), p. 223.

2.   Dietrich Bonhoeffer, *Prayers from Prison* (London: Collins, 1977), pp. 17-18.

3.   Richard John Neuhaus, *Freedom for Ministry: A Critical Affirmation of the Church and Its Mission* (San Francisco: Harper & Row, 1979), p. 210.

4.   Johannes B. Metz, *Followers of Christ: The Religious Life and the Church*, trans. Thomas Linton (London: Burns & Oates, 1978), p. 12.

5.   Ibid. p. 15.

6.   David W. Johnson and Frank P. Johnson, *Joining To-*

gether: Group Theory and Group Skills (Englewood Cliffs, New Jersey: Prentice-Hall, 1975), p. 139.

7. There is absolutely no implication intended here that religious life is harder. It may, in fact, have more built-in escape routes. It may also be *easier* to see and recognize change in a person after a period of separation than it is with lifelong daily contact, as in marriage. It can be like perceiving signs of aging in another whom we haven't seen for a long time, signs not so easily perceptible to those who have been consistently present.

8. The material on pinches and crunches is derived from a paper by John J. Scherer and John J. Sherwood, "The Dating/Mating Game: How to Play Without Losing," *Institute for Research in the Behavioral, Economic and Management Sciences*, Paper No. 460, May 1974, Purdue University, West Lafayette, Indiana.

9. Jerome Murphy-O'Connor, *What is Religious Life?* (St. Saviour's, Dublin: Dominican Publications, 1975), p. 37.

10. Some of this material is derived from Joan A. Stepsis, "Conflict Resolution Strategies," *The 1974 Handbook for Group Facilitators*, eds. J. W. Pfeiffer and J. E. Jones (Iowa: University Associates, 1974), pp. 140-141.

5
FORMATION:

Shaping and Blending Our Stories

It is largely by default that I use the word *formation* throughout this discussion. I find it difficult to fix upon a single word to
adequately contain the complex of meanings that I should like
to include within a single symbol. My dislike stems from a tendency the word has to evoke for me the notion of one or several people perpetrating something upon others, a kind of instrumentalism that has overtones of coercing growth, of
determining life-directions for, or of shaping someone independently of his or her co-operation and free choice. The initiative
and creativity, the spontaneous responsibility of the other to his
or her own life story is somehow not covered by the word *formation*. One way of overcoming this semantic problem is to say
what I *do* mean by *formation* and assume the reader will hold
this in focus while reading what follows.

Formation is a process of assisted growth into life. Growth,
development, deepening, seeking meaning, espousing values,
choosing directions for life, moving toward self-transcending
love—none of these movements of the spirit takes place in a
vacuum. They are always located within a network of influences, some of them conscious, many of them buried in the unconscious or in a historical past of which we have little or no
memory. They are always being impinged upon, confirmed,
challenged, redirected, speeded up, slowed down by influences
in the present, events, learnings and relationships that bombard
us. Sometimes these influences confirm old learnings and ways
of seeing the world while at other times they create new horizons of meaning—which may be disjunctive with those of the
past.

It is, therefore, true to claim that formation is a universal
process and that some further distinction must be made when
referring to religious formation, that is, the particular form of
"assisted growth into life" designed to facilitate an individual's
assimilation into and continued growth within a religious community. As such, religious formation is an invitation to locate
our personal growth within the communal matrix of a religious
institute, to see the world in ways that are colored not only by
our own personal history, but also by the accumulated wisdom,
customs, insights and values flowing from the institute's past
history and present involvement. Religious formation, then, is
concerned with the confluence of stories, individual stories and
corporate stories. It is about the compatibility and convergence
of these stories as well as about the challenges and conflicts that
are inevitably part of the meeting.

Assisting the convergence of individual and corporate stories is not a simple task. Each is powerful in its demands for centrality. Each contains both creative and destructive potential. To help a person to find a certain "at-home-ness" within both stories is the task of those directing the formation. Fowler speaks of an "unavoidable tension" in this of which formation directors and new members of religious communities are only too aware. In the transition to individuating-reflexive faith (Stage 4 in Fowler's stages of faith growth),

> The late adolescent or adult must begin to take seriously the burden of responsibility for his or her own commitments, life-style, beliefs and attitudes. Where genuine movement towards stage 4 is underway the person must face certain unavoidable tensions: individuality versus being defined by a group or group membership; subjectivity and the power of one's strongly felt but unexamined feelings of critical reflection; self-fulfillment or self-actualization as a primary concern versus service to and being for others; the question of being committed to the relative versus struggle with the possibility of an absolute.[1]

At times, real reconciliation within the personal story is necessary before a person can handle the newness of the corporate story.

Each of us deals with the present and is impelled into the future out of the energy generated by our past. The past of our stories is enormously influential in determining how we view our world and how we behave in it in the present. This influence is so strong, in fact, that sometimes we make the mistake of seeing ourselves as totally and exclusively the product of an unchangeable past. We see ourselves as having been created moment by moment out of that history. Our capacity for growth and the direction of that growth, the balking and the fears, the hopes and aspirations inherent in the total process owe a huge debt to the past. But the other shaping influence is written in another tense. The story is unfinished, still evolving in the present.

Right now I am embedded in a network of relationships, events and circumstances that also have an enormous impact on who I am and who I am becoming. Sometimes the tension between past and present seems unbearable. Sometimes the way I handle present relationships and events draws on old scripts written for me in my family or school, neighborhood or novitiate, and I react to someone now, not in the immediacy of this rich and promising moment, but out of a way of putting meanings together that dates back to earlier times and raises echoes of old loyalties, fears and interpersonal strategies. It is possible that I am not relating to this person concretely here before me, but to the ghostly face of another, conjured up from my past in the now. The tension is to live in the now moment, sharply aware of the riches and challenge of it, open to being broken in upon by the total reality of this other, while simultaneously holding in balance as another and different reality the path I have followed, the route of my past history, knowing its myths and its deep and tenacious hold on me.

A friend unwittingly illustrated this tension of the tenses to me the other day when he said:

> "It's funny, you know. There's an old tape in my head that switches on from time to time and colors everything. Someone offers a critical suggestion about something I've said in a homily, and immediately I hear the harsh and complaining voice of my mother comparing me to my younger brother and finding me not good enough. Even now at the age of 42 I cringe inside when anything even slightly negative is said to me. My head knows the speaker doesn't mean to cut me down, but my mother's handwriting on the *tabula rasa* of my life and memory is still so big that I find myself feeling hostile to people who care about me and have my best interests at heart. The memory and the angry feelings happen automatically, and it's only later that I know what has happened and feel ashamed of the way I behaved. If only I knew how to switch off that damned tape!"

Past and present interact in other ways too. A present experience can reach way back into the past and touch a harsh memory with real healing. I know many a religious who recalls a lifetime of faithfully living up to external expectations, of internalizing the belief that personal worth comes from achievement and work performance. The historical evolution of meaning in such a person's life produced a sense of self as valuable-only-if-useful. Then, somehow, the transforming moment of being loved for one's own reality, for one's own *present* reality quite unrelated to productivity, penetrates the mists of those past learnings with the warm sun of a new revelation: I am lovable and worthwhile! This is not just a remedial awareness that I have *always* been lovable and worthwhile and that someone has just entered my life and revealed to me an enduring truth hitherto hidden from me by the dark clouds of my history. It is more. I am lovable in that generic sense, yes. But I am lovable and worthwhile in the now moment precisely *because* this person is here loving me, because between us something new is created. It is no merely bringing into conscious awareness something that was previously hidden. It is the *creation* of a new valuing, a new knowledge and a newly found capacity. It is partially redemptive, but deeply it is an act of creation.

When we speak of formation within the religious life, the process just described becomes more complex. An individual joins a novitiate that itself is shaped and formed by the history of the religious order as well as by the personal qualities of those entrusted with running it or overseeing its directions. Its story is studded with the biographies of previous members who have embodied its traditions and challenged its growth. Tales are told, too, of a somewhat picaresque nature. The stories have villains as well as heroes.

So we are speaking now of multiple stories, the corporate story of the institution, the folklore woven from the stories of the heroes and heroines, the theology that developed from the accumulation of lived experience, the many individual stories of those now living in the community. All of this, of course, is embedded in the story of the wider church, which itself receives from and contributes to the stories of many cultures.

This conjunction of the one and the many gives rise to formation-related questions. Implicitly or explicitly a new member may ask:

- Will my story find some kind of fit with theirs?
- Will my story be seen as good or bad?
- Will my story help me be a religious?
- Can our stories join each other in a single story, and if so, will mine become submerged?
- Must I lose something valuable in order to belong here?

Continuing members, faced with a new member, may well ask:

- What does this new story demand of us?
- Can we make room for this new story to become part of ours?
- How will the advent of this person change us?
- What do our stories have in common to unite us?
- What will the differences mean?

The challenging question that must be faced by all, new and old, may be put like this:

> Can all of us live creatively and appreciatively in the new moment of this new confluence of stories and allow the transformation that it will bring, or are we so entrenched within the powerful memories of our past histories that we are resistant, impervious even, to the cutting edge of the present?

It is these questions, among countless others, that I believe form the warp and woof of religious formation, and I would like to try and give them sharper focus in the rest of this discussion.

Old Stories and New Stories— The Present Context of Formation

Postulants to religious life join congregations that have not just an old story, but a story that is in flux. There has been a great deal of movement in the church in the last 25 years, some of it deep and significant, some of it the mere illusion of change created by adopting a new vocabulary to cloak old and resistant realities. Religious life, a product of the church, reflects the same movements.

Preserved and enshrined in this story is the spirit and original vision of founders who saw a particular gospel emphasis relevant to prevailing conditions of their time and set about giving their vision a pragmatic shape in social action. The vision thus gave birth to a public proclamation of the relevance of Christianity through active service in many of the dark places of human existence—illness, ignorance, death, poverty, loneliness and practically every form of human brokenness.

> In our growth as persons, our personal past history feeds into and shapes what we are now, what we have become. We might reject what we have done in the past, undergo a change of heart, follow a new course; but we never throw off our past.[2]

Some of the insights of Vatican II grew out of a grass-roots awareness that not only had many religious orders never thrown off the past, they had indeed preserved it in stultifying ways. In their efforts to be faithful to the founding vision, now referred to as the charism of the founder, they had petrified and fossilized old *expressions* of this charism.

Enough prophets were present just prior to Vatican II to

challenge religious communities to a new awareness that the culture had changed and that the demands for service and the proclamation of gospel values were coming from different places and asking for new modes of religious witness. The meanings of old symbols such as the medieval religious habit and the separateness of enclosures, had lost their meaning or had even taken on negative messages of remoteness, superiority and aloofness. The tense commonly used began to shift from past to present, from "how we used to do things" to "the needs all around us right now."

One possible movement stemming from this change of tenses is the likelihood that religious orders sensitive to the signs of the times will begin to abandon merely cosmetic changes. Some groups will make the difficult transition from institutional ministries to corporate ministries

> so that by common concentration on major important issues— peace, poverty, minority concerns, hunger and human rights—they may bring gospel influence to bear on social development at large no matter what the individual works of their individual members.[3]

One of the tasks of formation, then, will be to assist members to become future-orientated, rather than to remain rooted in the secure but increasingly irrelevant past. This is not to imply that the learnings of history are anything less than critically important. However, they are an important trajectory into the future, not a museum of dusty memories.

The poets and prophets of a congregation will reiterate in word and deed their recognition of and response to the urgent invitation to move from conformity and uniformity in the direction of plurality of involvement and multiformity. They will hear and proclaim the "call to individual giftedness within a common charism."[4] The pragmatists will give shape to the vision and the charism by modelling new behavioral shapes for religious life and ministry.

The greatest pain in this will be experienced by those who have become strongly dependent on institutional security. Formation in earlier years reinforced this, and if they are explicitly invited to be different, to "leave their boats behind," so to speak, their present ways of seeing their world are likely to be tumultuously disturbed. This may indeed happen even when the invitation is not directed to them, but when some of their companions begin to act differently and to reconceptualize religious life in new and "dangerous" ways. Those who are responsible for continuing formation may find that their task, which was once the poor sister of initial formation, has taken a central place in the revitalization of the group. I believe that, because of all this, religious life is on the brink of a new and deeper polarization than it was in the 1960s and 1970s.

Shifting from a past focus to a future focus implies that formation must have a strong remedial component. Many memories cry out for healing. Meanings must be transformed. Old stories must be retold and re-examined. I became sharply aware of this recently as I listened to a sister recall her initial formation experience (which happened in the 1950s):

"There was a kind of sexless, martial quality about it. Everything went to schedule and we were a bit like sausages out of a machine. Not that I'm blaming anyone, mind you, just remembering what it was like. Our training was strict and sometimes crushing. Our worth was judged pretty much in terms of how successfully we did our work. Generosity was preached to us as a reason for working till we dropped. It was also used to praise us. Our novice mistress, God bless her, totally ignored the differences among us. I'm a small and rather weak individual and I was even worse then. I can remember scrubbing floors beside this huge Amazon with arms as thick as tree trunks! She could do physical work all day with a smile on her face! Imagine how I felt when urged by the novice mistress to imitate the generosity and zeal of this monster! I felt like an ant beside her, and many's the time I wanted to kill her!

"I still have some anger about a lot of that. Usually I feel it when I'm alone or when I see the confidence of the younger people these days. When our novitiate group gets together we do now what we did then—we make a joke out of it. I join in with it but privately I still feel that we canonize some things that were unjust.

"But it wasn't all bad. In a lot of ways life was simpler then. We had joined religious life to sanctify ourselves and to teach the children of the poor. So all we had to do was say our prayers, turn up in the chapel when the bell rang, do our spiritual reading, work hard at being good teachers and die with our boots on! Nobody talked much about relationships and community life, though these things were mentioned. Relating wasn't so difficult when feelings weren't important and we were often told to pay no attention to them. At most we had to curb our tongues and be charitable. I remember going to confession and saying I'd been uncharitable when all I had done, in fact, was experience a feeling of dislike for another person. We weren't allowed to talk about whole areas of life, so what we could talk about was narrow and safe. Needless to say, I still found it hard to like some people and to keep myself from showing distinct preferences for others. Clashes could and did happen, but they were largely resolved by appeals to authority or confessing them as lapses or temptations. A lot of religious and moral language was used to take the steam out of it all.

"I suppose the main difference between then and now was the certainty. The rule and the directions of the superior were the will of God. That was clear and unambiguous. These days it's not so plain. Discernment and community discussion are more important and I sometimes wonder if we fool ourselves a bit. . . call discussion discernment. . . but most of the time I wouldn't want to go back to the old days."

For this sister there is a fairly healthy level of self-awareness and a down-to-earth recognition of some of the tensions change has brought for her. However, the learnings of the past are not so easily dealt with for many others who seem embittered and embattled and deeply resentful about damage they see themselves to have sustained. They are a constant reminder of the age-old tension between past and present, recognizable even in the beginnings of Christianity and intrinsic, therefore, to our deep and sacred story:

> The gospel message is a promise of a new future, a future that has broken in upon us in the person of Jesus. But a tension regarding the value of the past runs through all the New Testament writings: the "fulfillment" accomplished in Jesus involves continuity as well as discontinuity with what went before.[5]

The candidate for religious life, therefore, comes into a milieu struggling with the tension between its own past and present, the traditions hallowed by generations of selfless religious and the contemporary cry of a world that hungers for meaning. Those who remain in religious life after some years are perhaps even more acutely aware of this struggle. They, after all, were acculturated and socialized into religious life, for the most part accepting its values and traditions, only to find that deeply rooted and dearly held ways of being in the world are being challenged yet again. For some, the religious life that attracted them for a variety of reasons closely connected with family background, personal needs and personality characteristics no longer exists. They are confronted with a story whose last chapter has not been written, and whose plot has taken an unexpected turn.

It is the gift of the poet in these days to discern in the past of our story the live and vibrant spirit of adventure and insight, of energy for good, which can invigorate the present and inspire the future. It is the province of the prophets to juxtapose with this a sharp and challenging recognition of the needs of the present and the call of the future. It is the work of the pragmatist to marry the insight and the challenge and build practical possibilities for action.

Present Trends

Perhaps the most reliable way to anticipate the future is to understand the present. Formation, which looks to the future, must therefore be clearly predicated upon the directions that are emerging in a kaleidoscopically changing world. I mention here merely a few of the observable trends. I assume that for the most part changes in religious life will lag behind social and cultural changes, and thus if the cultural changes are identified, some of the implications for religious life and formation will become apparent.

1. *From Certainty to Ambiguity*

In a world of scientific questioning, the church itself has had to abandon the stance of absolute certainty that it is the sole possessor of the truth. Pluralism of moral values in the world at large has pushed the church to re-examine its stance on a variety of issues, sometimes reasserting old positions, sometimes making no clear proclamation (an indication to some of uncertainty), sometimes revising and changing (albeit, at times, grindingly slowly). Even when there has been a proclamation of the official stance of the church on a particular question, pastoral practice varies, generating tensions that may be either creative or potentially destructive—or both. The debate and pastoral variance stimulated by *Humanae Vitae* is a clear example of this.

The church is no longer a monolith, but shows the face of a struggling and sinful human institution. Within it and within religious life there is new emphasis on discernment, an ac-knowledgment that all is not immediately and infallibly clear, that not every movement, not every spirit, is good or desirable. There is a new search for poets with eyes to see, prophets with voices to proclaim, and pragmatists with wisdom to point out new directions.

Such ambiguity permeates the whole of life, touching the systems in which we live, our values and deepest beliefs, our education, marriage, the very existence of a future. As one young brother commented recently:

> "I don't look ahead much. The world might be blown apart in the very near future. We're here today but we might be gone tomorrow. So what's the use of long-range planning? All I want to do is get the best out of my life right now and give the best of it too, because tomorrow may be too late."

The pluralism introduced into religious life by such ambiguity is indeed a challenge for formation teams. On the one hand are the recruits to religious life who were born into and are part of a world where even future shock is passé, where the continu-ance of life itself is questionable, where change and uncertainty and the wistful need for stability are part of the landscape. Ini-tial formation reaches out to people with a passion for justice, an insatiable need for knowledge rather than information, and a history of immersion in pluralism, which often means that en-trants to religious life may be at a pre-catechesis stage of faith-development!

Alongside these are members whose history is one of sta-bility now under siege. They are challenged to reflect and re-consider and reconceptualize when their habit has been to obey without question. The very institution they joined may be showing cracks in the foundations, and its existence, hitherto believed in as dogma, now demonstrates its finitude in practical ways such as increasing average age and diminished intake. In a situation of such dramatic and obvious change, constantly re-conceptualizing may well prove to be a central task of forma-tion.

2. *From Garrison Mentality to Open System*

Closely related to the experience of ambiguity and pluralism is the movement that has gone on in the last few decades and which represents a shift from what Andrew Greeley once re-ferred to as the post-Tridentine garrison mentality to greater openness to secular learning and indeed to being part of, rather than separate from, the world.

> Thus the Church, at once a visible assembly and a spiritual community, goes forward together with humanity and experiences the same earthly lot which the world does (*Gaudium et Spes*, No. 40).

Once buttressed against secular knowledge, the church now, willingly or unwillingly, is a melting pot for myriad learnings, speculations, opinions, intellectual discoveries and hypotheses. Having moved from a classicist world-view that left little room for uncertainty, it is now an arena within which the influences of existentialist thought, phenomenology and personalism challenge and change Catholic thinkers.

> In a real sense a new theory has developed with permits and even fosters a plurality of theories, of theologies and of understandings. Pluralism constitutes a keynote of such "new theory." Disappointment may well await those who urge and expect some new univocal theory in the sense of an all-comprehensive and wholly coherent system of goals, values and models of appropriate behavior and assumptions for the church at large. Such a theory seems unlikely to appear on the horizon in the foreseeable future, if at all. What seems far more plausible and realistic to expect is an acceptance of pluralism in theology, philosophy, church structures and social customs and laws.[6]

I believe that this statement is equally valid when it is applied to a single religious institute and its local communities. The challenge to formation, then, is not to find single answers to questions that may allow of multiple answers, not necessarily to replace outmoded structures with new single structures. Rather it is to envisage institutes where differences are allowed to exist and encouraged to exist, with ways of holding the whole complex reality in some sort of dynamic balance.

Some of the possible outcomes of the shift to greater openness within religious life include:

- alienation and depression among those who cannot make a similar *internal* shift
- impatience among those for whom the change is experienced as incomplete and slow
- more frequent questioning and challenging of closure whenever and wherever it occurs

- structural changes such as more open houses, less emphasis on privacy and more on hospitality
- divestment of some of the larger and more institutional buildings in favor of smaller neighborhood dwellings
- new challenges to the openness of greater hospitality of heart and intimacy
- greater psychological openness, perhaps manifesting itself in mixed communities, lay involvement in formation and so forth.

3. *From Immortality to Finitude*

Many religious congregations are being forced to face the issue of their own decline and make choices about their survival or death. Some members fear that all the available apostolic energy may soon be swallowed up in the geriatric nursing of their older members. For older members there is a personal concern about security and welfare as they are rendered less and less active by age and infirmity. They wonder who will take care of them.

For new members or those contemplating entry into religious life, there is consideration of the question "Will my ministry be entirely inward (to other members of the community) or is it possible for me to work for the kingdom in areas of social concern where the challenge and hope of the gospel need to be proclaimed?" There is yet another group, dwindling I think, who refuse to admit that present trends may continue. They wait in constant hope for an upturn in the numbers entering religious life. Often this group includes those who cannot yet accept the value of lay apostolic activity; they see in the large numbers of men and women who used to join religious life a pattern that, in the providence of God, will soon repeat itself.

Over the past few years I have had the experience of working as a facilitator with a number of religious groups coming to terms with their own demise. The pain of struggling to an acceptance of this is overwhelming. Long periods were spent in swinging between denial and grinding efforts to say yes to what seems indeed to be taking place among them. Once the minimal acceptance took place, groups experienced the stages of grieving often associated with individual death. Their acceptance has in some instances been expressed in courageous planning of the limited work they would take up as their institute died. I have been deeply impressed by the dignity of this.

The important thing for this age to remember is that there is nothing wrong with death with dignity, provided that it is ringed with resignation rather than with denial. In fact, this acknowledgement may be the last great gift these groups can give.[7]

4. *From Superiority to Equality*

The past is studded with stories of the enormous sacrifices made by Catholic laity for the priests, sisters and brothers who serve them. At its best this was a genuine recognition that religious came among them with neither purse, nor scrip, nor shoes, dependent but serving. At its worst it represented a kind of elitism that set religious life above the lay state and above marriage as a vocation. I remember that during vocation campaigns in my own school days I was indoctrinated with the superiority of religious life as a calling. Much of this has, of course, been put to the sword by new awareness in the church about the basic dignity of the person, the nobility of marriage, the quality of lay involvement in the church, and of the church itself as people of God. I believe, however, that religious are still struggling to internalize this in practical ways.

As we move through the 1980s and 1990s, contemplative and monastic spirituality will need to be balanced by an apostolic spirituality, cultivated in the midst of active service for others. Such a spirituality (sometimes called "incarnational") will emerge only when laity and religious enter into serious dialogue, bringing to the discussion the spiritual insights that result from the experience of both groups. If religious continue to function with a spirituality that only runs parallel to that of the laity, they will become an increasing enigma to them.[8]

It is claimed by many that we have already entered into such a dialogue. This may be so. My own observation suggests, however, that we do a lot of talking together, but the religious are frequently the givers and the laity the receivers. This is aided and abetted by many lay people who have been taught an exaggerated respect for and distance from religious. Many religious cite their participation in Marriage Encounter, prayer groups, and the like as instances of their dialogue with the laity. While I do not want to call this into doubt, I do want to point out that the religious are often the "teachers" or the most articulate persons in these encounters. Perhaps the challenge is to silence and receptivity rather than to pseudo-dialogue.

Recently it has been a deeply educative process for me to

conduct courses on spiritual direction at St. John's University, Collegeville, Minnesota. I was surprised by the large number of lay people enrolling in the courses (discovering in myself a hidden expectation that spiritual direction was largely the province of clergy and, more lately, of religious) and moved by the intensity of their faith life. The openness and simplicity with which they were able to share their stories and the wisdom that flowed from their reflective experience of life made me aware at the end of my term there that I had learned far more than I had taught.

I believe that messages of superiority, intentionally or otherwise, will continue to be given as long as we do not involve laity in our planning, education and formation. It is still a somewhat shocking idea to suggest that lay people become more than occasional visitors to our formation houses, chapters, council meetings. If compassion and ministry are defined as giving, and the laity are the "poor" to whom we give, we have not begun to understand that dialogue is a form of asceticism.

> Genuine dialogue is simply sincere exchange whereby people endeavor to share the truth, to search together for what is truly human and good in life, to be in touch and relate to one another in an honest and caring fashion. Such dialogue is implicit prayer. It is also real asceticism.[9]

5. *From Subservient Helpmate to Assertive Partner*

The changing role of women deserves some attention here as part of the matrix of formation. It must be noted at the outset, however, that behind the changes in the status of women in western society are reasons much deeper than the mere assumption of different roles and a slowly evolving equality. Developmental studies have been based on patterns of male development, and real understanding of the ways women grow and put together meanings is only recently beginning to be articulated. Carol Gilligan, for example, hypothesizes a radicality of difference that, if taken seriously, will have an impact on methods of formation and continuing education in religious life as well as elsewhere.

> As we have listened for centuries to the voices of men and the theories of development that their experience informs, so we have come more recently to notice not only the silence of women but the difficulty in hearing what they say when they speak. Yet in the different voice of women lies the truth of an ethic of care, the tie between relationship and responsibility, and the origins of aggression in the failure of connection. The

failure to see the different reality of women's lives and to hear the differences in their voices stems in part from the assumption that there is a single mode of social experience and interpretation. By positing instead two different modes we arrive at a more complex rendition of human experience which sees the truth of separation and attachment in the lives of women and men and recognizes how these truths are carried by different modes of language and thought.[10]

It is neither my task nor my intention to attempt here an exploration of all the implications of this, but a number of glaring facts spring to mind in relation to religious formation. In the first place, those currently entrusted with overseeing the work of formation in many religious congregations have been brought up with little real appreciation of femininity. All too often their understanding is limited to a "femininity" that is shut in on itself by mere lack of maleness and passively collaborates in the continuance of an ideological patriarchalism. I am not sure that we can speak of formation without currently giving consideration to the re-formation of the formation teams and to a revision of the very notion of formation itself. If formation is indeed assisted growth into life, scrupulous attention must be paid to seeing that life is not crippled by injustice or oppression, that masculinity and femininity are not seen as rungs on a hierarchical ladder. Then new partnerships between male and female formation directors may model for a sinful church a mutuality and reciprocity that celebrate likeness and difference bonded together in the richness of equality.

Traditionally, education of formation personnel has envisaged a program in which they receive teaching in the general areas of human development, scripture, theology, spirituality and pastoral practice, with the possible addition of canon law. In all of these areas, current insights from feminism are revolutionizing or at least challenging old models. Distortions in the area of self-image, images of God, language within ecclesiology, worship, ministry and religious life need transformation. Formation personnel need education to dream new dreams, so as not to perpetuate old injustices. This is as true of men as it is of women.

The church has a long road yet to travel in this respect. The journey has just begun. Perhaps it may be powerfully assisted by those hundreds of men and women throughout the world who are in the process of restructuring their own identities and are in positions of influence, not necessarily formal ones, out of which they may assist similar growth into more wholesome life among those to whom they relate.

Formation must now take account of new faces of pluralism. Social shifts in the way women and men see themselves are still in flux. It is likely, therefore, that those joining religious life will bring with them a degree of unresolved confusion. Caught in the maelstrom of feminist arguments, diverse opinions, and encouragement to assert themselves, many young women bring with them to religious life an uncertainty sometimes masked by assurance and poise, sometimes by a barely contained belligerence. Others have achieved a fluid sense of self that is comfortable with independence as well as hungry for interdependence and intimacy. Similar observations are made of young men joining religious life.

Thus new pastoral questions arise. New conflicts arise between the generations, as older religious observe the behavior of the young with scepticism and lack of understanding, knowing that their own path to development followed a different route. Different degrees of freedom create their own conflicts. The ongoing and the initial formation processes in religious groups of both men and women must take account of this new reality in new and creative ways.

Formation—For Whom?

If formation is assisted growth into life, it is for everybody. Sometimes the often-used categories of initial and ongoing formation create an unfortunate dichotomy implying that a single group has two formation policies with little relationship between them. This is even more pronounced when different personnel are assigned to the two areas with little or no expectation that they will collaborate in ways that build continuity. One of the challenges of pluralism in religious life is surely to help make it possible for young and old, like and unlike, free and less free, to live and work side by side in healthy mutuality.

When an individual joins a religious community he or she enters a group where there are enshrined values, customs, beliefs, ways of seeing the world and of participating in ministry. These have more or less long and hallowed histories, and so they resist change, assimilating rather than adapting to a new individual. Perhaps one of the most often spoken but least internalized challenges of this is that when a new member is received, the group becomes a *new* group. The one and the many must join hands in the creation of a new reality.

This is no small challenge. Coming from a social milieu that is qualitatively different, young candidates bring disturbing qualities. Often their search for self-fulfillment seems to translate into a search for immediate gratification rather than to lead beyond the need for fulfillment to self-transcendence. The powerful sense of finitude that they derive from being born into a world poised on the brink of self-destruction expresses itself at times in a "get your pleasure now" mentality even when, paradoxically, they are in the act of committing themselves to live with eschatological vision.

They come, many of them, with a more tenuous sense of identity arising out of pluralism itself, having fewer certainties and greater ambivalence. It may well be that they come with more fragility and psychological immaturity, even though they wear the mask of brash confidence. As a result, they move more rapidly from hope to despair and back again than their older companions in community. Often they come with more experience of sex, drugs, social life, poverty and materialism, justice and injustice than did former candidates to religious life. It may be a mistake on the part of the community to assume that they therefore understand the *meaning* of their own experience and can move from it purposefully into ministry.

How, then, do formation people decide which candidates are suitable, whom to admit, whose admission to postpone or refuse? For the incoming candidate these days batteries of psychological tests have become the order of the day. In the hands of skilled and insightful practitioners, these are extremely valuable. It is my opinion that anyone who has not given evidence of minimal completion of the developmental tasks of adolescence should not yet enter religious life. Negotiating the adolescent tasks of separation from home (personal autonomy and responsibility for one's own life), independent work (capacity to sustain and financially support oneself as well as to see work as part of adult expression) and coping with sexual relationships (love as a dynamic of adult formation)[11] appear to me to be prerequisites for an informed undertaking of vows of obedience, poverty and chastity.

The process of screening candidates for religious life ought not be limited to psychological testing. There is no substitute for ongoing relationships over time with those who want to join us. It is well-known that test results may vary with the physical or emotional state of the person at the time of testing. A headache, a cold, a rift in a relationship, or even the weather and other environmental factors are known to have possible effects on test performance. Apart from this, however, I believe that there are movements of the human spirit that cannot be measured. Beneath the empirical facts is a deeper reality, which I hesitate to describe as motivation, because of the limitations placed on that by psychological interpretation. I am referring to the deep "I want" that flows from the graced spirit of a man or woman on the brink of a life choice, an "I want" that is deeper than feeling or conditioning, that resists discouragement from the opposition of others and climbs over obstacles placed in its way. An intuition by screening personnel of this deep "I want" can be experienced only in continued relationship that is far more than mere evaluation and which is characterized by mutual trust and sensitive listening. Many congregations stipulate that entrants be in contact with one or several members of the formation team for a prescribed minimum period of time before they join the institute. Others set up pre-postulancy programs which give the candidates opportunities to work with the members of a community in their usual day-to-day routines. This allows the candidate to test the flavor of the community's mode of life, and the community to see the person in relationship with them and their work and those to whom they minister.

Following the recommendations of the Sacred Congregation for Religious and Secular Institutes in the *Instruction on the Renewal of Religious Formation* (1969), those engaged in screening processes try to establish that the person seeking admission is "endowed with such elements of human and emotional maturity as will afford grounds for hope that he [sic] is capable of undertaking properly the obligations of the religious state and that, in the religious life and especially in the novitiate he will be able to progress to fuller maturity." What this means when translated into specific qualities must be determined by policy-setting groups. More will be said about it in the section "Formation—For What?" later in this chapter.

If life is seen as a developing process rather than as a thing to be possessed, it is clear that formation does not finish when novitiate is ended. The stages of life now entered into call for information, understanding, ministerial involvement, flexibility, direction, companionship and spiritual nourishment. New ministries may need to be prepared for, old bitterness abandoned, burnout healed, aging faced, retirement planned, death accepted, emotions long repressed given space, time and encouragement to be expressed and explored, old theologies and theories of religious life replaced and re-educated. The call for integrated programs that cater to all these needs is clear. It cannot happen unless congregations examine sensitively how they understand the process of formation.

There is no adequate understanding of formation predicated upon unilateral power. Zeal can lead directors to want to change those who are not yet ready for change, or who do not see the direction of change proposed by others as possible or appropriate for them right now. Plans for the re-creation of religious life must take into account that the primary responsibility for a person's growth belongs to that individual, and that each person's history and present networks are unique. Formation policies and programs aim at providing stimuli, opportunities, challenges and directions for such growth along with efforts to create an environment in which it is increasingly safe to *want* to grow and change. The demands on formation personnel are daunting.

Formation—By Whom?

I have already intimated in many places that the talents and insights of the poets, prophets and pragmatists must be brought to bear upon all the directions of religious life. Few individuals are gifted with a combination of all three, so it seems appropriate to speak of a team effort, this team being understood to include the persons whose growth and development is the particular focus of formation as well as those appointed to guide and facilitate the process. Most novitiates these days are either empty or have only a few members, and numbers in congregations are diminishing. This makes it difficult to support full-time formation teams when there is a critical shortage of personnel for other ministries. It would seem, then, that teams for formation must cross the boundaries of religious congregations. Existing institutes do share personnel, but often do little more than impart information to groups. By their nature these institutes can attend to little in the area of individual needs and to nothing at all in the area of ongoing formation of those in active ministry. I am proposing an "ecumenical" approach to formation which would go further than the existing institutes.

The Sacred Congregation's economical and generalized list of qualities required of formation personnel are the following:[12]

- human qualities of insight and responsiveness
- a certain experiential knowledge of God and of prayer
- wisdom resulting from attentive and prolonged scripture meditation

- love of the liturgy and understanding of its importance in formation
- necessary cultural competence
- enough time and good will to pay individual and not merely group attention to those in formation.

To this I add my own interpretive and more specific list, with the caveat that not every individual can hope to possess all these qualities, but that it should be carefully determined that they are present in a *team*.

1. *Ability to Relate*

This should be a characteristic possessed by every member of the team. It is a prerequisite for the internal dynamics of the team itself as well as for the credibility of the team member to those he or she serves. Hence I am not speaking merely of the ability to engage in small-talk or pious conversation, or to entertain and amuse. Rather, I refer to the ability to communicate meaning, to be vulnerable enough to engage in appropriate self-disclosure, to offer understanding and empathy, to challenge and confront, and to know when and how to do this in creative ways, as well as knowing how to face interpersonal issues with immediacy.

2. *Attractiveness As a Person*

Mere knowledge is insufficient to qualify a person for the work of formation. It has been said of spiritual directors that hanging out a brass plate listing their degrees does not mean necessarily that they will be effective. People tend to gravitate in the direction of some people and not others. A quality of inner wisdom, trustworthiness and experience of life attracts. I am sure that in formation also this is important at the level of trust-building. I am not speaking of soft quasi-parenting, but of a clean quality of openness difficult to define in the abstract but easily recognizable in the concrete. Clearly, some persons on a team will be more attractive in this sense than others. This will make demands on the rest of the team for largeness of spirit that recognizes and encourages this gift when it is present. The temptation may be to compete.

3. *Appreciation and Valuing of Differences*

In a discussion of pluralism, this is self-evident. The absence of prejudice—or at least the honesty and self-awareness to admit it when it occurs—is imperative both with the team and in relation to the varied personalities and backgrounds that are the receiving group of their ministry. A single definition of a "good religious" can be a subtle but deeply entrenched form of bigotry which allows no departures from a single norm.

4. *Enough Ego-Strength to Challenge and Live With the Consequences of the Challenge*

I have already referred to this, but take it up here in the context of assessing suitability for religious life. Some candidates in the past (and from my counselling experience, in the very recent past) have been allowed to take vows and to eke out an unhappy existence in religious life when there were early signs of unsuitability, cries for help from the person that were dealt with by superficial encouragement and soothing noises and a sickly, inauthentic sort of compassion. When a team can combine its strengths and compassion in consultation with an individual about his or her future, wise and timely decisions are possible.

5. *Experience of Life and In-touch-ness With That Experience*

Personal reflection among members of formation teams will highlight their strengths and weakness. I want to ask potential team members if they are *weak* enough to engage in this task. Are they sufficiently in touch with their own brokenness to be involved in the direction of others who bring, not perfection or the possibility of perfection, but incompleteness to their commitment? Can they hang in there with their own brokenness and value it as a commonality that is the potential ground for compassion. Do they have faith in their experience of weakness?

6. *Adequate Professional Knowledge*

Is the team equipped with appropriate working knowledge of human development and spiritual growth, models of adult education, models of the church and images of God, differences between super-ego and conscience, signs of psychological disturbance, a variety of prayer forms, approaches to discernment, and so forth? All too often, under the pressure of time, ignorance and economic necessity, religious congregations skimp on the training of formation personnel. Frequently a course in spirituality of relatively short duration and questionable quality is deemed sufficient, and the person thus trained assumes a task that reaches into all the dimensions of a person's life. Perhaps it is merely my own bias, but I fear preparation for formation work that does not at least provide trainees with adequate understanding of the linkage between spiritual growth and the ordinary steps of human development. I am not demanding here an exhaustive knowledge of all of these things, but enough shared knowledge to know when other talents have to be co-opted onto the team to deal with specific issues beyond the team members' own competence.

7. *The Ability to Make Referrals*
In special instances professional consultation may appear necessary or be requested by a person in formation. Formation teams should have available a whole network of contacts for medical, psychological, spiritual and organizational issues. Sometimes these will be called in for consultation or case-study discussion with the team to facilitate its own growth or provide help in particular situations. Sometimes direct referrals will be made to them.

8. *Understanding of How a Team Works*
There is an abundance of information available about goal-setting and goal-seeking on teams, about functional and dysfunctional behavior on teams, and about ways of ensuring cohesiveness without sacrificing creativity. Regular self-evaluation, evaluation by those to whom the formation team ministers, and in-service sessions with outside facilitators will help avoid dysfunctional patterns of behavior hardening into practice and stimulate creative change. If I were to single out one feature of team-functioning as particularly important, it would be the necessity of sharing all the information necessary for the team to work as a unit. Unnecessary secrecy and the punitive or bargaining withholding of information can rapidly kill a team's effectiveness. I am not, of course, referring to confidential personal disclosures made to individuals, but it is important that the team members make clear contracts with each other about what information can and cannot be exchanged. The persons in formation should also be acquainted with this. The area of contract-making needs a good deal more attention in religious groups, not for bureaucratic reasons so much as for the best possible relating.

9. *Non-possessiveness*
Formation team members should be sufficiently able to deal with their own personal needs for love and affection and esteem and belonging so that they do not transfer these into the

formation process, muddying the waters of other people's growth. If observation is correct, there has been an inclination recently to choose younger directors than formerly. I am of the opinion that while chronological age is relatively unimportant in team members, their stage of development is highly significant. They should have reached a sufficiently generative stage of their development to be able to cope with the demand that they

> avoid projecting some of their unsolved personality problems on to their vocationers and/or falling into some of the inordinate demands which the latter may make subconsciously. . . . Aware of their inner strivings, they should be able to love unselfishly, to give without getting.[13]

It is important, therefore, that members have a life outside the team—friends, colleagues, directors and helpers who provide other avenues for expression and need-satisfaction and personal growth. The team itself is also an important arena for confronting inhibiting personal baggage. I risk the suggestion that those who have successfully negotiated the developmental task of intimacy and have well and truly demonstrated the capacity for generative caring make the best team members and that these people are usually middle-aged.

10.   A Mature Spirituality

Formation directors should be in the process of growth in a healthy spirituality that does not demand to be foisted on others, and which is lived deeply enough not to require constant justification in religious verbiage. This same healthy spirituality provides an awareness that others are in different places and do not have to be hurried to another place. Particularly dangerous in this regard is a spirituality that emphasizes progress and measurement as if growth were a simple linear process.

12.   A Love of Life, Creation and World

I read a statement from a major superior to a province recently that was motivated by a sense of appreciation of the work and self-sacrifice of the province and urged even greater commitment to ministry in the future. Unfortunately the superior inadvertently advocated an insular and separate notion of religious life. She listed at length the evils of the world in which young people struggle to survive, painting a picture of religious life as a small and besieged island of good in a huge sea of evil. She apparently overlooked entirely the fidelity and strength of these young people themselves, originating as it does in their families and networks. She did not mention the enormous dedication of laity in a variety of services. In listing the marriages that come unstuck, she made no mention of those that struggle through poverty, loss, grief and all manner of difficulty and manage to preserve love and fidelity.

As I read, I found myself hoping that this was an exception, and that leaders in general love life, and that their love of life *creates* life and hope.

I would add to this list other more obvious qualities, knowledge and skills such as capacity for discernment, understanding of leadership styles, an ecclesial rather than insular view of formation, awareness of the lacunae in past formation that may require remedial attention now, intelligence and a working knowledge of systems and how they operate and how they may be constructed, real respect for personal friendship, both homosexual and heterosexual, the ability to communicate simply and to listen deeply.

I would like to see the blossoming of formation teams that value wisdom over gimmickry and are sufficiently non-defensive to envisage the possibility that they themselves might submit to some form of assessment or screening for their job as routinely as they suggest screening for applicants to religious life. In this context I find myself wondering how many religious orders have policies for formation team members listing the particular requirements they seek in their appointees.

In all of this I think we should reach for the stars but keep our feet on the ground.

Formation—For What?

A friend who for many years guided a province through the troubled waters of change was sharing a meal with me recently and suddenly asked, "What is the most important quality you would hope to see forming in the young religious if you were on a formation team?" Quickly, as if the answer had been lying ready on my tongue, I shot back, "Flexibility." My friend registered surprise, and when I asked him his own question, his answer was "Fidelity." What follows is merely a beginning of some reflection on these two qualities.

It was possible once to anticipate the future much more accurately than it is now. When someone joined my own religious congregation, for example, it was almost a certainty that she would spend six months as a postulant engaging in limited apostolic work among students in the boarding school nearby.

Then she would proceed to the novitiate where she would endure the rigors of the canonical year followed by the training and teaching experience offered during the second year. At the end of this time, unless she had been recalcitrant enough to be asked to add another few months to her novitiate before making first vows, she was admitted to religious profession and, usually within days, she would be assigned to a local community of the congregation where she would engage in teaching. There were very few exceptions to this. On rare occasions a candidate with nursing or domestic skills was admitted, often expecting to be later employed in situations where she would use these skills in ministry. Sometimes this happened, but often the expectation gave way to demands that the person become a teacher and use the other skills incidentally. Entrants usually expected to spend their whole lives teaching, until death or incapacitating illness put an end to the process. There was no recognized retirement policy; younger average age, larger numbers and vigorous membership no doubt masked the necessity to think about it. Added to this was the glorification of work from which most individuals derived their sense of personal worth, thus making it unthinkable to withdraw from active work, even though there was already a thin but audible cry of "I want to be valued for me, rather than for what I do!"

Fidelity in this situation meant continuing to do the things assigned, to keep the Rule and live a regular religious life, avoiding singularity and adhering to the common life. There was real heroism in the midst of this, and the history of the group is studded with stories of women who grew to great spiritual stature and warmth of humanity. However, flexibility was not a human characteristic much called upon since the situation in which people lived was relatively stable, secure and predictable. Much of the brittleness and pain of the 1960s possibly came from the fact that external and systemic change was beginning to occur before many people had the capacity to bend to it.

The attrition that occurred at this time may indicate that the tensions of this, along with many other variables to be sure, was beyond the endurance of many whose fidelity had hitherto expressed itself in remaining punctiliously true to injunctions to "keep the Rule and the Rule will keep you." The fidelity was a systemic fidelity, a rigorous obedience to the demands of the structures. Flexibility also was within the confines of a foreseeable life rhythm and consisted largely in learning to bend to the multiple demands of the system—to move from teaching third grade to teaching sixth, to cook and clean as well as being an administrator, to study for a degree at night after teaching in the classroom for six hours during the day, to be supervisor of athletics programs, financial organizer for fund-raising efforts while being literature teacher. I believe that many of the sisters whom I most admire in my own congregation and in others with whom I am associated emerged from such a background with a strong sense of dependence on God, a fidelity to prayer and a tenacious loyalty to one another and to religious life that are overwhelming in their beauty. Others did not survive so well. Times have changed. The world of which religious life is a part stands on the threshold of enormous re-creation and simultaneously on the brink of catastrophe and total destruction. Armed with nuclear power strong enough to blow whole countries off the map and destroy every remaining living thing with radioactive fallout, we hold in our hands the technology and wealth to feed every hungry mouth on the earth. Paradox and ambiguity are in the air we breathe. We cannot be sure what tomorrow will bring, either for good or for ill. This is the matrix of formation now.

Flexibility in such a world means the ability to live with ambiguity, to hear the cry of the poor from wherever it comes, not necessarily in the narrowly defined area of traditional apostolates. It means to take new and different risks, cut new paths. Perhaps we have passed the time for specialists and are entering a time when adaptable generalists are needed. Specialists—like dinosaurs—become extinct. At a time when the work of our own hands has become frighteningly large and destructive, we need to avoid the narcissism of self-preoccupation or survival-orientation and focus as sensitively as we can on the needs of the church.

Fidelity means, first of all, living faith. It is therefore a process to be followed rather than a thing to be held onto. It is a journey embodying common elements of

(a) conversion, (b) a struggle to internalize and act on that conversion experience, (c) a call to integrity, (d) a call to reality and (e) a call to radicality.[14]

It is for me a vision that has its origin in Jesus the man of faith, center of the deep story of Christianity out of which religious life has grown—a man who was unerringly faithful to the authentic demands of his own humanity, even when these demands drew him into death. Faith in Jesus does not mean for me slavish imitation of a person who lived in another time and culture, but an appropriation of his central and prophetic vision that love can transform a world. This means an effort to locate this faithfully in conditions that call for new heights of living and new translations of Christianity for our time.

Further reflection on the directions in which formation is called to travel suggests emphasis on developing the hunger and thirst after justice called "blessed" by Jesus. The inequalities spawned by pluralism have resulted in the accumulation of rights, riches, privilege and power for some, and the utter deprivation of others.

Religious life stands as a living witness to the beatitudes. A lived search for justice is therefore intrinsic to its very nature. The question arises, then, how is this to be inculcated. I believe that the answer lies in the process of educating to a life of relationship and service which begins at home. For the young there is a stage-specific readiness to espouse causes and to expostulate and demonstrate about various forms of injustice. Formation is about more immediate and less spectacular things than these. It is about sensitivity to personal differences and needs within the community first of all. It is about a spirituality that recognizes the importance of prayer for those who are in need, but which does not then consider duty satisfied.

> If one of the brothers or one of the sisters is in need of clothes and has not enough food to live on, and one of you says to them, "I wish you well; keep yourself warm and eat plenty," without giving them these bare necessities of life, then what good is that? In the same way faith: if good deeds do not go with it, it is quite dead (Jas 2:15-16).

A contemporary reading of this within the context of increasingly pluralist religious communities might read:

> If one of the brothers or one of the sisters is lonely or unbefriended, troubled or in need of befriending, and has not enough affirmation to live on, and if one of you says "I hope things improve for you and that you'll be happy; take care," without offering human warmth and care and companionship, then what's the use of that? You are offering verbal concern only and that does not come from lively faith at all.

Formation, then, teaches people to notice needs, to be aware. It then proceeds to educate to appropriate ways of expressing attention and empathy in action and service. At times the service involving personal engagement and companionship is more demanding than a service that requires only material contribution. Once again it is plain that a spirituality of empathy is the foundation of this, and that a process of mutuality is at the heart of appropriate action.

Planning the Future

I would like to see groups of formation personnel and others with the gifts of poetic insight, prophetic daring and innovative pragmatism gather together to brainstorm wildly and creatively directions for formation, ways of sharing gifts and understanding. There have, indeed, been gatherings to discuss formation. They have taken the familiar shape of sharing problems, questions and knowledge and as such they have been valuable as reservoirs and sources of information as well as of new motivation and energy. Yet I believe that it may prove advantageous to dream new dreams or re-story the old ones in the present tense, to allow right-brain creativity to romp about in the forum that has until recently been the exclusive territory of left-brain logic and reasoning.

I would not limit this to novitiates and the planning of initial formation. Hopefully it might also give new shapes and breathe new life into continuing education and growth on every level of human functioning. I would love to see some of our already existing programs thrown open, inviting clergy (often sadly neglected in terms of their need for further growth), laity and religious from other congregations to share the riches we have and to offer us theirs. It seems sadly insular that in houses within easy reach of each other we duplicate resources instead of combining and enlarging them.

I would like to see those who plan for ongoing formation think outside the limits of existing opportunities (such as institutes that provide courses for older religious) and, instead of fitting individuals into whatever is offered, plan with them the directions that they might take. This might open possibilities wider than merely attending lectures or taking on study projects, laudable and necessary as they may be, which are often referred to as "taking time off." Continuing formation should not be regarded as a vacation, a sort of sabbatical from religious life. It ought to be time for trying out new and unaccustomed behavior in forums where this can be evaluated. It may be time for joining in the work and community life of other congregations, for being in contact with other forms of poverty, for being in touch with the church's action in a new way.

Such ideas may well prove unsettling for some, especially for those who are committed to maintaining their institutes and preserving a clear continuity with the past. I would remind them that to be a Christian is to be and remain unsettled.

> Jesus' wineskin-breaking ministry was unsettling to his Jewish co-religionists for the same reason it must be unsettling to us. For the logic both of the parables he spoke and the parable he is reveals just how upsetting and destabilizing is his God.[15]

Belief in a surprising God, then, makes it impossible to believe in or perpetuate a church that digs itself into and remains entrenched in old ways of seeing and doing. Such an institution has nothing to do with the kingdom Jesus came to found. Perhaps in our own small and local ways of breaking through and beyond our tunnel-vision and fear of risk-taking, in our efforts to preserve the wisdom of the past while responding with novelty to the challenge of the present, we may be helping to build and renew a church true to its mission of creatively transforming the whole of life.

For community consideration

A.   In what ways is your present communal group visibly formative? How does it encourage and enlarge life?

B.   How are differences dealt with in this community? Indeed, what are the differences that are allowed to flourish in the community? (Be as concrete as you can in discussing this question.)

C.   To an outsider looking in at this community, what evidence is there of a respect for variety? Of a love of life, of creation, of world? Of genuine appreciation of individual gifts and talents?

For individual consideration

A.   How much conscious responsibility do you take for your own growth as a person and for the growth of others in your communal group? What shape does this responsibility take?

B.   What areas of important learning for you have been neglected in the past and now need nourishment?

C.   How committed are you to reading and gathering knowledge by your own efforts? What *daily* energy goes into your continuing formation (as distinct from occasional re-treats, seminars, and so forth?)

D. How comfortable or uncomfortable are you with the dif-ferences existing in the church, the congregation, the com-munity? What is easiest for you to accept? Why? What is hardest to accept? Why?

E. Looking back, what have been the most significant forma-tive experiences of your life so far? Tell the stories. How were you changed by these persons or events? Remember that formation may have both positive and negative results in your experience of growth. Get in touch with the crea-tive ones first, but do not omit attending to the negative ones.

Notes

1. James Fowler, et al., *Trajectories in Faith* (Nashville: Abingdon Press, 1980), p. 28.

2. Tad Guzie, *Jesus and the Eucharist* (New York: Paulist Press, 1974), p. 128.

3. Joan Chittister, "Religious Orders Must Offer Future Vi-sion, Not Memories," *Sharings*, 14:1 (January 1984), p. 20.

4. Ibid.

5. Guzie, op. cit. p. 129.

6. George M. Regan, "Pluralism and Polarization Among Reli-gious," *Review for Religious*, 32:2 (March 1973), p. 250.

7. Chittister, op. cit. p. 18.

8. Paul Michalenko and Loughlan Sofield, "Are Religious Or-ders Irrelevant?" *Human Development*, 4:4 (Winter 1983), p. 11.

9. Ernest E. Larkin and Gerard T. Broccolo, eds., *Spiritual Renewal of the American Priesthood* (Washington, D.C.: United States Catholic Conference, 1973), p. 31.

10. Carol Gilligan, *In a Different Voice* (Cambridge, Massachu-setts: Harvard University Press, 1982), pp. 173-174.

11. I borrow the set of three tasks from Jack Dominian, *Cycles of Affirmation: Psychological Essays in Christian Living* (London: Darton, Longman & Todd, 1975), p. 101. However, I have deliberately omitted his qualification, *hetero-sexual*, since I believe the sexual component of *all* relationships, both homosexual and heterosexual, to be of dramatic importance in the transition from adolescence to young adulthood.

12. Patrick Sean Moffett, "Formation of College-Age Religious," *Human Development*, 4:3 (Fall 1983), p. 32.

13. Luigi M. Rulla, et al., *Psychological Structure and Vocation* (Dublin: Villa Books, 1979), pp. 195-196.

14. Katherine Marie Dyckman and L. Patrick Carroll, *Inviting the Mystic, Supporting the Prophet* (New York: Paulist Press, 1981), p. 13.

15. William R. Burrows, *New Ministries: The Global Context* (Melbourne: Dove, 1980), p. 50.

6
COPING WITH
STRESS AND
BURNOUT:
The Experience of the Overloaded Story

A friend with a mild cynical streak commented to me the other day, "In the last few years the fashion has been to have a mid-life crisis. Just when I thought I had escaped the peril of that I find that the new fashion is burnout, and I'm in danger again!" New it may be. Fad it is not. I believe that burnout, a phenomenon for which a term has had to be coined over recent years, is a sign of the times with connections to pluralism and change both inside and outside the church.

Burnout is not an illness. Neither is the term a psychiatric one. It is a descriptive term rather than a scientific label. For the past 15 years I have been counselling religious both at home and abroad. For the last five or six of those years I have been noticing the frequency with which many of them, especially those in positions of authority, leadership or other helping ministries, have been reporting a cluster of experiences that together form a recognizable pattern, a pattern that develops out of unrelieved stress.

Patterns of Burnout

"I'm not sure if anyone can help me. I'm bone weary, but it isn't the kind of tiredness that goes away if I get extra sleep. In any case it's hard to get extra sleep in my job. Everybody expects me to be available almost the whole time. I try, but lately it's more and more of a chore. It wasn't always like that. I *enjoyed* work once and poured my whole life into it. Right now all I want to do is stop the world and get off. I'm kind of bored and low. I went to the doctor the other day thinking I must be sick because I have so little 'get-up-and-go.' He says there's nothing organically wrong with me. And that's why I'm here. If there's nothing organically wrong, then there must be something psychologically wrong. I must be neurotic or something."

This introductory statement from a new client reveals some of the symptoms of burnout. The following experiences are interlocking pieces of the pattern:

1. *Weariness*

Physical and spiritual weariness blanket the individual. There may be some efforts to rectify this by taking holidays or extra rest and relaxation, but the effect is minimal or temporary. To cope by attempting to assuage the weariness is to treat the symptom rather than the cause, and even if there is a slight amelioration of the tiredness, the individual quickly finds that old ways of dealing with life produce a return to the worn-out and depleted feelings.

2. *Boredom*

Life loses its savor. Tasks that once were creative and energizing challenges to be looked forward to, now become chores to be performed. Ingenuity and initiative give way to a grindingly perfunctory doing of duty. Ministry is a succession of obligations rather than cheerfully undertaken service. Every day looks the same and holds no excitement. As one client put it,

> "I used to spring out of bed at the crack of dawn and greet the day with a smile in my heart and a 'Good morning, God!' on my lips. Now I turn off the alarm clock, groan with tiredness and say, 'Good God, not another day!' Every day is like the previous one. I don't want to face it."

Even previously joyful relaxation—a game of tennis, a movie, a meal with friends—feels like a major effort. Food seems tasteless and even unpalatable. The salt of life has lost its tang.

3. *Guilt and Self-blame*

When it becomes apparent that there is no direct physical cause for the feelings of exhaustion, many individuals begin to say in a pejorative way, "It must be all in my head." They label their experience as lack of generosity, selfishness and even hypochondria. They compare themselves with their still happily functioning peers and find themselves inferior. The unfortunate fact about this is that it spins the already turning wheel still harder. In an effort to pull themselves out of the depths and to reassert their "virtue," they deny their feelings or discount them as unimportant and make superhuman efforts to work harder. Much of this effort is directed toward feeling better about themselves and rescuing themselves from their own disapproval. It creates further stress and digs them more deeply into the mire of the burnout. This is neurotic guilt for it does not attach itself to a clear, freely chosen wrong. It is free floating and destructive.

4. *Anxiety*

Many burned-out individuals report a fear of their lives slipping out of their grasp, being carried like flotsam on the tide of a life that is in flood. Meanings on which they previously founded their lives and daily action fade, and nothing is there in their place. An indefinable and unanchored panic sets in. This may not be a permanent state, but is often experienced in recurring episodes.

Lawrence Kolb defines anxiety as "a painful uneasiness of mind, a state of heightened tension accompanied by inexpressible dread, a feeling of apprehensive expectation."[1] This is spelled out in more detail by E. James Anthony:

- It is diffuse or free floating and not restricted to definite situations or objects.

- It is not accompanied by any degree of insight into its immediate cause.

- It tends to be experienced in terms of its physical manifestations, but these are not recognized as such by the person concerned.

- It is prompted by the anticipation of future threats, against which current avoidance responses would not be effective.

- It is not controlled by any specific psychological defense mechanisms, as are the other neurotic reactions.[2]

I heard one sister describe her experience of anxiety thus:

"I'm afraid. I don't know what it's all about, but I have the feeling that my deepest meanings, everything that holds my life together, are in jeopardy. And I have no resources. I'm paralyzed, unsure and totally helpless, like a baby in a carriage that has been left unattended and is running downhill. I look around for someone to save me and I don't see anybody."

5. *Anger*

As the individual feels his or her meanings drying up and efforts at self-redemption prove ineffective he or she begins to uncover layers of frustration, bitterness and anger, which are often displaced onto other community members, colleagues at work, authorities, the "system" or the church itself. Some people go searching in their early history and uncover real or supposed grievances with some significant person of influence. Unprovoked angry outbursts are not uncommon. These, in turn, feed back into the guilt that is already accumulating and which reciprocally fuels the anger. Efforts are made to "attach" the anger, and this may lead to unwise decisions affecting future career choices and even vocation. At a time when help is needed, angry individuals discourage attempts to help them, holding helpers at bay with their hostility. This is usually consciously recognized along with a helplessness to control or understand it.

"What's happening to me? I let fly at Margaret today when all she did was tell me I looked tired. She was trying to offer me some time off, I think, and all I could do was snap at her! I know that in my head but the message takes too long to get to my tongue and prevent me spitting out hateful words."

6. *Loss of Meaning*

Along with the anger and hand-in-hand with it is the experience of loss of meaning. Questions without answers surface. What am I doing here? Have I worked all these years for nothing? What if it's all a big hoax anyway and the person I should have been caring about all along is myself? Has my vocation crumbled to dust? How can there be a God who lets me wander in this desert?

Appreciation of beauty, a sense of the body's litheness and reliability, connectedness with the rest of creation, spiritual values, prayer—all of these dry up. Even the capacity to sit down and read a novel disappears. Enjoyment is a thing of the past. The fires of the burnout are reducing the pleasures and the meanings of life to ashes.

7. *Apathy*

Finally, when hope seems to have vanished, the individual gives up. There is a sinking back into a tacit unwillingness to make an effort at living or relating. It may be that the person goes on working, but it is working like an automaton rather than as flesh and blood. At this stage there is even unwillingness to investigate the causes of the person's state. What is left is a flaccid passivity. Describing a colleague, a psychiatrist friend told me recently,

"He's resigned from living. We had a barbecue at our place on Saturday evening and he came and brought two of his kids. He sat on the patio with a beer in his hand all evening and conversation went on all around him. He answered when he was spoken to with the fewest words he could scrape together and not once in the whole time did he take the initiative in a conversation. He's scraping the bottom of the barrel and nothing I say seems to reach him."

These days many religious recognize in this the portrait of themselves or one of their fellows. Sadly, when burnout gets as deep as this, it may last for years; chronic depression may be one of the outcomes.

It is no doubt possible to add other experiences of burnout to this list, but these are the ones that I most often encounter in the therapeutic situation. It is important to point out, however, that burnout is a progressive process. Not all of these seven symptoms are experienced suddenly or simultaneously. People are often well into the slide into burnout before they are conscious that anything beyond simple tiredness is wrong with them. It is easier to halt the process in its early stages, and the list of symptoms may help to alert both the sufferer and his or her companions to its beginnings. Of course not all weariness is incipient burnout, but a good test is whether or not it yields to adequate rest and relaxation, and whether or not other early symptoms accompany it. Duration is another indicator of danger.

I have an unexplored hunch that the phases of burnout may be tied at least partially to life stages. Huge energy expenditure in ministry is a feature of young adulthood when intimacy and competence are major developmental issues. If proving competence is dominant and formation for intimacy neglected or downgraded, a door into burnout is opened. Situational expediency (such as loading a religious with added responsibility because of demonstrated competence, lack of alternative man/woman power and so on), may lead to inadequate space in midlife for the interiorizing proper to that stage to happen in a quiet and relaxed way. Asking for the same work output as previously from an individual (whether the demands emanate from self, others or both) at a time when energies need to be redirected may well lead to an inner depletion of energies that deepens gradually into the chronic fatigue and ennui so characteristic of well-advanced burnout. If there is no relief and no assistance, the final retreat into chronic apathy may take place. My hunch is substantiated by the evidence that almost all of the people I meet who present burnout symptoms are middle-aged.

Where Does Burnout Come From?

Burnout is related to ineffective ways of dealing with stress. Stress is a fact of life; it cannot be totally removed. Indeed, it would be harmful to do so even if we could, because stress impels us to greatness. Everyone knows the creative inner tension that comes to our assistance at times—reaching into what we thought was forgotten knowledge for a lost fact necessary to pass an exam, quelling initial nervousness in order to give our best performance in a public appearance of some kind, finding the energy to meet a demand that we thought we were too weary to handle, having the calm required to meet a crisis or a deadline effectively, summoning the courage to effect a difficult reconciliation, dredging up a last burst of energy in the competitiveness of the playing field when the team needs us. All of these are responses to stress.

Most of us know the other kind, too, the stretched-to-breaking anxiety that destroys creativity, deadens ingenuity and impairs our ordinary resources for coping. We know the paralysis, the irrational fears. And we know the after-thoughts that suggest that we are losing our grip or are not in the right place or want to escape or hide.

My thesis is that *both* these forms of stress, *eustress* (positive stress) and *distress* (destructive stress)[3] may lie behind burnout. The early stage of an endeavor is not a period in which individuals experience distress. For religious, this is often a time of enormous commitment to ministry. The fields are white for the harvest and the hand of the Lord is upon us. We are called irresistibly to be laborers in the vineyard. The demands of ministry clamor all round us, and we experience in ourselves the feisty yes to its call, pouring out energy and inner resources to meet it. If there is no balance, no sabbath mentality, the chances are that we are entering the first phase of burnout without knowing it and without awareness of any distress. We often, at this time, need to be needed and, as we succeed in our given ministry, success reinforces success and spurs us on to greater effort. Our conscious motivation for this is good. We would die for the sake of the kingdom. Beneath this, however, may be a subtle and hidden need to gratify our need for recognition and importance. Unconsciously we are expending such effort in proving something. There is an inner contradiction and incongruence which we do not at first perceive. Only as we move into the deeper stages of burnout do we begin to re-examine motives and ask ourselves questions. Those of us fortunate enough to have close relationships which challenge and confront us early may be assisted to see what is happening a little earlier.

Stress, like beauty, is in the eye of the beholder. It is known that the same chemical changes are effected in the body by eustress and distress. The chemical neurotransmitters in the brain, norepinephrine and epinephrine, are suppressed somewhat and endorphins (morphine-like chemicals) increase. Corticotropin releasing factor (CRF) is produced in the hypothalamus of the brain. This triggers the pituitary gland to produce ACTH (Adrenocorticotropic hormone), which sends a series of chemical messages to the body, speeding up heartbeat and raising blood pressure to produce the familiar sensations of excitement and "on alert." Since the same chemical reactions are at the basis of both kinds of stress, it is likely that it is the human perception of the stressor that renders it positive or negative. For this reason, emphasis should not be placed on reducing the cause of stress (stressors) in a person's life as much as it should be directed to re-educating people's perceptions and interpretations.

> What no treatment programs attempt to do, however, is eliminate stress entirely. Nor should they. Hans Selye made a career of studying the ill effects of stress, but he nevertheless believed that it was "the spice of life." Falling in love, catching a ride on an ocean wave, seeing a great performance of *Hamlet*—all can unleash the same stress hormones as do less uplifting experiences, sending the blood pressure soaring and causing the heart to palpitate madly. But who among us would give them all up? "A certain amount of stress is a positive and pleasurable thing," says neurochemist Barchas. "It leads to productivity in the human race."[4]

The distinction that needs to be made is that eustress is the stress of winning (bringing a sense of achievement, triumph, exhilaration) and distress is the stress of losing (accompanied by loss of feelings of security and adequacy).

Common Stressors in Religious Life

A stressor is any event, inner or outer, which provokes a stress reaction. I shall list common stressors for religious under the following headings:

1) Historical stressors

2) Environmental stressors

3) Stressful expectations

4) Stressors of an affirmation desert

5) Body stressors

6) Affective stressors

7) Stressors from spirituality

1. *Historical Stressors*

Every human being has learned to look at life in particular ways shaped by culture and environment. If the myth of sexuality in a family was that it was secret, private and not discussable, a child born into that family may grow up uncertain about his or her sexuality, afraid and reticent and even somewhat ashamed. If particular patterns of relating in the family emphasized survival at the expense of others, win/lose games, retaliation and manipulation, it is likely that the traces of these formative influences may be tracked in the life of an adult whose childhood was colored by such attitudes. If the message about self-expression was freedom and spontaneity, then the chances are that the child will grow into a creative, open and spontaneous adult. If conflict was regarded as a fact of life to be negotiated reasonably and kindly and with compromises, it is likely that these historical origins will leave their mark on the maturing adult.

While it is true that our history is not the whole story, and that influences in the present are another powerful source of learning, few of us have total awareness of the multiple ways in which we act out of our past. It is only as we remember and recognize the patterns of learning and conditioning that we take charge of our responses in the present. We are not prisoners of our history when this happens. What has been learned can be unlearned, albeit often painfully and with grinding effort.

It is true to say, however, that most of us never discover all the historical shapers of our present responses, and that some of our reaction to stress now may have its roots in what we learned consciously and unconsciously in the past. One sister, aged 50, who had battled for years with high anxiety and inability to cope with what for many would have been only moderately stressful situations, began to trace patterns in the past:

> "My mother was neurotic, now that I think about it. She was afraid of her own shadow. What the neighbors might think was always desperately important to her. She wouldn't go out into the back yard to hang out the washing if she had curlers in her hair because the neighbors might see her. For crying out loud! *I'm* like that. . . always afraid of what others will think of me, and sure they'll think the very worst . . . that they'll look at external things and judge what's on my inside. And so I hide myself. I'm scared to go into a group or appear in the common room if there's a stranger there."

As she began to identify the source of her learnings this sister began—fearfully and tentatively at first—to take risks, gradually reducing the fear of rejection and the stressful inner state she had carried for so long.

For another religious, a middle-aged teacher, community meetings were experienced as stressful and potentially damaging. He found some traces of this in his family of origin:

> "We didn't fight in our home. Dad was the boss and if any disagreement flared up he quieted it immediately with a look or a word. . . (long pause). . . I guess no real conflict was ever allowed to surface, at least not in any detail. If you felt angry, you sat on it.

> "That's a bit of how it is for me at community meetings. The others see them as times for airing grievances, and when they start to lay it on the line, something happens in my guts. . . . I want to get out of there, or I keep willing the superior to close the discussion, put the lid on it. . . . I guess I'm wanting him to be Dad all over again."

Not all historically learned stress goes back as far as family of origin, of course. For many religious who claim a healthy and generally quite positive family learning climate, the significant period in which stress originated was the novitiate:

> "I lived in fear in the novitiate. It was bad to make a mistake, so I learned to take no risks, and now when I want to take a risk I go cold and paralyzed."

or

> "Teaching about celibacy was all negative—no sex, no marriage, no closeness, no physical touching. As things change all around me and I see the younger men able to befriend one another and be close and express affection I'm full of futile anger. I'm threatened by their overtures of friendship and their expression of care. It's too uncomfortable. . .dangerous even. I don't know how to respond, and I'd feel silly if I tried."

Learning to deal with the effects of the past, recognizing transferential learnings in the context of the open now, is imperative for dealing with a huge amount of experienced stress.

2.   Environmental Stressors

> Everyone knows the world today is significantly different from the one of even fifteen or twenty years ago. Clear, too, is the fact that the Church is significantly different. Every believer within the Church finds his or her life affected by these changes. . . .

Yesterday's stable world, which Catholics sometimes recall nostalgically, is now gone. Catholics seemed to have more answers then.[5]

The most significant and powerful environmental stressor for many religious is change. It has affected the very fabric of religious life. Religious who learned to cut themselves off from the world in a variety of ways are now aware of new insistence that religious life is not an escape from the world but an entrance into it. Change, therefore, strikes at their mode of being in relationship with their world and alters the way they are expected to see and understand themselves in it.

Among the many shifts of focus that affect religious deeply, I list the following:

(a) *A shift of tenses.* Instead of preoccupation with the past and with tradition there is a new emphasis on appropriating the spirit and charism of founders in the present as a trajectory into future life and ministry. This is perceived by some less as fidelity and continuity than as betrayal and fracturing of relationship with the past.

(b) *A shift of values.* Poverty is currently being interpreted not only as material poverty, but also as a surrendering of time and space. We become "public property," available for service to the local church and neighborhood.

Celibacy is seen as warm and open loving, risk-taking in the modelling of a new way of loving that is at once humanly credible and countercultural, witnessing to the fact that love does not necessarily equal sex. Celibacy is deeply relational and allows of close and intimate personal friendship as well as of intensely committed and loving ministry. For individuals who were taught *not* to be close, *not* to befriend, to be separate and somewhat removed, there is an enormous challenge. Many are looking around for credible teachers; others have chosen to cling to old values.

Obedience has become less of a giving up of the power to deliberate, to choose and to decide, and become a redirecting of the will into accountable personal initiative for the sake of the kingdom. For individuals conditioned to be dependent and to regard this dependence as virtue, the challenge to take initiative and to be responsible for individual choices within the context of the aims and values of the group demands radical rearrangement within the psyche. This is not to suggest that such individuals do not embark on such a process, but to point out the magnitude of the potential stress involved in doing so.

Charity is no longer seen as simply acts of charity but as moving in close to love personally, reflecting the all-embracing love of a God passionately involved with creation.

(c)   *A shift of structures.*   The shape of life itself has changed for many. Reliance on external rules for the validation of behavior has diminished. Authority structures have shifted from monarchical rule in the direction of collegial rule. Built into new understandings of authority, reflected gradually in the structures, is the conviction that

> in a profound way we are responsible for ourselves. Only we can live our lives and die our deaths. No one can do either for us. To the extent we forfeit that responsibility, we relinquish being human.[6]

For some the stress lies in pressure to take personal responsibility for their lives when for many years they have been accustomed to parenting by authority figures. For some in leadership positions, there is the stress of having in their communities chronically dependent people who regularly seek parenting and seem unable or deeply unwilling to be otherwise.

The expression of authority has shifted from command to consultation, from organization to humanization, but the shift is not total in many cases. Thus people experience some incongruence between the language of consultation and the hidden dynamic of manipulation and coercion:

> "I don't really see much point in going through the motions of a discernment process about what I should do next year when my term of office as a school principal is over. I get a strong impression that the decision is already made and that I'm being edged toward doing something that is already decided."

The shape of life together has shifted, or is shifting, from being all together under one roof, most of us sharing a single, institutionalized apostolate, to dispersal and individual apostolates. For those living in the latter situation there is often the loneliness of greater isolation to be dealt with. For those in a more heavily institutionalized situation, where such change does not appear to be imminent, some experience the pressure to change and a desire to change without the power to effect the change.

Relationship with church and laity has changed. There is a shift from a sense of superiority to the laity to partnership in ministry with them, and there is an initial shift from a sense of inferiority to the clergy to a deep wish to be partners also with them. This is partly a structural shift, but it might also be listed under the heading of relational stress.

3. *Stressful Expectations*

Every human being is at the center of a nexus of expectations and demands. Even if we were to insulate ourselves totally from the demands of others, we would be left with our self-expectations, at times the strongest and most imperative of all.

Almost any expectation can be a stressor depending on the amount of freedom we perceive ourselves to have about meeting it. The expectation may come from the nature of ministry itself, from within the self, or from others.

(a) *Stress from ministry.*   It is the nature of many forms of ministry to be open-ended. Teaching in a classroom is no longer a task extending from 9 a.m. till 4 p.m. with a few hours of preparation outside those hours. More professional approaches to education now demand the attendance at meetings, upgrading of qualifications, constant proof of standards being maintained and a host of ancillary, and for some, primarily important, helping relationships with troubled students, lay teachers and parents. Being a parish minister involves new approaches to sacramental programs, the ability to work as a team member, liturgical skills, skills for spiritual direction and counselling, organization and leadership skills. Being a helping person in ministry, whatever shape that may take, is not seen as a purely professional and therefore time-limited job, though professional standards are expected. The professional competence is seen to be hand-in-hand with unlimited availability and generosity. The minister runs from one task to another with little thought about priorities. The clamor for his or her presence and service is never quiet. The job is never finished. The sheer exhaustion that eventually results from trying to satisfy the voracious demands of such an apostolate may end in burnout.

In addition, it is the nature of some ministries more than others to have intangible results. How do helpers or parish ministers, superiors or formation people, measure success? If they worked on an assembly line in a factory they could look at their paycheck at the end of the week or the number of objects assembled in an hour. They could compare this with previous productivity and assess performance. This is not so in ministry. I know from my own experience of counselling that many people, when they begin to get their life together fairly constructively, do not come back any more, even when contracts for a specific number of counselling sessions have been made. They feel better. They cease to feel any further need for help. They go away. It is as simple as that. For me, there is no clear recognition of how I have helped, if indeed I have done so. All I know is that apparently our mutual search has ended. It is rare (and immeasurably rewarding!) to have someone come back feeling whole to inform you of the fact and to say thank you. It is a well-known fact that we are energized and rewarded by tangible successes. New motivation is created, new springs of energy well up. For clergy and religious and, more recently, for laity in ministries of this kind, it is possible to feel depleted and enervated in the absence of such rewards. The exhaustion may—but need not—lead to burnout.

> To work with the psyche, the spirit, the world of words, and people and their problems, is to run the risk of becoming psychologically thin.[7]

Sanford calls this the "airy nature" of ministry and recommends balancing the abstract work with more tangible compensatory hobbies where the results are solid and the satisfaction may feed back into new life for ministry.[8]

The abstract, never-ending, multiple demands of the work do not, however, produce burnout or depletion in everybody. Why some and not others? Clearly, the attitudes and self-expectations of the person in relation to the work are at the core of the burnout. It is questionable whether sheer quantity of work ever broke anybody. The way they see it is another question entirely.

(b) *Stress from self-expectations.*   Surrounded by the mass of demands of the work itself and impelled by a conditioned sense of obligation to accomplish it, many religious overcommit themselves. They are simply unable to say no. There is an unnatural suppression of the instinct for self-preservation in their ceaseless activity. Worse, there is a life-deep disjunction happening. The external, generous yes continues to be said, but in the inner core there is a secret no gnawing away at vitality and spontaneity and interest. The no is not always conscious but manifests itself in the weariness and dullness that herald burnout.

In the name of Christianity many religious feel obligated to give until they drop, forgetting that the founder of Christianity himself had a mountaintop, a desert place, a chosen few, dinner companions, conversation partners and a rhythm of life that withdrew, ministered, recreated in the congenial company of friends! It is a peculiar definition of virtue that does not allow for human growth, for recovery, for recreation, especially when the core of the Christian imperative is to become more fully human moment by moment, day by day.

Associated with this is the expectation that ministers are always to be givers and not receivers. It is for this reason that I have placed emphasis on the primary *receptivity* of empathy. To give without first experiencing personal poverty and need is to give condescendingly, invulnerably. The denial of human weakness, the expectation that by some magical transformation religious vocation makes us super-people is a lie, and a serious one, for it may lead us to destroy the gift of creation that we are to ourselves.

I recently spoke with one sister whom I have known for many years and who has lived with enormous fidelity to a set of exorbitant self-expectations. A quiet person, she always went where she was sent, took on jobs outside her desires and competence without a murmur, dealt with her feelings by suppression, served her sisters with gentleness and apparent serenity, but now has recurrent psychotic episodes and must be hospitalized at regular intervals. I noted how often in our conversation she said, "I have to rise above the way I am feeling." Recognizing the harshness of this, I invited her to come to a meal with me, see a movie with me, just to have fun. But she had to "rise above" her sense of obligation to work ceaselessly in order to accept my invitation. Having fun felt somewhat sinful, and so what I had envisaged as relaxation and fun became for her another source of tension, an exercise in futility. I really love this woman and feel tears of sadness in me that she has embarked with enormous commitment and good will on an apparently unbreakable cycle of self-destruction.

I am sad for my friend that she never learned to dance. There is a tragic little echo in my head, from Kazantzakis I think, that the person who has not learned to dance has not learned to live. I grieve that this beautiful woman surrendered her dream, heroically gave primacy to conformity in life, and now lives out her remaining years shuffling along the corridors of a psychiatric institution.

Rest and relaxation are not luxuries but imperatives. A sabbath mentality is not only for the cloistered or retired; the whole of creation needs to take time to tune the instruments of their symphony of life. To take time for self is not selfish. It is growth-producing and regenerating. But time taken grudgingly, with a sense of being lazy, uncommitted or unfaithful cannot be called relaxing. It has to be undertaken with the joyful recognition that it is a human right, a participation in ongoing creation, to be enjoyed and celebrated with as much gladness as conversion and healing. Indeed, for many of us, to relax and take time to savor life may indeed be a form of conversion and healing. There are some religious who rush from one task to another as the demand arises without any attention to setting priorities. But not every task has the same degree of importance as others. It may help lift burdens if people list the things they customarily do in a busy week of ministry and rank items in order of importance. It might be salutary also to consider what can effectively be done by others or omitted altogether from the list.

(c)   *Stress from expectations of others.*   Many religious confuse goodness with trying to meet most of the expectations of others whether these tally with inner capacities and attitudes or not. For those who have little sense of their own worth as persons, to meet every demand of community members, friends, colleagues, pastors, superiors, clients, students and of the institution itself is a way of demonstrating worth, proving it to themselves and others.

Clearly there are many who have developed enough self-assurance and assertiveness to know that they have an intrinsic worth that does not demand from them efforts to achieve the impossible. They have an inner realism that allows them to be selective, to recognize conflict between expectations and to make prudent choices. If this is also accompanied by the skill of immediacy, they will be able to make their attitudes known. They will be able also to refuse to meet a demand in ways that are enspirited by empathy and sensitive to the effects of their refusal on those who make the demand or request. They will at times choose to put aside their own comfort and stretch their limits a little for the sake of the common good, knowing that dying is a part of living. They do not, however, constantly choose death over life in a suicidal fashion, and they know how and when to say no. They carry life's imposed crosses, but do *not* nail themselves to crosses.

For others, the freedom to make such choices is not yet established. Insufficient affirmation in their lives, or the inability to allow it space, has not yet built in them a reverence for themselves and their own life. They cannot yet extend to themselves the same care as they profess to offer others.

The real choice for persons with a poor self-image is to stop trying to earn others' love and accept the fact that others love them for who they are. With this realization these persons begin to let go of impossible ideals, to ignore the negative voices, and to trust successful experiences of a loved and loving self. Gradually they begin to see themselves as persons who are limited yet gifted and unique.[9]

This is more easily said than done. It cannot be accomplished alone. Such a process of journeying from self-doubt to self-valuing implies significant unlearning. Once again the potential impact of a spirituality of empathy in the community is obvious. The co-creative invitation to move constantly in the direction of greater freedom issues only from a communal group that empathically understands the binds and unfreedoms, the caution and the fear of such movement, a group that faithfully and appropriately challenges the individual in small doses, principally by its unconditional love.

All this being said, it is nevertheless a fact of life that we at some time or another find ourselves caught amid conflicting demands. To expect to meet them all is to ask the impossible. To do this constantly is to set up a pattern of stress that will eventually take its toll in the form of psychosomatic symptoms or other expressions of depletion eventually crashing down into the collapse of burnout.

(d) *Systemic expectations.*   Systemic expectations are another powerful set of oughts and shoulds for many religious. Where institutional ministries are still a way of life, it is often an unwritten norm that if another person is ill, on study leave or for some other reason is absent, someone else will readily step in and fill the gap thus created in the workforce. This is becoming a more and more unreasonable expectation as numbers decline within religious life and as specialization and the discrimination of gifts assume greater importance. The meek, gap-filling religious is often a person who has a need to meet the expectations of those in authority.

It is a joint responsibility of leaders and potential gap-fillers to ask what the individual's capacity to accede to the request is and what the honest motivation behind asking this particular person is.

Systems are powerful. The pressures on leaders and administrators to find personnel to meet particular needs are greater than they have ever been. It becomes imperative, therefore, to fight passionately to preserve the core virtues of empathy and compassion in the process, to resist instrumentalism at all costs, to close down commitments in particular areas rather than crucify people who do not yet know how to say the fearful no that burns for release in them. For the systemic decision-makers there are conflicting expectations here too. On the one hand, they see the needs of a particular area and are pressured by the demands of pastors, laity and so on. On the other hand, they recognize the foolishness and even the cruelty of laying more burdens on the backs of those who minister. When the clamor of the system is louder and more insistent than the "I can't" of the individual, it is easy to obey the louder voice. The pain of this kind of decision-making for leaders is great. It is a potential source of stress, depending on the strength and clarity of their priorities, their assertiveness in the face of demands and their own definition of leadership.

One further stressor is a common one these days and is experienced sharply by superiors. Caught in the process of changing understandings of authority, superiors often do battle with old learnings they themselves have had about the meaning and shape of authority. Beginning to experience their authority as leadership from *among* rather than from *above*, they often find themselves at the mercy of opposing demands. On the one hand, they recognize the dependence of some who have not yet been able to move beyond a childish expectation of parenting by the superior and who ask permission for every minor detail of their daily activity. On the other, they sometimes feel completely irrelevant in the face of the assured independence of others, while recognizing that their task is primarily a modelling one. It is often possible to make a clear statement defining their role to their own satisfaction, but it is difficult to translate this into behavior that does not bring upon them the wrath, or at least the tacit disapproval, of some members of the communal group. How to be empathic with and yet simultaneously educative of their critics is a dilemma. The stress of this is often apparent in their need to escape for a time from the pressures of the community, to have a life outside it and to give themselves permission to do so when old expectations still insist that the superior is always there and always available.

I believe that we are at a time when solid and strong insistence on a power that serves concrete needs is necessary. Superiors need support systems to sustain them in this, peers who share their values, and means of communicating this understanding of authority to those whom they serve, so that even those who disagree at least are informed of what to expect. Superiors these days are also people who have to understand the meaning of compromise and patience, because those who do not understand, who are by long history dependent, cannot be changed merely by good communication.

Superiors must have inner fibre, a capacity to roll with the punches, the separateness to get lost at times as well as to stay with. It is no longer virtuous reliance on Providence to dump people untrained into a role that is not as clear-cut and linear as it used to be. Superiors must be trained. Then they must be nourished, sustained and supported. To do any less is irresponsible.

4. *Stressors of an Affirmation Desert*

An earlier chapter has laid heavy emphasis on the significance of affirmation for freeing people from old bonds and for calling them to greater fullness of humanity. Where there is an affirmation gap, individuals exist in an affective desert. Like children who suffer from malnutrition, they will scrape at whatever surfaces contain possible nourishment, taking refuge in work, finding false comfort in fantasy to hide the emptiness of reality.

At a recent seminar on sexuality and celibacy a young male religious commented:

> "Sometimes I wonder what's going to happen to me. I really want to belong to this community, and I believe it's where I belong. It's right for me. But there are questions for me, all the same.
>
> "I see my old classmates, men who were at school and university with me, making a life for themselves. Most of them have good jobs. Some of them as young as myself have made quite a bit of progress in terms of success and promotion. Many of them are married and have several children by now. I see them with a wife who clearly loves them and I watch them hugged and loved by their children and I begin to envy them. What about my fathering needs? Who loves me as much as that?"

Although this statement was prompted by a discussion of the nature of celibacy, it contains many other ingredients besides an awareness of sexual need.

It is true that in religious life there is no such clear hierarchy of progress. How, then, does an individual have his or her competency recognized and affirmed? Where faithful and persevering effort is taken for granted, there is a danger that individuals will lack any clear confirmation that their efforts are appreciated. Where positive feedback involving affectivity is sparse, doubts about competence may develop. In such a climate the sap of commitment and energetic dedication may dry up.

If it is also true that in religious life the value of person *as person* is ignored, insufficiently recognized overtly, or displaced by instrumental valuing on the basis of performance for the sake of the system it can happen that the person never knows deeply that he or she is loved. The young brother's comment, it transpired, was less about sexuality and celibacy than about a perception that many religious communities are affective desserts. The question becomes, Who will love me just for myself? Who will let me know that there's warmth and belonging and intimacy for me here?

The discussion ranged over a number of issues. It was claimed in this particular group that conversation in the common room was limited to discussion of work and sport. It was admitted that there was some affection for one another, but its only form of expression was jocose camaraderie which never *directly* expressed affection. I sensed in this group, as I have in many others, a thirst for demonstrated affection. I believe that this is frequently greater in male communities where the cultural norm reinforces the religious custom of reticence.

I know of no greater and more penetrating stressor than this. Celibacy was never meant to be a life of unfulfillment. To expect this of anyone is sinful, for it is a crime against nature as well as a denial of what lies deep in the heart of Christianity. Religious life is neither a denial of intimacy, nor a desert in which human needs must be totally sublimated. It is not a place where rich and poetic and beautiful religious language and ideals somehow camouflage a huge chasm of loneliness.

The unaffirmed person cannot minister effectively. He or she is too preoccupied with questions of personal self-worth to be able to reach out and affirm the value of the poor, the halt and the ignorant. Or, on the other hand, the person may deaden the clamor of avoidable loneliness by plunging into work and being an efficient, and perhaps officious, minister whose service is lavish, visible and even compulsive, but lacks the warmth of blood and flesh and sinew. It comes not from someone who is prized but from someone who needs, consciously or unconsciously, to buy esteem.

> In order to overcome or escape our loneliness, we often throw ourselves compulsively and anxiously into an endless round of activity. Or our fear drives us to withdraw from human exchange. Either way, we are reacting to life out of fear

and anxiety, which leaves us less open to what life offers. Our fear shapes our attitude and expectation and only serves to attract that which we wish to avoid.[10]

The American Bishops' Committee on Priestly Life and Ministry made this comment on the experience of priests:

A priest many times experiences his morale undermined when he perceives that he is receiving little or no affirmation from those who are likely to be for him "significant others." Among these are his family, fellow priests, and especially his bishop or major superior. Although he may be receiving affirmation from other sources such as his friends and the people he serves, if he does not sense support from his superior and fellow priests or if he believes that his superiors will not take steps to lighten his burden, confidence in his own ministry begins to erode. For this reason priestly fraternity and unity is of critical importance in the life of a priest today.[11]

5. *Body Stressors*

Whether from the pressures of a constantly demanding ministry, from a spirituality and asceticism that denies the body attention or from sheer forgetfulness, many religious neglect their physical health. Because our response to life is holistic, if any aspect of our life is ignored, the chances are that depletion of one kind or another may be felt, not always with clear recognition of its source. In fact, the symptoms of bodily neglect may be felt first not in physical pain or discomfort, but in psychological malaise, boredom with religious exercises and a general loss of taste for life. The limp muscle tone of the spirit may be perceived long before it is attributable to a physical cause.

Asceticism is often defined by religious and clergy in terms of work dedication and fidelity to prayer. But we are bodily persons. The condition of the body affects the whole person—vitality, relationship, ministry, prayer and outlook on life. There is need for a new look at asceticism, a redefinition that includes attention to daily or at least regular exercise, control of diet, adequate sleep and leisure, spiritual nourishment, regular medical check-ups and work. I am unimpressed by statements that suggest that, as a matter of daily practice, most of these concerns are put aside in the interests of working for the kingdom. When this does indeed happen, working for the kingdom may be a very short-term enterprise, or operate according to the law of diminishing returns, as weary bodies and saddening spirits lose their engagement with the exhilaration of a life lived fully.

Smoking and excessive alcohol consumption are currently being decried socially as detrimental to health, but many clergy and religious seem to regard themselves as somehow immune to the evils that beset the rest of humanity. New attention must be given to these things, both by the individual and the organization.

The physical effects of life's developmental stages also cry out for attention. Women undergoing menopause without adequate information and education about the normal and abnormal functioning of their own bodies may be subject to unnecessary worry and stress exacerbated by reticence born of long years of not mentioning their feelings or bodily functions. The effects of aging on the body and its energy ought also be explored in a public fashion so that not only the aged but also their companions in communities may understand and accept limits without underestimating the enormous potential that also exists at this time. Such education is highly significant since ignorance can be a powerful source of stress, rendering individuals helpless in the face of processes that seem outside any personal control.

Religious recovering from surgery also need education and assistance. Not only the physical realities of post-operative convalescence but the hidden fears and the grief associated with loss of some part of the body or trauma to the body need to be recognized. These require as much quiet attention as does the feeling of loss and desolation associated with the death of a loved one. To ignore this process and the need for understanding companionship at such times is to ensure that the stresses simply transfer to another level of consciousness producing neurosis, psychosomatic problems or even chronic invalidism.

Perhaps one of the first positive actions to be undertaken in the face of gradually encroaching burnout is to have a frank talk with an understanding doctor. Perhaps, also, one of the best ways of preventing burnout in the first place is an asceticism that recognizes that the body is as great a gift as faith is, and prizes it as such.

6.   *Affective Stressors*

Among religious and clergy emotional neglect is as common as physical neglect, and perhaps more difficult for them to handle because of their history in relation to intimacy.

I believe that for many religious there has been a sad neglect of the functioning of the right brain. Brought up in a left-brain, intellectual, logical, problem-solving tradition, where truth was to be found in law and norm and commands of the higher powers, many have grown to late adulthood without the normal flowering of that imaginative, creative and appreciative faculty referred to as right-brain activity. In association with this, there has been an overeducation of animus at the expense of anima. That is to say, the coping, organizing, thinking self has been given pride of place, and the more tender and receptive aspect of the person has been underplayed in importance. I believe that this is true of women religious almost as much as of men. Culturally, as well, men have been expected to be left-brain, animus-inspired copers with life. The conditioning is doubly reinforced for them. There are very good arguments in favor of male liberation. For women in religious life, although there have not been such cultural expectations, early novitiate formation for many has played down the natural, anima-generated capacity for emotional tenderness and the free expression of right-brain creativity. I remember being instructed that we women had to have a "virile spirituality" and thinking to myself, not without a twinge of guilt at entertaining the thought, that it would be easier if we had the appropriate hormones to go with it!

Many hopeful signs indicate that a lot of religious, both male and female, are being freed of such impossible and narrow restrictions. Renewal courses, approaches to spirituality, more open mixing of the sexes and increasing understanding of and engagement in growth-producing relationships, all play their part in the liberation process. From the number of religious whom I meet in the capacity of a counsellor, however, I recognize that the stressors of emotional inadequacy or fear are far from gone.

One issue involved in all of this is celibacy. For too long celibacy and lack of intimacy have been connected. Emotional distance and fearfulness have been the result for some. There has been a failure in formation programs to examine the process of growth into celibacy. Celibacy has been frequently presented as a thing, a finished condition, an obligation which once undertaken, is simply thereafter a matter of fidelity. I have heard individuals say that for them celibacy means loving everybody in general and nobody in particular. If anyone who reads this can explain how that may be, I would be grateful for an explanation! It appears to me that growth toward a totally generous, self-giving and all-embracing love proceeds from healthy self-love through individual loves to all-embracing love, and that all-embracing love is the peak of a life of growth to maturity which does not ever rule out the presence of intimacy and closeness.

Where closeness and a healthily positive view of celibacy as a chosen way of living and loving are absent, the individual may experience tension, the need to escape, a kind of desert where the only feedback is from those ministered to and relates to performance, an inner longing for closeness that is unsatisfied because it is accompanied by fear of possible sexual involvement.

Inability to handle strong feelings of any kind is common among religious, especially those whose initial formation took place in fairly restrictive regimes. For younger religious who are better equipped to handle their emotions, the lack of reciprocity from their older companions and colleagues can be a source of stress if they cannot at least occasionally spend time with their peers to recoup the energy lost in one-sided relating.

At seminars and workshops religious are now exposed to programs of education that indicate ways of recognizing, naming and directly reporting their feelings. However, much of this knowledge remains at the level of intellectual data unless there are enough fairly confident people in communities to model appropriate disclosure of emotions and to create the safety for those less accustomed to this to take a risk or two. It is difficult to risk being open to our emotions where there is little interpersonal trust. The conundrum is that the very climate of trust can be created only by some disclosure of the risky feelings. Hence the need for models, the prophets, who by the quality of their own responses and at times by the pain they are willing to take on can challenge their companions to an alternative way of being. It is for the poet in each person to discern with empathy the extent to which individuals are willing and able to trust, each coming as he or she does from a unique personal story with unique limits, chains and ways of understanding.

7. *Stressors From Spirituality*

Where there are still remnants of an "it's no good unless it hurts" spirituality, there is stress. In the interests of fearful fidelity to a demanding God, those tainted with such a belief cannot allow themselves what appears to be the luxury of leisure, time with friends, stillness for reflection, fun, or even enjoyment of work. Everything is obligation. If it *feels* good, it cannot *be* good! This is, of course, something of a caricature, but there are old tapes that play in the minds and hearts of some religious; they switch on as soon as the individual begins to relax or to enjoy, and engender automatic guilt. This is closely related to the heresy of good works, the belief that we are worth something in the eyes of God and of others only in so far as we are accomplishing good works. The gratuity of the love of an all-faithful God is intellectually acknowledged, but practically ignored.

The most obvious expression of all this today is in the urgency of work exacerbated by fewer numbers and apparently undiminishing need for ministry. In this context it is easy to submit to the urgency and ignore the nourishing of the spirit. I mean time on a regular basis for prayer and reflection. I also mean time for "wasting," time for letting the sand on a beach sink under our toes, for tree and leaf to speak their timeless language, for the noise of passing traffic to sing of life, for wind and wave, color and shape, tone and timbre to register on the senses and the spirit. I mean time to ingest new ideas from reading and talking. I mean time to think new thoughts, dream new dreams. I mean sloughing off the obligation to work all the time, to be seen to be productive in order to justify our existence.

One common confusion experienced during burnout is expressed in the complaint that God seems unheeding and distant. There is an expectation that God will fill the gaps created by human imprudence. But this is not prayer and this is not God. If God is immanent in every moment of our life process, drawing us with subtle invitation toward wholeness and harmony, prayer first admits who we really are and issues in hopeful anticipation rather than forlorn daydreaming. It flows into appropriate and responsible action.

A central recognition in all this is that it is not primarily by performance that we bear witness to a life of fullness, but by the quality of a life lived faithfully and deeply. Paradoxically, when we do this, the work itself is more alive and productive because our spirit sings through it. It is work that is *one* expression of a contemplative spirit appropriately nourished.

Finally, the sharing of faith is intrinsic to spiritual health. Where it is absent, one lives in a stressful vacuum.

> Many religious houses are the last places to hear the good news shared with infectious enthusiasm. Yet, one can hardly imagine a greater healing power for burnout than this.[12]

Above all, nurturing the spirit requires a form of kindness to ourselves that is unashamed and generous with the same prodigality we offer to the receivers of our ministry.

Handling Stress and Burnout

Stressors abound in life, but burnout is not inevitable. A healthy sense of realism which identifies the risky areas of living and ministering will assist in the prevention of burnout before it happens and recognize the process before its grasp takes too tight a hold. It will push us to make constructive decisions and to choose life. It is a realism that involves our own poetic, prophetic and pragmatic gifts. A self-directed empathy is in touch quickly with the heaviness and discouragement of the first stages of burnout. Our prophetic desire to model and to live a life that is vital and faithful and committed will take hold of false desires and ambitions to be endlessly productive and recognize that these are a projection of a worldly need for success rather than a genuine form of service for the sake of the kingdom. Our pragmatic realism will not allow us to be carried along by flaccid acquiescence on the tide of our incipient burnout but will plan ways of working, playing, relaxing and nourishing that ensure a life lived to the full. These gifts will be put to the service, not only of our own potential or actual burnout, but will also be brought to bear on the same process in our companions.

A number of common sense tactics may reduce the risk of burnout or help to cope with it once it has begun. I offer a few suggestions here.

1.   *Develop Adequate Self-knowledge*

One of the great advantages of living in this time is the availability of many ways of gaining insight into ourselves. There has been a resurgence of interest in spiritual direction. Counselling has attained new respectability and does not necessarily label one as neurotic or "on the way out." Personality tests and other associated instruments are readily available to offer help with self-knowledge. Journal-keeping, self-disclosure in dialogue with community and friends, helpful reading material and skilled leadership offer opportunities for growth. Adequate self-understanding that leads to happier and more effective living is no longer seen as narcissism. New approaches to prayer emphasize listening to the sound of the current of our own life.

One important and at times neglected recognition in all this is that self-awareness at any moment is only a step in the journey. Life is movement and process. It is not merely a succession of identical beads on the string of time, but qualitative change as well. Thus it is well to be aware that even reliable test-results represent a moment that is the result of past patterns, but also a stepping-stone to a future over which one has control. These days when it is a fashion to undergo batteries of tests, or to "do" the Myers-Briggs or Enneagram, a yawning trap is to assume that whatever descriptive facts these things reveal are fixed and unchangeable. I am at times uneasy at the way such results are interpreted, possibly less by their practitioners and exponents than by their subjects. In particular, I meet individuals who canonize the Myers-Briggs and the Enneagram, freezing their results, adopting a language that issues from them, judging and comparing in terms of them in ways that are less than helpful. I believe such things are very helpful indeed when seen as instruments to be used among other things that are also enjoying their moment in our experience. When they begin to shape the whole of a person's consciousness, I believe that they are dangerous.

So, adequate self-knowledge is important. It is important also to see it as process, and not to let it be a freezer in which we become coldly immobile.

2. *Establish a Rhythm*

The synoptic gospels present a Jesus whose life flows from the solitude of the mountaintop and a deep, quiet immersion in the relationship with the Father to the energetic ministry of teaching, healing and life-giving to time for recreation with a chosen few. Establishing such a life rhythm is a way of ensuring that the whole of life is attended to and that no single aspect of it grows into a devouring monster.

Patterns like this require planning and an asceticism of time. In the old days we shot out of bed in the mornings at the first stroke of the bell and had half a day's work done by breakfast time! In the interests of peace and the prevention of burnout—in the interests, perhaps, of preventing cardiac arrest!—it may be helpful to ease gradually into the day. I sometimes suggest to friends and clients that they wake up gently, stretch like a cat, *enjoy* the sensation of waking, of showering and dressing, feel the morning air on the skin with gratitude and pleasure. Bursting into energetic action immediately after waking from the immobility of sleep is a kind of violence.

Knowing the time of day when our energy is at its peak will help us plan activities suitably so that we are not making exorbitant demands on energy, attention and concentration. Having a fairly accurate knowledge of our attention span for particular activities will also let us know when a short break is advisable. Far from diminishing performance, there is evidence to show that this picks up and heightens performance. It is false guilt to believe that a five- or 10-minute break at regular intervals is lazy or slack. Everybody is different. I have my rhythm and you have yours. I do not need to feel ashamed that I am not like you.

3.   *Establish Buffer Zones*

Ministerial life is full and active and demanding. It is prudent and helpful to have a few stable and predictable life spaces where you can take refuge from time to time from being in the thick of things. For me these are simple. I make a short phone call to a friend, call on my family, talk with one of our retired sisters who exudes a sense of restfulness. Or I build periods of reflection into the schedule. Sometimes I read, sometimes I sit and think and sometimes, like the proverbial old gentleman, "Ah jest sits."

Other religious report that meal times are special for them. They do not accept phone calls at this time. They eat slowly and deliberately, savoring taste and textures. Still others tell me that their time in the car or train going from one place of ministry to another is personal space. One teacher tells me that she deliberately walks from one class to another slowly, deepening her breathing and, as she puts it, getting back in tune.

What all of this does, no matter what its shape, is set up a small area of stillness in the midst of daily turbulence. The turbulence loosens its grip.

4.   *Know Your Priorities*

Stress mounts when every detail of a day or week becomes imbued with the same urgency and importance. It may be helpful to list all the things you do over a given period of time and then rank them in order of perceived importance. This does a number of things to reduce stress. It shows the relative values of the tasks and thus overcomes stress' tendency to make everything an imperative.

Knowing our priorities does not mean that crises will not change our plans, but it is helpful in reducing the feelings of guilt or discomfort that sometimes happen when someone makes a demand that we see as low on the priorities list. If there *is* such a list, it may be easier to refuse or postpone action or refer the demanding person to someone else. Listing our priorities reduces the pressure that originates in conflicting expectations.

Establishing priorities presupposes a clear awareness of

some criteria for the process. I have a few questions I ask myself:

- Is this central or peripheral to my ministry?
- How urgent is this?
- What will happen if I do not do this right now? Will I relieve pressure or build more?
- Is this within my competence?
- Is it within my role-definition?
- Am I the person to do this or should someone else do it?
- Does it need to be done at all?

5. *Try to Break the Type-A Pattern*

Two American cardiologists undertook research into the kind of personality characteristics that predispose individuals to heart attack and other cardiac illness. They found a set of qualities that, if taken in conjunction with other behavior such as neglect of physical fitness, excessive alcohol consumption or poor diet, indicated such susceptibility. The cluster of characteristics became known as Type-A personality. Broadly characterized by the twin qualities of time urgency and free-floating hostility, people with Type-A tendencies are often overprogrammed, with no emergency space or relaxed time built into their day. They prize success and work for it incessantly, carrying a fear of failure into all they do. They compare themselves with others constantly and are highly competitive. They make enormous demands on themselves in terms of accomplishment and perfection. They are the people who listen to one person on one phone with someone else on hold while they scribble a note to a secretary or colleague with one hand and glance at the clock to see if they are keeping to schedule. They are often chronic clock-watchers and at times alienate people by the habit. Delays for these people create foot-tapping anxiety. They are task-centered rather than person-centered; when their job involves others, those others are seen as facets of a duty to be completed. Empathy is very difficult for people with Type-A personalities.

Breaking such a pattern may require the help of another person. Whether it does or not, it involves slowing down, thinking of one thing at a time, doing one thing at a time, learning to waste time without guilt and to listen to other people without a nagging impulse to find solutions or offer premature advice.

Essentially, breaking the Type-A pattern means giving oneself permission to be still, to relax, to take time, to sense and be aware, to slow down thought processes, to imagine, to read and explore, to touch and to feel, to be different from rather than better than. One of my friends, a successful convert from Type-A, speaks of creating "temple space." In a corner of his office he has a low table. On it is a fat candle with lots of wax drippings around it. A plump cushion is nearby on the floor. He says that when his impulses rattle off in the old and familiar Type-A direction he retreats to his temple. He sits lotus-fashion on the cushion, closes his eyes and consciously gives himself permission just to be. Another friend who is a social worker, and not so completely a convert, says that she has altered her tea-drinking habit from rapidly gulping scalding liquid while reading over a set of adoption papers and listing phone calls to be made, to sitting quietly in a chair away from her desk and inviting someone in to join her for the tea-break. She has gone to the extent of preparing the tea more carefully and setting it out on a tray. Even the domestic task of washing up the cups and saucers afterward is seen by her as a way of cutting across time urgency and success needs.

6.   Learn to Relax and to Attend to the Body

Care for the body and indeed for the whole of life invites times of relaxation. For individuals brought up in a tradition of working till they drop, this facility may have to be learned. Religious are in an excellent position to do this. They have, built into their life, periods of prayer and reflection that cry out for stillness. Even so, if this has been undertaken as a duty or another task in a busy daily schedule, there may be new need to learn centering prayer, to be taught progressive relaxation of the muscles and parts of the body.

For some, yoga is a helpful discipline and most cities and towns have classes that meet in the afternoons and evenings to accommodate working people. Such learning is not a luxury. If it prevents or halts burnout, it is a worthy investment of time and money. Transcendental meditation and the use of mantras may help some, while for others physical exercise is of prime importance in relaxing the body and emptying the mind of stressful preoccupations. One of my colleagues describes running as a religious experience for her.

In addition to factors of health care already mentioned, avoiding excessive weight gain (or unhealthy weight loss), attending to sensible dietary needs (avoiding patterns of snacking or consumption of junk foods and alcohol habitually) and ensuring sufficient sleep are matters for concern. Such body-care is simultaneously care for life and a concern that recognizes that a vital body contributes to a lively spirit.

7. *Fight Only for What Is Worth It*

At times I feel like a modern day Don Quixote, tilting at windmills, fighting to the point of exhaustion to achieve the unachievable. This is often in the arena of relationships. I find myself working at building relationships with persons who quite clearly indicate that they couldn't care less. Perhaps it may be less stressful and more creative in the long run to accept the fact that, while remaining open to possibility (and dreaming the impossible dream, perhaps), I need not try so hard. I might be better advised to put my energy into relationships that already hold the promise of growth and development.

At times, also, I expend huge energy trying to change institutions and rules when it would be simpler, and possibly as effective in the long run, to live my life honestly (at times in contravention of institutional expectations and rules), saving my energy for those small daily battles that require and merit it.

8. *Balance the Abstract With the Concrete*

Because much of what we do is in the realm of faith, belief, coping with life problems, and so forth, it can be a healthy redress to do something concrete and measurable. The danger of making such a recommendation is that some will seize upon it as another obligation and add another "ought" to an already huge list, thus increasing stressors rather than combating their effect.

To make a cake, paint a landscape, polish a gemstone, build a hen-house, plant a tree or fix the plumbing, is to experience welcome relief from the intangibles of ministry for those who enjoy these activities. To watch a loaf of bread rise or to see something take shape is to be in touch with earth in a different way. It is novelty, relief, sanity and preservation in the midst of often unrewarding effort.

9. *Dispel Your Myths*

Most of us have ways of rationalizing our sense of stress and the creeping depletion that encroaches on us. We say, "I'll have a good night's sleep and things will look better in the morning," knowing that we have said this before and it does not come true. We continue to preserve the belief because if we don't we may have to undertake more radical and difficult change and disturb the accustomed pattern of our life.

We say, "I'm too tired to cope any longer, and so I'll take a few days off and come back refreshed." Or somebody else advises us to do this. If the fact is that such a tactic is only a temporary expedient and we quickly revert to weariness, boredom and lassitude, we are well in the grasp of burnout and change at the level of attitude is imperative. To avoid this by constant days off (which some call "legitimate malingering") is to live out of a lie and gradually to stop living.

Some say, "The system is to blame," and abdicate responsibility for themselves. Indeed expectations emanating from the system, or more precisely from authority figures within it, may be insensitive and even cruel. More often, however, they are ignorant and ill-informed precisely because the individual complies out of a sense of obligation that thinly disguises hostility. To know and admit limits, to dialogue about these and even, at times, in the interest of survival, to flatly refuse to take on any additional commissions is to speak inner truth. This is more effective than shucking off responsibility by displacing blame on an abstract system.

Others become professional workshop and seminar goers, attending every lecture at home and afar as a way of drinking in temporary energy for more effort in the workplace. It is false and evanescent energy which wilts quickly under the hot sun of work-stresses and soon needs refuelling. Hence, the individual again takes refuge in the quick fix of another seminar.

At times when an individual is under acute stress or in the grip of escalating burnout, superiors or friends misguidedly suggest a transfer to another place or another work. If, in fact, the stress is founded in dysfunctional attitudes to work or self or relationship or a combination of all of these, moving from one place to another is a temporizing tactic. It treats a symptom rather than a cause and adds the extra stressor of rootlessness. The help that is called for from superiors and friends is the challenge to re-examine motives and beliefs, to build a self-image that is sustaining, to change and to grow. This can happen only in a climate of affirmation and empathy that is more costly for the friends and the superiors since it calls for heavy investment from them.

In all that has been said so far, there has been no clear warning that burnout may happen not once but many times in a person's lifetime unless there is a real change of attitude. If the problem is dealt with by addressing symptoms, the chances are that some recovery may indeed happen, but when stresses mount up again, the problem will recur.

Help From Poets, Prophets and Pragmatists

At the level of the organization, it is clear that deep insight into the personal gifts and limits of individuals is called for. Genuine poets will never assume that because somebody had energy for a particular task five years ago, he or she still has it now. Like Peter at the Council of Jerusalem they will be reluctant to lay burdens that are too heavy on backs that are tired or weak. Thus dialogue will be prized as a way of ensuring that stresses are not created by the organization.

In their preoccupation with challenging and energizing to an alternative consciousness, the prophets will call their congregations away from emphasis on performance and the numbers game to a life lived deeply and cheerfully out of a common vision. They will criticize the sinfulness of institutions while simultaneously energizing by their repeated challenge to live true to the founding vision with creativity and adaptability.

Taking their cue from this the pragmatists will constantly seek ways of protecting and enhancing the quality of life. They will program ways of being in touch with everyone in their corporate ministry, of consulting and planning. They will look for ways of attending to appropriate education in the various life stages. They will search for ways of keeping life meaningful and whole for those who are beginning religious life and for those who are retiring, at the same time attending to the life-shape of the middle-aged who are often the major work force. They will pay attention to the pragmatic details of health care such as health funds, opportunities for holidays and professional and spiritual renewal. In conjunction with poets and prophets, they will ensure a system that, like the kingdom itself, is built on love rather than on utility.

In local communities, the poetic gift of empathy pushes individuals to notice signs that other people are getting worn out. They will communicate this and challenge prophetically and positively. In the spirit of empathy those with practical insight may be able to help individuals undertake planned change.

Above all, it is incumbent upon individuals to reach into their own capacity for empathy and to care for themselves out of it; to delve into their own ability for self-challenge to admit the signals of stress and the false attitudes that make them susceptible to burnout; to take hold of life and voluntarily seek ways of changing those falsehoods, self-deceptions and historical learnings that are ingredients in the process. In doing so they will have to rely not only on their own resources but open themselves receptively to the ministering help of others, since creation happens in relationship. It is a faith process as well and involves faith in *life*, a choosing of life rather than a preference for the dark places of obsessiveness, anesthetic activity and self-destruction. It is the worship of a God who calls to life, "out of darkness into everlasting light."

For community consideration

A. How are people valued in your community? Who gets the greatest attention, the best feedback? Who is seen as most "important"?

B. What are the clearest and most frequent messages to those who have retired, or who are ill, depressed or lethargic?

C. What is said of and to those who take regular time to go out and share a meal with friends, to engage in recreational pursuits or hobbies?

D. How would you describe attitudes toward work in the community? How much guilt is there about times for *not* working?

For individual consideration

A. List the activities that you engage in throughout an average week. (Include everything—time spent dressing, sleeping, praying, doing nothing, working, etc.) Now establish priorities on the list. Under pressure, what is less important? What can wait till tomorrow or next week?

Divide the activities you have listed into three groupings: play, pray and work. How happy are you with the balance? What would you like to change? Is there anything that stops you from changing? What? To whom should this be made known?

B. How do you feel about your work? Circle the appropriate words from the following list:

obligation	all-consuming
weary	self-expression
fun	creative
enjoyment	chore
competition	boring
time-bound	stimulating

C. Re-read the section of this chapter entitled "Try to Break the Type-A Pattern," pages 237-238. What signs of Type-A personality do you have, if any? Plan a few ways of changing this.

D. What creative activities do you have that are absorbing and different from the mainstream of your ministry? What would you like to take up or learn?

E. If you are a retired person or an invalid, how does it feel when the others in the house go out to work each day? What would you like others to understand about you? How do you spend your time? How peaceful do you feel about this? Are there any changes you are willing and able to make?

Notes

1. Cited in James J. Gill and Linda Amadeo, "Celibate Anxiety," *Human Development,* 1:4 (1980), p. 7.

2. Ibid. p. 7.

3. These two types of stress were identified and named by Nobel prizewinner Hans Selye in *Stress Without Distress* (New York, Signet, 1974).

4. Claudia Wallis, "Stress: Can We Cope?" *Time*, June 6, 1983, p. 70.

5. The Bishops' Committee on Priestly Life and Ministry, *The Priest and Stress* (Washington, D.C.: United States Catholic Conference, 1982), p. 5.

6. Martin C. Helldorfer, *The Work Trap: Solving the Riddle of Work and Leisure* (Winona, Minnesota: St. Mary's Press, Christian Brother's Publications, 1981), p. 84.

7. John Sanford, *Ministry Burnout* (New York: Paulist Press, 1982), p. 23.

8. Ibid. p. 22.

9. Gerald R. Grosh and William E. Creed, "Dealing with a Poor Self-Image," *Human Development*, 4:1 (1983), p. 23.

10. Kelley Kelsey, "The Gift of Loneliness," *Spirituality Today*, 36:2 (Summer 1984), p. 101.

11. Bishops' Committee, op. cit. p. 9.

12. Norbert Brockman, "Burnout in Superiors," *Review for Religious,* 37:6 (November 1978), p. 815.

7
CONCLUSION:

Endings and Beginnings

The story of religious life must stand within the story of contemporary society like yeast in the bread dough. It is there not to call attention to itself but to point to an alternative view of reality—to inspire, to lead, to enable, to heal, to give life. It exists to make known the incomprehensible fact that behind every event, encounter, tragedy and success, indeed behind every individual or corporate story, lies the face of the God in whose image we are shaped. The *how* of doing or being a sign of this is the continuing challenge to religious life. It raises questions less related to numbers than to credibility. The crisis of religious life today is in the area of relevance rather than of vocations.

Crisis there is, however, and every crisis carries simultaneously the possibilities of both death and life. Right now religious life is faced with the possibility of making death-dealing or life-engendering choices. To focus on survival as numbers dwindle and aging increases is to become self-preoccupied and myopic, ignoring the assurance that "whoever loses his or her life for my sake will find it." Such a focus opts for decay. To be concerned only about the internal dynamics of religious community is to become inward-looking and religiously incestuous. This, too, is death. To embark on a quest for self-fulfillment reminiscent of the Me-generation is a deadly refusal of the gospel imperative to self-transcending love of neighbor. To translate the church's call to renewal into an invitation to pursue the luxury of incessant self-nourishment is to espouse a form of spiritual gluttony that merely replicates in a more "religious" mode the inequalities and injustices of the world's story. To fossilize the past as a way of remaining separate from the dangerous challenges of the present is to repeat the disobedience of Lot's wife, freezing fertility, cutting off the possibility of creating a new future. To choose a childlike bondage to a parented, safe existence is ultimately a choice of ennui and atrophy, where the echoes of the gospel fade to a whisper and finally to an entombed silence. To regard ourselves as "the good guys" and the rest of humanity as "the baddies" is to deny that we have anything to receive, and as soon as this choice is made empathy is dead, and, when empathy dies, so does community and the possibility of love.

Religious life may, however, choose the other path at the crossroads where it now stands, for crisis is also possibility. Individuals and systems facing crisis can summon up all their energies, pull together all their resources, renounce all their enmities in order to move toward novelty, to deal constructively with threat and to generate new creativity. It is the suggestion of this book that religious are currently being challenged to re-story themselves. The call to relevance invites them to reach back to the birthing of their story in the founder's charism, to strip this of historically accumulated frills and ancient devotional tarnish, so that its stark and original message is clear again. The next step is to appropriate this vision and struggle in the pangs of rebirthing it in a new place and time and culture. The story is not finished. We are writing the next chapter. Developmentally, religious life is being called beyond the self-preoccupation of its adolescence and young adulthood into the self-transcending generativity of its maturity. It has to forget itself to live. It has not only to choose life, but to choose to be a bringer of life. It is my belief that religious life has entered a new phase of its history where mission and ministry require new attention. Tossing aside concern for survival, religious are being asked for new forms of involvement, new closeness and dialogue, new trust in Providence, new courage to walk out trustfully into the dark. Concern for the meaning of community is less about making life serenely comfortable and conflict-free than about liberating life and energies, empowering each other and sustaining each other in life, faith and mission. To challenge each other to move beyond the narrow quest for self-fulfillment into the sometimes lonely, often painful world of self-transcending love is a call to life that paradoxically involves little deaths— death to the nesting instinct, death to the temptation to set up our tents on Tabor, death to old definitions of prayer, of service, of authority, of community, of piety and of tradition. Self-transcending love refuses to be tied down by legalities. It goes where the cry for love is raised. At the same time it is also profoundly receptive. Those who are fired by such love allow what is "out there"—the cry of the poor and the displaced or dispossessed, along with their privileged access to the gospel—to reach into them, to enter their world and shake them to the roots. They themselves are constantly being re-created.

The flames of such a life-opting vision need constant fuelling, and it has been the thesis of this book that the gifts of poets, prophets and pragmatists provide impetus for this. Together they offer the light, heat and kinetic energy of their insight, passion and practicality that together constitute an empowering form of wisdom. It should be noted that only some especially gifted individuals carry these qualities in visible and public abundance. This book is about other people as well. It is about those of us who recognize that there are times when we can be poetically empathetic, or prophetically energizing or pragmatically helpful. There are times, perhaps only moments, in our lives when a situation or an encounter creates those qualities in us. The reference to poets, prophets and pragmatists is about those moments too, moments out of which come permanent learnings and new belief in our own giftedness. So, the leadership of poets, prophets and pragmatists operates on every stratum of religious life and, indeed, of church and social institutions. Religious do not have a monopoly on it. Chapters, I believe, must seek out these gifts as they deliberate about appointing formal leaders, but formal leaders in their turn must look for the same gifts at grass-roots level, themselves avoiding a proprietorial sense of giftedness that quickly becomes self-devouring and narcissistic. Those entrusted with formation tasks must ask whether the same qualities can be developed and trained, and devise ways of doing this. Those in formal positions of leadership (and those who appoint or elect them) need to recognize that the three groups of gifts do not automatically sit comfortably together. Poets, prophets and pragmatists can irritate and anger one another as well as mutually enlighten one another. It is the very gifts that abrade one another that must be mobilized to deal with the conflict they produce.

But, I repeat, this book is not just for those who are superiors or formal leaders. It is for everyone in ministry, because every minister is in some sense asked to be a leader. For this reason every person in ministry is obliged to reflect upon what gifts he or she recognizes or needs. Full use should be made of mentors and models, spiritual direction and friendship, all of these providing essential feedback about talents and propensities that may be overlooked or unrecognized. There are questions that must constantly be asked:

How may I in my situation exercise these gifts?

How receptive am I to these gifts when they are exercised by others?

How may these qualities in people be developed and maximized?

What forms of support should I offer those who formally exercise the gifts?

Where must we place our poets, prophets and pragmatists so that their call to conversion may be most audible?

How may we combine the gifts into a corporate wisdom that incessantly calls to life and witnesses to life?

For ultimately we exist as religious to echo the voice of our Author who promises: "I have come that you may have life."

Our beginning and our ending is in this.